THE DYING OF THE TREES

ALSO BY CHARLES E. LITTLE

Challenge of the Land

Green Fields Forever

Louis Bromfield at Malabar (ed.)

Greenways for America

Hope for the Land

CHARLES E. LITTLE

VIKING

THE DYING OF THE TREES

THE PANDEMIC IN AMERICA'S FORESTS

Ila

VIKING
Published by the Penguin Group
Penguin Books USA Inc., 375 Hudson Street, New York, New York 10014, U.S.A.
Penguin Books Ltd, 27 Wrights Lane, London W8 5TZ, England
Penguin Books Australia Ltd, Ringwood, Victoria, Australia
Penguin Books Canada Ltd, 10 Alcorn Avenue, Toronto, Ontario, Canada M4V 3B2
Penguin Books (N.Z.) Ltd, 182–190 Wairau Road, Auckland 10, New Zealand

Penguin Books Ltd, Registered Offices: Harmondsworth, Middlesex, England

First published in 1995 by Viking Penguin, a division of Penguin Books USA Inc.

3 5 7 9 10 8 6 4 2

Grateful acknowledgment is made for permission to reprint excerpts from the following copyrighted works: "We Vainly Wrestle with the Blind Relief" from *The Poetry of Robert Frost* edited by Edward Connery Lathem. Copyright © 1962 by Robert Frost. Copyright © 1969 by Henry Holt and Co., Inc. Reprinted by permission of Henry Holt and Co., Inc. Letter from John Flynn to the author. By permission of John Flynn. Letter from E. Gerry Hawkes to the editor of *American Forests.* By permission of E. Gerry Hawkes.

LIBRARY OF CONGRESS CATALOGING IN PUBLICATION DATA
Little, Charles E.
The dying of the trees : the pandemic in America's forests / Charles E. Little.
p. cm.
Includes index.
ISBN 0-670-84135-8
1. Forest declines—United States. 2. Forests and forestry—United States.
3. Forest ecology—United States. I. Title.
SB762.L58 1995
634.9'61'0973—dc20 94-46136

This book is printed on acid-free recycled paper.

Printed in the United States of America
Set in Minion
Designed by Katy Riegel

Contents

Preface

This book, as its title quite explicitly states, is about the dying of trees, and of a related phenomenon that ecologists call forest decline. I do not mean by this simply that *some* trees are dying—in, say, the forests of Brazil, where they are felled by the buzz saws of international greed, local poverty, and ecological ignorance. That's a part of the story, to be sure—as is the destruction of trees in Europe and Southeast Asia—but it's not all of it. For the trees are dying everywhere, including everywhere in the United States of America. They are dying on the ridges of the Appalachian chain and in the sugar bush of Vermont. They are dying in the mixed mesophytic of the mid-South border states, in the thick forests of central Michigan, on the mountainsides of Colorado and California, on the gulf of Mexico, and in the deserts of the Southwest. And they are dying in the Northwest, too—even before they are cut.

Despite some lingering protestations to the contrary, including some recent books that aim (wrongly, I believe) to minimize global environmental challenges, the present-day phenomenon of dying trees in America cannot convincingly be explained in terms of the normal rhythms of natural forest decline and regeneration. We are almost certainly witnessing the accumulated consequences of some 150 years of headlong economic development and industrial expansion, with the most impressive of the impacts coming into play since the 1950s—the age of pollution.

My purpose here is to bring the manifold events of tree death in the United States into focus: to aggregate the incidents of death and decline so that their implications, both globally and nationally for Americans, can be accurately and honestly assessed. For reasons that may be of interest to those who study mass psychology or politics, the stories of tree death in foreign lands are rather better known here, and certainly better understood, than the story of what is happening right in our own country.

The first part of the book describes, in eight chapters, the discrete, seemingly unrelated examples of tree death in various regions of the United States. It begins with what is quite likely the extinction in its native range of the lovely Eastern dogwood. Then, in two chapters, I describe how acid rain has eaten through the forests at high elevations in the Appalachians—from Camel's Hump in Vermont to Mount Mitchell in North Carolina. Thence to California to examine the once-mysterious "X-disease," a deadly man-made killer of Ponderosa pine. A subsequent chapter relates how a century of logging and fire suppression has changed the composition of the forest in the Rockies and the intermountain West generally, and for the worse: It is now a forest of torches. Changing forest composition, courtesy of Paul Bunyan–style logging, is also implicated in the virulent spread of the gypsy moth, now so prevalent in northern Michigan that it is dangerous to drive a car during caterpillar season—the roads are slick with the mashed corpses of the larvae. Then there is the tragic tale of the last of the old-growth timber in Oregon and Washington, where for every ancient tree that is cut, two others die from changes in the microclimate. Finally, in a chapter entitled "Lucy's Woods," about the forest of the hollows of West Virginia and eastern Kentucky, I describe how one of the two oldest woodlands on earth is simply falling down—dead—the effect of a whole range of human-caused maladies, exacerbated (here as elsewhere) by the perfidies of the U.S. government.

The final chapters show how tree death and forest decline have become widespread in the United States, even beyond these examples, and what citizen organizations and others are trying to do about it. In a phrase, their efforts are brave, but quixotic. The last chapter, "On

Crossing the Threshold," suggests that the dying of the trees is an ecological phenomenon that simply cannot be ignored, for it is not just a set of local symptoms; it may actually become a *cause* of a potentially catastrophic failure of global ecological balances. Ecologists have described nightmarish biochemical and atmospheric feedback loops wherein the more trees die, the more they will die.

Despite the foregoing gloomy synopsis, I did not set out to be alarmist in this book. I am a writer whose usual topics deal with the affirmative aspects of what Barry Commoner calls making peace with the planet. I had hoped to find affirmative aspects to this story, too. But I did not. I can only speak plainly here—not only about the environmental causes of the dying of trees, but also about the consequences, for us and for whatever generations may ensue.

Let us go, then, to the woods, and see.

1

In This Sign

Henceforth it shall be
slender and shall be bent
and twisted, and its
blossoms shall be in the
form of a cross . . .
—from an Appalachian
folk legend

Let me begin with the Catoctin woods, a wonderfully profuse Eastern deciduous forest, with impressively tall oaks and hickories and maples and tulip poplars that cover some Appalachian outliers near my former home in Maryland. Indeed, anyone who comes from the cold North or the dry West (such as I, who have lived for long periods in both places) cannot fail to be amazed at how fast and how big the dominant hardwood trees in the Middle Atlantic states can grow.

The massive energy transfer, the gaseous exchange, the movement of googols of molecules of moisture and nutriment that such rapidly attained size implies, is almost too much to comprehend. The trunks of trees no older than I am are thick enough to hide behind. In height, or perhaps I should say elevation, even the most ordinary specimens reach well over a hundred feet and intermingle their topmost branches at such a great distance from the ground that the canopy seems almost a kind of intermediate sky. When one walks in woods like these, the scale and sheer numbers of the big trees is such that their presence merges into a kind of forest *atmosphere*, where the "stems," as foresters call them (stems sometimes three feet through!), lose their individuality.

As a result of this phenomenon, the woods walker is actually more aware of the *smaller* trees. An architectural analogy may be found in the great medieval cathedrals where despite the magnificently soaring naves and buttresses, one's attention is nevertheless drawn to the altar. Just so, in our deep woods there are "altar trees," which in fact is an apt title for the most striking tree of any size in the Catoctins—the Eastern flowering dogwood, *Cornus florida.*

With its graceful branches and luminous leaves, perfectly suited for a life under the overarching canopy of the oaks and hickories (or, sometimes, most beautifully, beneath the deep green tent of an old hemlock grove), the dogwood is a human-size tree. It serves our needs in ways that the giants cannot, which is spiritual rather than practical. The economic value of dogwoods in their native habitat is nil these days, though the Indians used the bark as a remedy for malaria, as did colonists who added it to whiskey as a specific for the ague. The tight-grained wood was also once carved into smooth shuttles that would glide back and forth between warp and woof on old-fashioned looms. But these employments are no longer important to us. And so in modern times the tree became famous for its own sake. Now the function of the dogwood is to be found in its sheer beauty. Indeed, in the vicinity of the Catoctins—an hour's ride from both Washington, D.C., and Baltimore—thousands of families would load up the children in the station wagon and drive up the windy roads to witness the burst of bloom lighting the winter-locked woods in early spring.

Of all those who have ever written about trees, perhaps no naturalist-writer has provided as affecting, and as exact, a one-paragraph description of the dogwood's gifts as Donald Culross Peattie. In *A Natural History of Trees,* Peattie writes:

> Stepping delicately out of the dark woods, the startling loveliness of Dogwood in bloom makes each tree seem a presence, calling for an exclamation of praise, a moment of worship from our eyes. On the almost naked branches the blossoms shine forth like stars, and these blossoms are borne in long flat sprays of bloom along the boughs, turning their pure faces up toward the sky with a suggestion of the most classical traditions of flower arrangement. It is a botanist's quibble to point out that the four white "petals" are not petals indeed but bracts; by any name, they make a clear and pleasing design, in detail as in mass. And the little tree bears them with a royal grace, tier upon snowy tier, the slim trunk often

leaning slightly from the hillside, as though to offer its burden of blossom, princess-like, to the spring world.

I now must make it clear to those who do not know it already that this is what families once journeyed to the Catoctins to witness, but no longer. The showy bracts—the creamy white leaflike coverings for the blossoms themselves, which are less significant—no longer gleam in the deep woods, for now the dogwoods are mostly dead in the mountains, victims of a virulent form of fungal infection called "anthracnose" that has been killing off *C. florida* as the dominant understory tree in natural woodlands throughout its native range—from southern New England to Alabama. The term *anthracnose* is a combination of the Greek words for coal (*anthra,* as in *anthracite*) and disease (*nosos*), and describes the dark brown blotches on infected leaves.

I shall return to a fuller discussion of anthracnose pathology in due course. For now, in the Catoctins, the significant datum is this: Just a half dozen years after the anthracnose was discovered here, a comprehensive study (first conducted in 1988, with later updates) revealed that 79 percent of the dogwoods were dead, and the rest were dying. A few still hang on today, but in large sections of the mountains a living dogwood is nowhere to be seen.

Having long known of, but not personally witnessed, the dying of the dogwoods in the Catoctins, I arranged to meet with a forest pathologist named James Sherald, who was conducting dogwood research at Catoctin Mountain Park, a unit of the National Park System located near Thurmont, Maryland. He said that he would be pleased to show me the damage, though he added that a better time for viewing dying trees in the mountains would have been earlier in the year, in the spring—or better yet several springs ago.

This was not a trip I was looking forward to, for I too had been a sojourner to the Catoctins in pre-anthracnose springtimes. But since it was late summer, not bloom time, I did not expect to be struck with the absence of the "burdens of blossom" as Peattie so poetically described the dogwood in flower. In fact, as I drove up into the park, I could even see some living dogwoods along the roadside, where (I was to learn later) a few trees were able to withstand infection somewhat, owing to a dryer and sunnier location. On the road to the Park Service's field experiment area, I passed the forbidding entrance to Camp David, the presidential retreat that is located here, with its sign promising severe reprisal for any sort of intrusion. The area was devoid of dogwood survivors, so I don't suppose the anthracnose paid much attention to the sign. I wondered if any president of the United States or any of his visitors had paid any attention to the anthracnose. (I was to discover that one of them had. Ronald Reagan, though not known as a tree lover, had complained to park officials that something was wrong with the woods.)

As I drove along the park roads, the woods seemed pretty much like woods anywhere, at least at first. Then (like President Reagan before me) I realized that something was wrong. There was something odd about the look of the place that I couldn't quite figure out. It seemed gloomy, though this was a bright summer morning. I put it down to an overworked imagination, stuffed with too many of the plant pathologist's statistics.

I met Sherald, a tall, athletic-looking scientist, in a parking lot, and after an exchange of amenities he took me for a brisk walk in nearby woods. There was nothing to see in the way of dogwoods, of course, except a few diseased-looking branches that were taking longer to die than their compatriots. In the dim light of the summer forest, I felt a sense of uneasiness, as if I had intruded in some place I did not belong. I took several pictures, but without much sense of what they were supposed to show, except an absence. Then it struck me: I could see too *far* into these monochrome woods through the camera viewfinder. There was nothing to focus on except the trunks of the tall trees. Between them were just empty distances unrelieved by the luminous green leaves that had once created an understory to give a human scale to the forest. Before the scourge of anthracnose, the dogwoods, with more than four hundred medium to large trees per acre, had provided primary definition to the woods. But now a whole layer of life had been extinguished. Questions arose: What of the plants and creatures that live below the understory—the mosses and grasses and lovely ground covers, the mayapple, ferns, and violets? What of the birds, such as the cedar waxwing and robin, who love the bright fall berries of dogwood—would they absent themselves from these woods? What of the big trees themselves—will some subtle change in the chemistry of the forest soils make their own survival more difficult?

Sherald said that in addition to the loss of the dogwoods as an understory plant, whatever shrubs and small trees of other species—sassafras, spicebush—remained were being totally consumed by the local deer, which were altogether too plentiful owing to a string of warm winters. They had stripped the lower forest of anything resembling a leaf or blade of grass. It was a kind of desert, then, that I was walking through, and silent, except for the soughing of a summer breeze far above in the dark canopy that hid the sun.

Out in a cleared area, Sherald had made a kind of garden of tiny survivors—seedling dogwoods collected from various places throughout the park to see if any might be possessed of some genetic characteristic that would permit them to elude the virulent disease that had taken their parents. If one such seedling could be found—just one—then a new generation of resistant dogwoods might be nurtured, and hard-hit areas replanted. But even in the warm, full sun (the fungus likes a cool, moist environment), the seedlings looked stricken, with the telltale leaf spots and "necrotic blotch"—from the Greek again, *nekros,* meaning a dead body. Said Sherald, "My interest is in trying to find resistance to the disease, but there's something unique about this organism that makes it difficult to handle. We've got trees here and there that are not succumbing, but we don't know whether they are resistant or just escapes." And so James Sherald and his assistants scour the mountains to find any living trees to transplant to his garden. One graduate student is trying to figure out some new way to inoculate the test seedlings with the anthracnose fungus—other than simply applying a culture medium of the disease to leaves—in order to shortcut the time required to determine resistance. Meanwhile, Park Service naturalists are concerned that the loss of the dogwood will have a local impact on wild turkeys, wood ducks, cedar waxwings, bluebirds, gray squirrels, and the scores of other species that use the tree. As for human visitors, a species that is also part of the Park Service's responsibility, they don't come to the Catoctins in the spring to see the dogwoods in bloom anymore anyway.

The first notice taken that something might be amiss with the dogwood occurred some three thousand miles to the west, when in 1976 Ralph Byther and Roy Davidson, plant pathologists with the Western Washington Research and Extension Center in Poyallup, Washington, received a diseased dogwood branch (it was *C. nuttallii,* the native Pacific dogwood, which is much like *C. florida*) from a correspondent living near Vancouver, Washington, across the Columbia River from Portland, Oregon. The following year, similarly diseased trees were found a bit downriver from Vancouver, in Kelso, Washington, but also further north, near Olympia, on Puget Sound. And then the year after that the disease had spread throughout the Puget Sound region—northward to Tacoma and Seattle, where arborists estimated that at least 60 percent of the Pacific dogwood trees were showing severe symptoms from some sort of fungal infection.

What Byther and Davidson examined on that first specimen sent to them from Vancouver, and on the other infected trees they investigated, was an ugly, dark brown blotch on the leaves. The blotches were edged by a dark graying green, purple, or darker-brown margin. On some leaves, there were only dark brown or purple spots. But in either case, trees so afflicted would drop their leaves prematurely, and sometimes become completely bare long before fall. On a few samples, the disease, clearly caused by a fungus, looked something like the common "spot anthracnose," which routinely visits dogwoods without any permanent damage to the tree—just a few dark spots on some of the leaves at those times (cool, moist) when such fungi can get a toehold.

Anthracnose is the ordinary term plant pathologists use to describe a set of disease symptoms for a quite wide variety of trees—oaks, sycamores, even citrus—that are attacked by fungus. But the coal-dark dogwood leaves Byther and Davidson were investigating were caused by no ordinary fungus, in the rapidly expanding area of the Northwest where the disease was spreading. Thus, in 1979, they decided it was time to prepare some sort of scientific description of what seemed to be a new form of anthracnose. Their paper, scarcely a page and a half long, appeared in a regional information sheet for the nursery trade—the *Ornamentals Northwest Newsletter*—in the spring of 1979. It is the first published account of a disease that scarcely drew any attention then, but has now broken the hearts of all those who go to the mountains to admire the dogwood, whether in the Appalachians or the Sierra-Cascades or the Pacific Coast ranges.

What could be done? Byther and Davidson suggested that chemical controls would be ill-advised. In gardens one might prune off dead branches and rake up the fallen, infected leaves, since the fungus would have no difficulty overwintering; but in their natural locations, where *C. nuttallii* brightened the dark coniferous forests of the Northwest, the pathologists could only put as good a face on a bad situation as possible: "It should be remembered," they wrote, "that diseases are as much a part of these natural areas as are dogwoods, and that the diseases will be worse in some years than in others." The unspoken hope was that the outbreak would be temporary, and local.

But then, less than a year after Byther and Davidson's first paper, Pascal Pirone of the Brooklyn (New York) Botanic Garden sent a short article to the *New York Times* garden section. He, too, had discovered a strange new form of dogwood anthracnose. "The dogwood trees are in trouble," he wrote (of *C. florida,* the Eastern flowering dogwood). "Last spring [of 1979], thousands of trees in southeastern New York State and southwestern Connecticut were seriously damaged, some were killed, by a mysterious disease." Like his colleagues in Washington State, Pirone thought the fungus was *Colletotricum gleosporioides,* adding, "Why should such a fungus, usually considered to be a weak parasite, suddenly cause so much damage to one of our favorite ornamental trees? I am afraid I do not know the answer."

In the years since Pirone asked this question, many others have been answered regarding the form of anthracnose attacking dogwoods. The fungus, on both coasts, turned out not to be *gleosporioides* after all. Several researchers, including Craig Hibben of the Brooklyn Botanic Garden and Margery Daughtrey of Cornell University's Long Island Horticultural Research Laboratory, determined that the fungus causing dogwood anthracnose belonged to another genus altogether, named *Discula.* But there was nothing unusual about *Discula* fungi either. They are well-known to mycologists. What *was* unusual was that the particular species of *Discula* which was able to kill dogwoods could not be identified. It had never been seen before. In the literature it was simply described as *Discula sp.,* meaning that the species name was unknown.

Thus Pirone's mystery remained: a new virulent form of fungus had suddenly and unaccountably appeared on both coasts, at the very same time, and was wiping out dogwoods, particularly in the East, by the thousands, and spreading outward in widening circles like a silvacultural version of the bubonic plague.

The first signs of *Discula* anthracnose are small dark spots appearing on the leaves and flower bracts in the spring—tan with dark purple borders, according to an official Department of Agriculture brochure. Soon the leaves die, turning a dark, blighted gray and drooping limply from the branches like hung corpses. Then the infection spreads to the twigs and branches themselves. The tree, in a valiant attempt to compensate for the dieback of the lower branches that inevitably follows, sends out new "epicormic" shoots from the main trunk—water sprouts, they are sometimes called. This is the worst possible survival strategy for the dogwood, for the new shoots simply speed up the progress of the disease by providing easy access for the fungus to invade the trunk. On the underside of each *Discula*-infected leaf, masses of small brownish dots appear, about the size of a flyspeck. These are the conidiomata, the spore-producing structures of the fungus. The sticky microscopic spores are then dislodged by wind or water, which assist gravity to transport the disease to the new, vulnerable epicormic shoots below, and thus to the trunk; the trunk eventually becomes so girdled with cankers that the translocation of moisture and nutrients from the roots to the branches is slowed and finally stops, after which the tree dies. The fungus spores also move from tree to tree—so quickly in the Appalachians that the course of infection from New England to the deep South, a thousand miles or more, has seemed almost instantaneous. Furthermore, regeneration is well nigh impossible, for the disease strikes seedlings even more decisively than their parents. There are now too few mature trees to provide seeds in forested areas. And so, it would seem, that's to be the end of it.

In shady woods such as the Catoctins, the dogwood is on the margins of survival even in the best of times, struggling for light and moisture and nutrients in a land of giants. Accordingly, its method of subsistence was to develop immunity to the blights and plagues visiting other kinds of trees. For this reason, even discounting its pleasing shape and floral display, the dogwood's resistance to infection made it a favorite garden tree wherever it would grow. Now, with the most virulent anthracnose ever observed in nature attacking them, the formerly resistant trees have succumbed quickly in the forests, where competition is intense, but less quickly in gardens and parks where they do not grow as thickly and enjoy uncompetitive environments (sunny, dry, with plenty of moisture and nutrients) that make them stronger and able to resist the new anthracnose, at least for a time.

The failure of garden trees to die off as quickly as their brothers in the deep woods has led a good many magazine and newspaper articles to propose a "cure" for anthracnose. Prune off diseased branches and water sprouts, the writers prescribe, rake up the leaves every fall, mulch around the tree, spray with a powerful fungicide, and for heaven's sake don't hit the trunk with the lawnmower. Maybe all is not lost for the dogwood after all. Either in the garden *or* the woods. This is, of course, an example of the basic American tenet that anything broken can be fixed, if not now then just as soon as some super CEO in some corporate boardroom decides to invent the new cloning material or chemical that can be sprayed from the wingtanks of air force jets. The glass is always half full in our land of optimists.

But optimism is not much in the mind of Frank Santamour. A well-known plant geneticist with labs at the National Arboretum in Washington, D.C., Santamour was invited by Sherald to conduct a "provenance study" in the Catoctins shortly after the dogwood anthracnose had invaded the mountains. Fortunately, the arboretum was in possession of hundreds of native dogwood seeds from various areas in twenty Northeastern, Midwestern, and Southern states collected as part of a 1982 dogwood and cherry seed "exchange" between Japan and the United States. Seedlings from some thirty-eight sources were planted and allowed to grow for three years. Then, in October 1985, Santamour carted 120 dogwood (*C. florida*) seedlings from some twenty provenances up to Catoctin Mountain Park, placing them in their original containers (though opening the bottoms so that roots could move into the forest soil) within fenced plots beneath the fungus-infected overhanging limbs of mature dogwoods. In addition to the provenance seedlings, Santamour also brought along several controlled-pollination crosses of *C. florida*—such as those developed by nurseries for special qualities, shape, or color of bloom—as well as a kousa dogwood (*C. kousa*), an ornamental variety imported from the orient with bractlike blooms that appear after the leaves are out, rather than before, as with *C. florida*. Dogwood lovers are generally scornful of the kousa as a garden tree, but it is widely sold by plant nurseries nevertheless, so its resistance would be of interest at least to them.

Interim evaluations of how the seedlings were faring showed that virtually all the *florida* dogwoods quickly became infected, but Santamour held out some hope that those that were hanging on to their leaves longer than the others might be resistant due to some sort of genetic difference. For example, after the first year, leaf loss on samples from provenances in Arkansas, Missouri, and Oklahoma ranged between just 11 and 14 percent, even though more than 80 percent of the leaves were infected on these seedlings. Nineteen of these individuals showed no leaf loss whatsoever. Santamour wondered if they might pull through. However, after two full growing seasons, 73 percent of all the provenance seedlings were dead, and all the others showed serious infection. "The only green leaves on the surviving seedlings," Santamour wrote in his paper reporting the experiment, "were on the epicormic shoots"—the appearance of which, as those studying dogwood anthracnose have found, is the beginning of the end. The hope that some of the seedlings might demonstrate resistance by holding on to leaves longer despite infection was dashed. Of the controlled-pollination crosses, 65 percent were dead after just two years, and like the provenance seedlings, they had no green leaves either, except for the dreaded water sprouts. The kousa, otherwise known as the Japanese flowering dogwood, survived.

Santamour's cheerless conclusion: "These results indicate that there is probably little hope for the selection and development of anthracnose-resistant plants in *C. florida.*" As he told Charles Fenyvesi of *The Washington Post,* whose report brought these findings to a wide audience which included me (and set me off on my dogwood quest), the fungus had a one-hundred-percent fatality rate. Wrote Fenyvesi, "The sad news is that the fungus killing the native American dogwood is moving across the country with no reliable antidote in sight."

Since Santamour's paper was submitted for publication in 1988, it occurred to me several years later that new findings might have caused him to moderate this doomsday scenario. I called the eminent scientist for an interview. It was granted, but I was to be disappointed in the outcome. "Our studies show that there was not a lot of genetic variation throughout the natural range of the species in resistance to anthracnose," Santamour told me in his office overlooking the tidy lawns of the arboretum. "There may be some trees still hanging on up in the Catoctins, but I think it's a pretty tough row to hoe for the dogwood." Santamour did admit that you might save a dogwood by "spraying the hell out of it." But of course that would have no application for woodland trees, and possibly only limited value for garden varieties. (Horticulturists have told me that nothing less than weekly applications of fungicide will save a dogwood, and then only certain trees in certain locations.) We discussed Sherald's and others' ongoing effort to find a resistant tree somewhere that might provide a new beginning for the dogwood—an "Eve tree." "Well," said Santamour, "that's the 'hope springs eternal' game." His view was that finding a resistant dogwood in the wild "just ain't gonna happen."

Meanwhile, one mystery at least has been cleared up. Sherald got the National Park Service to provide a research grant to an accomplished young mycologist, Scott C. Redlin of the USDA's Agricultural Research Service in Beltsville, Maryland, to try to pin down just what kind of fungus species they were dealing with. Redlin first collected every bit of published scientific information available from the United States and abroad, scrutinizing it carefully to make sure there were no overlooked clues to suggest that the *Discula sp.* attacking the dogwoods might actually be identified, at least partially, as a known anthracnose fungus species. The search turned up nothing. Next, Redlin collected leaves and stems of infected trees from all over the United States and British Columbia. Then, following careful procedures, he began a laborious process of trying, in a sense, to "key out"—to organize the myriad characteristics of the fungus in order to determine exactly what he was looking at under his microscope (actually two of them—one a powerful electron microscope). He concluded that, without doubt (or at least not much of one), he was looking at an entirely new species of *Discula.* And that, of course, gave him the privilege of naming it. The agent that is destroying *C. florida* in the East, and a substantial fraction of *C. nuttallii* in the West (these trees, so far, show somewhat less mortality after infection), is now called *Discula destructiva* Redlin. "Conidiomata abunantia, acervulata, subcuticularia, saepe proxime infra trichomata hospitis evoluta . . . ," the formal Latin description begins.

I asked Redlin about choosing the name. Certainly *destructiva* was both vivid and accurate, but had he had any other ideas? In fact, he had, Redlin confessed. "I first thought I might use *enigmata* as the species name, since we still know so little about it," he said. But he settled on *destructiva* instead, for there would never be any doubt about the virulence of this deadly agent of infection.

But there are still enigmas: Where did this brand-new fungus come from? How come it appeared in locations three thousand miles apart at, apparently, the exact same time? How is it that it moved in just a few years, at least in the East, throughout the whole range of *C. florida*? The velocity has been faster than any other known blight. In what way are environmental factors involved—acid rain, photochemical smog, holes in the ozone layer, climate change? And does the demise of the dogwood have some sort of larger meaning for the forest trees with which it associates?

For these questions, the pathologists, ecologists, geneticists, and the other researchers whose articles I have read and whom I have interviewed have explanations, surmises, and assumptions, but no conclusive data. On the question of the origin of the new *Discula* species, some early researchers believed that it might have existed on this continent all along, and that it began killing trees in epidemic proportions as a result of some freak concatenation of weather or environmental pollution factors, or both. But that explanation seems unlikely in view of the fact that *Discula destructiva* appeared on both coasts at the same time. Could just the right meteorological variations—variations that evidently had never occurred before—have obtained simultaneously in Washington State and on Long Island? The improbability of such a coincidence has led many investigators to propose that the fungus is an import, perhaps one that came in on a shipment of nursery-stock kousa dogwoods from China, since increased trade was being developed with the mainland in the late 1970s, and since the outbreaks started in (or near) port cities—Portland, Oregon, and New York.

But then why not also Seattle and Baltimore? Or a dozen other cities? Why just two points of origin, with one of them—Portland—being rather remote in any case? And why did the disease then not appear in several places at once rather than in relatively localized areas—at least insofar as the first infections were found by Byther and Davidson on *C. nuttallii* and by Pirone on *C. florida*? Wholesale nursery stock is commonly shipped long distances, by semi truck to inland cities. Furthermore, if the virulent anthracnose originated with imported kousas, why did it take so many years for it to appear here, since kousas have been imported from Japan and China for decades? They are listed in my 1935 edition of *Hortus*, and doubtless they predate that emininent tome in American gardens by a good bit. Conceivably there's an explanation for the infected-kousa-shipment theory—as a sole cause—that can deal with such questions as mine, but none has been offered so far.

As for the rapid transmission of the fungus, plant pathologist Ethel Dutky of the University of Maryland suggested to me that the spores may have been carried by migrating birds, since the dogwood fruits as well as leaves, branches, and bracts can be infected. This does seem plausible, although it seems problematic in that the disease tended to travel northward from its point of origin on the West Coast, and southward on the East Coast. The late-fall seed would presumably be carried from north to south by migrating birds in both places. As for the matter of what are now called "anthropogenic" causes of tree death and forest decline, many experts have declined to consider them directly linked to the spread of anthracnose in the dogwood the way acid rain, for example, is linked to the decline of spruce and fir trees at high elevations of the Appalachians. More recent data suggest otherwise. One researcher, plant pathologist Robert Anderson of the U.S. Forest Service in Asheville, North Carolina, has found that when dogwoods are subject to simulated acid rain in a controlled greenhouse situation, the rate and severity of fungus infection is measurably increased. While acid deposition, photochemical smog, increased ultraviolet rays from the thinning ozone layer, or climate change due to the rapid buildup of greenhouse gasses in the upper atmosphere may not, singly or severally, be the *sole* cause of the dogwood anthracnose epidemic, it is probably mistaken and misleading to rule these out categorically as factors contributing to a dangerous buildup of *Discula destructiva*, wherever it may have come from.

Let me return to the mountains for a moment, and to what strikes me as the awful irony of the dying of the dogwood in this particular place. As mountains go, they aren't much, Maryland's Catoctins, named for an elusive tribe of Indians (the Kittoctons) that were rarely seen hereabouts and anyway preferred the lush lowlands along the Potomac River as a place of residence. It was the European colonists who discovered the riches, at least for their way of life, that this small piece of the Appalachian chain could bestow: charcoal for iron smelting, tannin for leather curing, and, in the high valleys, friable soil for crops.

But the mountains were asked to give of these modest boons too quickly. As the population grew in the cities of the mid-Atlantic coastal plain—Philadelphia, Baltimore, and the new federal city built on some swampy land along the Potomac just downriver from Georgetown—the woods and fields of the Catoctins were resolutely exploited on behalf of commerce, to the point of near-extinction. The offer of rent-free land by Lord Baltimore brought the first colonists to the Catoctin region, or more particularly to the Monocacy Valley, which runs along the eastern edge of the range. Then large numbers of Germans and Scots-Irish followed, moving from the valley lands into the mountains themselves, to clearcut the trees to make charcoal for iron smelting for cooperages and cannons; to fell the giant oaks and chestnuts for their bark, which could be sold to the insatiable tanneries to make saddlery and tack for the armies of both South and North; and to farm whatever land was farmable, logging it over and plowing and planting year after year until the thin topsoil had washed down into the Monocacy, thence into the Potomac, and finally out into the great Chesapeake Bay itself—the nutrients gone with it.

Thus was a great New World forest eons old reduced to a rubble of stumps and rutted fields in scarcely more than a couple of hundred years. By the early twentieth century, prosperity was long gone from the Catoctins, and those few old families left in the mountains could just barely piece together a subsistence living from the ruined land.

When Franklin Delano Roosevelt came to Washington as president in 1933, the devastated Catoctins, just sixty miles from the White House, seemed to him a perfect place to undertake a conservation experiment. The new president had two priorities. The first was to save the banks. The second, which turned out to be harder, to save the land. As he said of his own land in Hyde Park, New York, "I can lime it, I can cross-plough it, manure it and treat it with every art known to science, but it has just plain run out—and now I am putting it into trees in the hope that my great-grandchildren will be able to try raising corn again—just one century from now." What was good policy for Hyde Park, FDR figured, could be demonstrated to the nation as a whole, most especially on behalf of the starving owners of the "run-out" hill farms and woodlots all along the Appalachian chain. And he was, moreover, a lover of trees and forests for their own sake, not just as restorers of land. "The forests," he said, "are the 'lungs' of our land, purifying our air and giving fresh strength to our people." Accordingly, in 1935 the federal government purchased some ten thousand acres of the Catoctins as a Recreation Demonstration Area, to be administered by the National Park Service and the state of Maryland. The idea was simple: Do the necessary reforestation and erosion control; then let the land alone, using it only for hiking and fishing, and see if it would heal itself.

As it turned out, the strategy actually worked—and in half the time, even less, that Roosevelt had given it. The mountains were looking pretty good by the 1940s. And today, after nearly sixty years, the Catoctin woodlands seem to have been there forever, innocent of axe and plowshare, despite the remnant cellar holes and stone fences.

Indeed Roosevelt was so keen about the experiment and so optimistic about its outcome that he had the CCC (Civilian Conservation Corps) build a lodge in the Catoctins to which he and family and friends would repair on summer weekends to escape the heat of Washington in those pre-freon days when the stinks of the Potomac and the miasmic mosquitoes caused all who could afford it to flee the city for a bit of upland air. FDR called the place Shangri-la, after the mystical mountain realm in James Hilton's popular 1933 novel, *Lost Horizon.* Later the lodge would be renamed Camp David by President Dwight D. Eisenhower in honor of his grandson. Since then, much expanded and more luxurious, it has been the venue for high statesmanship—such as the peace talks between Egypt's Anwar Sadat and Israel's Menachem Begin—and has continued to provide a handy respite from the quotidian duties of presidents and their immediate staffs.

The lesson of the Catoctins, then, should be a reassuring one. Something to do with the inspirational timelessness of forests, with the capacity of nature to heal itself, and with the benevolence of presidents—at least some of them—who know of the goodness of woods and are inclined to look out for them. That it did not work out this way, given the hopeful origins of the Catoctins' renewal, is surely troubling for anyone who loves trees and the natural landscapes where they may grow. Given the sudden widespread appearance of this extraordinarily infectious disease—dogwood anthracnose—it is hard not to wonder if there may not be a metaphysical message in the physical events that the scientists have observed. Is the lovely dogwood, a tree without major economic importance, sending us a sign, a warning, as its last gift before it disappears altogether?

In Appalachian folk legend, it is said that at one time the dogwood grew to the size of the great oaks and other forest trees that now tower over it, that so strong and straight was its timber that the dogwood was used for Jesus's cross. Because of this, the dogwood felt shamed—deeply grieved that it should have been put to such a cruel purpose. And so the Lord took pity on the tree, saying, "Because of your regret, I make you this promise: Never again shall the dogwood tree grow enough to be used for a cross. Henceforth it shall be slender and shall be bent and twisted, and its blossoms shall be in the form of a cross—two long and two short petals. And henceforth this tree shall not be mutilated nor destroyed but cherished and protected forever as a reminder. . . ."

I suppose it *was* a sort of pilgrimage, our going to the mountains each spring to visit our altar-trees, or at least intending to. And every spring someone would say, "My, aren't the dogwoods lovely this year," as if this season's display had exceeded even the memory of all seasons past. "Yes," another would reply, "lovely." And of course that was always true. Only now, the dogwoods, those small beacons of hope, do not bring forth their gifts, despite the divine promise.

Have we been away from the woods for too many springs? Perhaps so. How did it happen? How *could* it happen? Who, or what, has really killed these trees so suddenly? Surely the causes are complex. Else how is it that so many other trees are dying, too? In the next chapter, the red spruce of Vermont is the victim, and the death of other trees is reported in chapters after that. So must we roam the dark and lonely forests to seek an answer, hoping that if there is to be one, it will be in a language we can understand. Or have not forgotten.

2

Vigil at Camel's Hump

We vainly wrestle with the blind belief
That aught we cherish
Can ever quite pass out of utter grief
and wholly perish.
—*Robert Frost*

In a red farmhouse in the hills of green Vermont lives a gentle botanist named Hub Vogelmann. For thirty years he has, with sorrow, watched trees die at a place called Camel's Hump, a dozen crow-miles from his farmhouse in rural Chittenden County. Hub (for Hubert) has the leathered lean face, the strong jaw, and the iron-colored hair of a man who has spent long years out of doors, which he has. He looks rough-hewn, which he is—in the sense that his manner is direct, unapologetic, unaffected. He carries his learning, which is considerable, lightly. Best of all, he is kind to strangers. "You are a gardener, aren't you?" he asked me as soon as I had told him that I wanted to know about the red spruce on Camel's Hump—that having witnessed the dying dogwoods in my Appalachian outliers to the south, I wanted to learn the how and why of tree death at this northern end of the mountain chain.

I was about to bring him back to the topic at hand, but he was ahead of me, just as he has been ahead of many of his colleagues in matters of acid rain (more exactly, "acid deposition") and its effect on trees. "You learn a lot when you garden," he continued. "You find out how subtle shifts in weather patterns, or the chemical balance of the soil, or the amount of sunlight and water, can make a big difference. But let me tell you, a forest is much more sensitive than that. Forest trees live in a very competitive environment, unlike your garden. They are forever hanging on by their fingernails. A forest is a very delicately balanced system that can be pushed very easily, can be dislodged very easily as an ecosystem. That is what a lot of people are missing when they say they cannot find a direct linkage between air pollution and forest decline, especially at a place like Camel's Hump."

On this matter, Vogelmann is in a position to know, for he has monitored the fate of red spruce as well as balsam fir (among other species) on the high-elevation slopes of this mountain—third highest in Vermont—since 1965. The work of Hub Vogelmann, and of the Forest Decline Program that he established at the University of Vermont, has produced, on a sustained, long-term basis, perhaps the most coherent understanding of the *mechanisms* of acid rain impacts on forest trees of any undertaking in forest ecosystem monitoring in North America. Significantly, the work has been done without U.S. government funds; the Vermont scientists have had complete freedom from subtle or overt pressures to modify their techniques or their conclusions to conform to politically inspired research objectives. I had thought this issue to be minor at the outset of my studies, but it turned out to be a central feature in the American tree-death story, especially in the East and the Northwest, as we shall see.

Camel's Hump is in a Vermont state forest in the northern part of the Green Mountains. At an elevation of 4,083 feet, it is nothing special as a dramatic peak, but because it lies in a northerly latitude the higher parts of the mountain contain boreal forest—the greenest of the Green Mountains. Moreover, Camel's Hump has great symbolic value for a state that values symbols, especially symbols of its independence. Vermont, not one of the original thirteen colonies, was originally called the Hampshire Grants, a "land between" New Hampshire and New York, both of which claimed the territory. The people living in this limbo, sick of the waffling of the Continental Congress concerning their statehood, declared themselves a republic and took the name Vermont, derived from the Latin root words meaning "green mountain." At length, after the machinations of Ethan Allen and the Green Mountain Boys, Vermont was accepted into the Union as the fourteenth state on March 4, 1791, the first of only two former republics to join (the other being Texas). It was dubbed "the Old Rooftop State" in the early days, in acknowledgment of its magnificent mountains, which are depicted in the state's seal. Specifically, what the seal reveals is the outline of Camel's Hump—the quintessential Green mountain. Camel's Hump *is* Vermont.

When Hub Vogelmann arrived at the University of Vermont to take a teaching job in the botany department in 1955, the forest cover on nearby Camel's Hump was green, dense, and seemingly healthy. As he wrote in a later article, "The red spruces and balsam firs that dominated the vegetation near the mountaintop thrived under high rainfall and cool temperatures. The trees were luxuriant, the forest was fragrant, and a walk among the conifers gave one a feeling of serenity—a sense of entering a primeval forest." Indeed, Vogelmann noted, the upper slopes had never been cleared, perhaps not even high-graded, the practice of logging off the largest trees. Certainly, the farmers round about shouldered an ax from time to time and trudged up the mountain to fell a useful maple for furniture, or skidded out a giant spruce for framing members for a house. But the forest up on Camel's Hump was probably, in Vogelmann's view, as close as you could get to pristine in Vermont. This was the forest as it was supposed to be—not the "forest of sticks," as he called it, the result of unremitting cutting and clearing in most parts of the state from colonial times forward. Here on Camel's Hump, some of the spruces stood a hundred feet tall and were over three hundred years old.

Once he had explored Camel's Hump, Vogelmann knew he had found a model mountain for comprehensive studies of a stable, largely undisturbed forest ecosystem with two different forest types: an upper-elevation coniferous zone with spruce and fir (and some birch), like the forests located in much more northerly latitudes; and lower down on the slopes, a more typical Northeastern deciduous woodland of maples and beeches and all the trees that in fall make Vermont such a riotous display of color. The idea was definitely not to find out what was *wrong* with the trees on Camel's Hump. As far as Vogelmann knew, they were fine. The idea was to provide primary ecosystem data so that natural scientists of all kinds would have baseline statistics to use, whatever their field of study—mycology, zoology, entomology, geology, or forest ecology.

Accordingly, in 1965, Hub Vogelmann, with a graduate student named Tom Siccama doing most of the legwork, conducted an exhaustive inventory, locating study plots at every two-hundred-foot rise along a line running to the mountaintop to provide an accurate census of the trees and other plants there, and to record their quantity, size, growth patterns, and state of health. In addition, they analyzed the forest soils; they set up instruments to measure precipitation, air temperature, soil temperature, wind speed; they recorded all the variables other scientists would need to know as essential background data for their particular studies. This was to be a contribution to pure science, altogether elegant. Dr. Vogelmann was at peace.

Then, beginning about ten years later, says Vogelmann, "We knew something bad was happening to the forest." He and his colleagues began to notice that trees—particularly the red spruce—were dying at the higher elevations. So Vogelmann and a new group of graduate students and assistants returned to the mountain to resurvey the plots that had been surveyed before. By comparing what had existed in 1965 with what they found in 1979 when they finished the second survey, they could tell, quite accurately, just how much damage had taken place.

In the 1965 baseline study, as well as in the 1979 assessments and those that came after, Vogelmann used three different kinds of measurements to determine the composition of the forest stands by species: the *density* of live trees of a given species on a per-hectare basis (a hectare being about two and a half acres)—in other words a simple tree count; the *basal area* of live trees expressed as square meters of "wood" per hectare, which is the aggregated diameter of live trees at "breast height" (a forester's terms signifying a measurement taken at roughly four or five feet up the trunk); and the total *biomass*, meaning the total weight of material per hectare expressed in kilograms. A "tree" was considered to be any "stem" greater than two centimeters (about an inch) in diameter. Vogelmann and his associates found that, where there had been 506 red spruce per hectare in their test plots in 1965, the number had declined to 261 ten years later, a drop of 48 percent. In terms of basal area, the red spruce had dropped from 8.21 square meters per hectare to 4.75, a decline of 42 percent. In total biomass, red spruce had started out at 37,000 kilograms per hectare in 1965, but by 1979 had plunged to 22,300 kilograms, a loss of 40 percent. Whatever way they sliced the statistics, the mortality of the red spruce was dramatic and frightening.

Not all species declined, however. The balsam fir did not appear to be affected at all, or at least not much. There was a significant decline in the numbers—though not of basal area and biomass—of white (or paper) birch, which grows among the spruce and fir at higher altitudes. Lower down the slopes of Camel's Hump, in the deciduous woodlands, the mountain ashes seemed to be holding their own, but not all the maples. The mountain maples were especially devastated, with some 73 percent of stems lost; the striped maple lost 49 percent. Less dramatic statistically but alarming in its implications was the fate of the beloved and commercially valuable sugar maple, whose numbers were reduced from 863 to 558 per hectare, a decline of 35 percent. (I shall return to the sugar maple in a later chapter.)

But it was the death of the red spruce that was so vividly alarming in the high elevations. As Vogelmann described it, "gray skeletons of trees, their branches devoid of needles, are everywhere in the forest. Trees young and old are dead, and most of those still alive bear brown needles and have unhealthy looking crowns. Craggy tops of dead giant spruces are silhouetted against the sky." As the big spruces died, Vogelmann noted, the strong winds whistling through the forest of Camel's Hump would overthrow the dead trees and create a kind of domino effect: other trees, newly exposed to the wind by the loss of a giant sheltering spruce, would themselves blow down, so that whole segments of the forest were laid flat.

After Vogelmann learned that the dying red spruce was a scientifically verifiable fact, through the statistically reliable comparison of 1965 data with that collected in the 1979 survey, it remained to determine what the problem was. For Hub Vogelmann the prime suspect was acid rain and other forms of air-pollution deposition—a logical enough deduction. By the time he and his colleagues had completed the 1979 follow-up study, acid rain was much in the news. President Jimmy Carter and the Canadian prime minister, Pierre Trudeau, were even then moving toward an accord (aborted later by the Reagan administration) that would reduce the impact of acid precipitation on the thousands of lakes and ponds of New England and Ontario, some of which had become utterly devoid of fish. Moreover, by the late 1970s, European scientists had begun to identify acid deposition as the likely cause of the decline of Norway spruce in the Black Forest of Germany and elsewhere.

And yet, practically the minute Vogelmann and his colleagues suggested that acid deposition might be killing the spruces and other trees at Camel's Hump, a chorus of dissent arose—for by that time acid rain had become a political issue in the United States, not a subject of scientific inquiry. In an exasperated article prepared for the *Journal of Forestry*—foresters being among those slow to grasp the significance of findings like those on Camel's Hump—Vogelmann complained about delays in strengthening air-pollution policies in the 1980s. "The common excuse," he wrote, "is that we don't have all the facts. This is ridiculous. We don't have all the facts about almost anything in our very lives. Such timidity is like the apples and oranges fallacy: If you can't prove statistically at the $p = 0.001$ level that apples are redder than oranges, then they aren't different. What has happened to common sense?"

Common sense depends to a large degree on taking the long history of forest decline into account—not just dealing with short-term phenomena. In fact, according to Robert Mello, a Vermont lawyer and author of a monograph on the decline of the red spruce in his state, the history has been longer than most realize: it dates to the early 1950s. It was then that a U.S. Forest Service plant pathologist named Paul V. Mook, stationed in Amherst, Massachusetts, learned that some big red spruces were dying up in the Green Mountains. At first he and his assistant thought that maybe their death was caused by a fungus disease, but ruled that out. Only 6.4 percent of the trees were dead anyway, so the Forest Service men put it down to "overmaturity," a catch-all term that people who cut trees for a living (or provide services to those who do, in the case of the USFS) use in order to rationalize logging off the biggest trees. The assumption is that "overmature" trees are going to die, so they might as well be cut. Of course, since any full-size tree that is dead or close to it can be judged "overmature," such an assessment can, and often does, conceal other factors that may be causing tree death or decline. Whether this was the case with Dr. Mook cannot be known, for he simply observed that, at high altitudes, on shallow, well-drained soils, trees are stressed, and he left it at that.

Ironically, when two preeminent acid-rain research scientists—Eugene E. Likens, then of Cornell, and Yale University's F. Herbert Bormann (in 1972 the first to call attention to acid-rain effects in the United States)—searched the databases for changes in rainfall from a normal acidity for Northeastern woodlands to something significantly lower, they discovered that such a shift did in fact occur shortly after 1950, at the very time when Dr. Mook was deciding that the dead red spruce in Vermont were overmature. And the shift was a significant one statistically. In northern woodlands normal rainfall (all of which is slightly acid) has a pH of 5.3. Likens and Bormann found that after 1950 the pH had declined from the normal level to between 3.8 and 4.0. In the scale of acidity, pH stands for "potential of hydrogen," a measure of hydrogen ion concentration in a solution. Perversely, the lower the number, the greater the acidity (pH 7 is neutral, i.e., neither acidic nor alkaline). In considering the Likens-Bormann findings, it is important to understand that the pH scale is logarithmic—that a pH of 4.3 is ten times more acidic than the normal 5.3, and that 3.3 is one hundred times more acidic than normal.

Despite Likens and Bormann's findings, however, a causative connection between acid rain and forest decline took another twenty-five years to be established in the United States, where the government has generally wished to suppress the idea. Nevertheless, scientific articles, at first a trickle, and then a flood, began appearing on both sides of the Atlantic during the 1970s and 1980s. In Europe they concerned tree death in the Black Forest of Germany—*Waldsterben,* "forest death"—and elsewhere in northern Europe. In the United States and Canada there were corresponding articles concerning forest decline in high-elevation sites in the northern Appalachians, such as Camel's Hump. On both continents, the findings were widely disbelieved. To admit to linkage might cost industry dearly in depolluting technologies, and international economic competition was beginning to heat up. Thus, when Vogelmann published an article in *Natural History* based on his rigorous measurements of dying spruce between 1965 and 1979, he was on the receiving end of a good deal of abuse, including a vituperative letter from a well-known and highly respected forestry professor in New York State. As Vogelmann (pacing in an agitated way before the fireplace in his Vermont farmhouse) told it to me, his colleague had said that he had hiked all over the Adirondacks, and that if the spruces were dying he would know it, and that Vogelmann was doing science and the nation a great disservice by being "alarmist," and, presumably, pushing the figures. "He just ridiculed me," said Vogelmann. Even ten years later, he felt the sting of the rebuke, the motive for which he still fails to understand. That he has been proved right—with the most recent data showing red spruce dying at the rate of some 75 percent in high-elevation areas—gives Vogelmann little comfort.

The European researchers had the same problem. "They didn't believe me," complained soils scientist Bernhard Ulrich of Göttingen University. "I went out into the forest to show them what I had been seeing, but it took at least two years to convince foresters that there was something going on. Now we realize that this has been going on for 20 or 30 years."

What was happening to the trees in northern latitudes, in Vermont and Europe, was complicated. Researchers found that the effects of acid deposition on whole forests, as well as on individual tree species such as the red spruce, were even more subtle, and more alarming, the more they looked into it. At the beginning of acid-rain research, only the hydrogen ion concentration was measured, simply to determine the degree of acidity. Early research, as Bormann and Likens have pointed out, dealt mainly with the effects of acid rain on lakes and ponds in northern Europe and in the northeastern United States and eastern Canada. However, they wrote, "With the discovery of *Waldsterben* in Europe and spruce dieback in the United States, further attention shifted to forests [and] as understanding and measurement ability have increased, estimates of the magnitude and severity of the air pollution problem have grown."

The upgrading of estimates of the pollutants' impact on trees and forests took two forms. The first was the recognition of a greatly increased number of toxic agents and their interactions—oxides of nitrogen and sulfur, ground-level ozone, and the deposition of toxic substances that did not occur in nature. But there was another factor that Vogelmann's research revealed: the number of years that these toxic agents had been building up in forest soils and in the trees themselves. When Vogelmann studied core samples of the oldest trees on Camel's Hump, he found that for most of their lives the trees showed varying amounts of growth, as revealed by the width of the growth ring, consonant with natural forces such as climate and cyclical insect attack. But then, at about 1950, the rings began to narrow. "A lot of trees don't show change," Vogelmann told me in describing his findings. "But a high percentage do show a slowing of growth in the 1950s." Something was happening besides bugs and weather.

At the University of Massachusetts, a team of chemists analyzed a core sample from a 200-year-old red spruce, and another from a 110-year-old sugar maple. They found that in both samples the "background chemistry" did not change at all until the early 1900s. Then, at about 1920, the tree rings were discovered to contain chemicals not present before—in fact not present in the natural environment. One of these, said Vogelmann, was vanadium, a by-product of the combustion of fossil fuels generally, but produced at a much higher rate by the burning of fuel oil as opposed to coal. As the great factories were built in the river valleys to the west of the northern Appalachians, which stand athwart the prevailing winds, the vanadium increased, year by year, but especially so when the change was made from coal to oil as the fuel of choice for factories and electrical generating plants. Indeed, one way to chart the changes in fuel use in the American Middle West would be to graphically compare the shipments of coal and oil to the region; another way would be to study the tree rings from an old red spruce and an old sugar maple from Camel's Hump, Vermont.

In a roundup article on the Camel's Hump research by University of Vermont scientists Richard M. Klein and Timothy D. Perkins, the coincidence of pollution products showing up in forest ecosystems in Europe and America is compelling. "Tree ring analyses and other studies," they write, "suggest that the initiation of forest decline in the northeastern United States, adjacent Canada, and Central Europe all date to about 1950–1960. . . . While making correlations is a dangerous game, this was the same period when alkaline fly ash was eliminated, when construction of tall stacks on power plants allowed pollution to be widely dispersed, when the high-compression automobile engine resulted in increases in nitrogen oxide emissions, when leaded gasoline became common, and when smelting and refining operations were greatly expanded."

Aside from oxides of nitrogen and sulfur, other strange elements (beside vanadium) showed up in the core samples of the spruce and maple—elements that do not occur in natural forest systems, such as arsenic and barium, both products of factory emissions carried long distances. In post–World War II tree rings, traces of highly toxic heavy metals—cadmium, zinc, lead, and copper—were found, too.

But there was yet another metal involved: aluminum, which could be the most toxic of all. To try to understand the mechanism, Vogelmann studied the research of Bernhard Ulrich, who had long been working on the puzzle. Ulrich had found that, instead of importing the metal directly from exogenous pollution deposition, as in the case of other metallic elements, trees were taking up aluminum directly from the very soil in which they grew. As it happens, aluminum is a common constituent of forest soils almost everywhere, but it is "locked up" in aluminum silicates, and in this compound form is not available to trees and other plants, and therefore is no danger to them. But after the acid rains came, beginning in the 1950s, the silicates were broken down, and the aluminum was freed to be taken up by trees and plants. The metal kills the roots first. This means that trees can no longer absorb and transport needed nutrients, such as phosphate, calcium, and magnesium—essential fertilizers that are themselves leached away from the soil by acid deposition. Thus the aluminum's effects are multiplied exponentially as the acidification increases. The trees are weakened and can be invaded by insects or pathogens or succumb to extremes of weather—or all of the above, in which case they die.

It was surmised, too, that the acidic compounds in the soils would likely affect the roots of trees in other ways. In fact, Vogelmann and his crew found that in areas with high levels of acid deposition, tree roots were devoid of a beneficial type of fungus growth—mycorrhiza—which covers tiny and fragile feeder roots with a corallike mantle that enhances the uptake of water and minerals by the tree. In an exhaustive sampling of Camel's Hump tree roots, Vogelmann's associate Richard M. Klein could find no mycorrhizal fungi anywhere on spruces. To confirm that the cause of this disappearance was likely to be air-pollution deposition, Klein exposed two different kinds of fungus known to produce mycorrhizae to acids and heavy metals in concentrations typical of those found on the mountain. He discovered that the growth of the beneficial fungi was significantly retarded.

Another soil-based effect of acid deposition the Vermont researchers studied was the disappearance of those beneficial organisms that chew up fallen needles and other litter on the forest floor into pieces tiny enough that they can break down, and their stored nutrients can be returned to the soil. As the acidified forest duff builds up, new seedlings, especially of spruce, are suppressed—not only because their roots cannot reach through the dead plant material to reach down to mineral soil, but also because the accumulated litter encourages the growth of ferns which give off substances that inhibit seedling growth of red spruce. This effect is yet another aspect of what Klein and Perkins alliteratively describe as the "complex cascade of causes and consequences [of pollution deposition] whose end is not yet in sight."

So far, then, the cascade of causes and consequences on Camel's Hump includes the effect of the acid itself in acid rain, cloud water, and in other forms of wet and dry pollution deposition; ozone, such as that produced by automobiles (the particularities of which I will describe at greater length in a later chapter); the deposition of toxic compounds, such as heavy metals, from Midwestern industries; the liberation of toxic aluminum from the forest soil itself and the leaching away of primary nutrients from these soils; the loss of mycorrhizae on feeder roots; and the loss of beneficial insects to break down the exponentially accumulating litter under dead and dying trees, thus suppressing the growth of new trees.

But there's more: a phenomenon known as nitrogen saturation. To a degree, the nitrogen, a primary component of industrial air pollution (along with oxides of sulfur), might even be thought a good thing. After all, to return to Hub Vogelmann's homely metaphor of the garden, it is nitrogen (among other fertilizers) that makes the tomatoes grow. And yet, as it is to tomatoes, an excess of fertilizer is harmful to trees. In a natural forest, nitrogen levels are ordinarily low, and this condition tended to mask the effects of nitrogen imported via air pollution—mostly in the form of ammonia—until the mid-1980s. According to John D. Aber of the University of New Hampshire, however, "In the past five years, evidence has accumulated suggesting nitrogen availability in certain forest ecosystems in excess of plant and microbial demand." Aber identified three stages in the process of nitrification. The earliest stage involves increased deposition with no ecosystem effects evident—indeed, the fertilization may result in increased tree vigor, at least temporarily. Then subtle negative effects begin, although they are largely nonvisual and difficult to measure. In stage three, the effects become all too apparent—as in the case of red spruce at high elevations in the northern Appalachians, with the loss of needles and of fine roots. Camel's Hump was stage three.

Aber and other scientists also believe that the imported ammonia is directly implicated in the killing of the beneficial creatures that help compost the forest duff. Moreover, the ammonia poisons the forest mosses that contribute importantly to the recycling process by breaking down the logs and limbs on which they grow. On Camel's Hump, in fact, Vogelmann found that the mosses had declined by 50 percent and that most of the earthworms were gone. The net result is not only that the trees are stressed, but that forest soils themselves become impoverished, with no way to break the vicious cycle of pollution impacts that holds them in a nearly permanent grip.

There is a final item in the cascade of causes and consequences, a retribution for pollution that seems almost biblically apt. Trees, as Franklin Delano Roosevelt was fond of pointing out, are the "lungs of the land." Every schoolchild learns how the green leaves take in carbon dioxide and other gases, and then release oxygen, the element that makes life possible. In recent years, we have learned that the worldwide emission of what are now called "greenhouse gases" threatens to exceed the capacity of the planetary biomass—including the trees' leafy lungs—to keep up. The trees that remain on the planet are, therefore, utterly necessary to our survival in this regard. And yet, in forests suffering the effects of long-term pollution, such as those in the northern Appalachians, the trees can actually *produce* nitrous oxide, itself a greenhouse gas. John Aber writes, in what seems to me a truly frightening statement in its implications: "Nitrogen-saturated forests may become net sources of nitrogen rather than sinks. The environmental effects of nitrogen saturation over large regions could then be considerable in terms of both nitrate leaching to streams and ground water and nitrous oxide flux to the atmosphere."

One searches for a human metaphor for the tragic irony of lifesaving, oxygen-producing trees becoming net producers of the very poisons they are intended to absorb—of the industrial emissions that, unless curtailed by resolute action, could unravel the web of life on the planet that has given *us* life. It is as if all the boats that have come to deliver us from the beaches of Dunkirk were designed to sink in midchannel.

There are demurrers aplenty, of course, for all these presumed causes and effects of air pollution as determined through the research at Camel's Hump and elsewhere. Recently, I heard a University of West Virginia forestry professor, who evidently had not read about nitrogen saturation, offer the view over a radio talk show that air pollution from the Ohio Valley was the best thing that could happen to the commercial forests of his state. He told the audience that pollution would make the trees grow, that all those environmental extremists were wrong, that air pollution was good for trees.

Other scientists, less willing to be Pollyannaish about pollution, suggest that the dying of trees at places like Camel's Hump is, despite everything, a predominantly "natural" phenomenon. Actually, they do not prove that the causes are natural, but only that they are not necessarily, or in every case, wholly *un*natural. Findings like these are unsurprising to ecologists like Vogelmann, whose approach tends toward the study of complex interactions rather than highly specialized findings. But such findings, seized upon opportunistically by those politically opposed to air-pollution legislation, succeeded in delaying legislative action for a decade. And even after legislation was passed (in 1990, with insufficient recognition of the role of nitrogen, many now believe), scientists and other experts beholden to industry continue to provide a rationale for legislators and government administrators who wish to delay and frustrate implementation of air-pollution regulations.

The 1990 Clean Air Act amendments, a significant achievement in environmental policy despite its flaws, provide for the annual reduction of sulfur dioxide by ten million tons by the year 2000 and of nitrogen oxide by two million tons by 1995. The reductions are to be managed via an EPA–administered air-pollution "credit" system, wherein the right to pollute can be traded from emissions source to emissions source, so long as overall goals are met. Almost as soon as the bill was enacted, however, Vice President Dan Quayle's star-chamber Competitiveness Council started dismantling it. Their first move was to allow individual polluters the "operational flexibility" to *increase* pollution so long as state authorities registered no objection within seven days of receiving notification of the increase. One effect of this was to cut EPA out of the loop, and let polluters deal with often more compliant and less well organized state government authorities that might easily find it convenient simply not to respond to the notification. The Competitiveness Council was abolished early in the Clinton administration, but the lesson is clear: Whenever scientific data are in dispute, even by a small minority of scientists, there's always a way to ignore the warnings of the majority and frustrate laws that are based on them.

Outcomes such as Quayle's effort to undermine the Clean Air Act amendments are not, of course, necessarily sought by the demurring scientists. In many cases they are motivated by a valid scientific interest in, and commitment to an understanding of, all the mechanisms through which air pollution might be operating to cause the death of red spruce and other trees in the mountains of the Northeast. Two such were Arthur H. Johnson, a University of Pennsylvania soils scientist, and Vogelmann's former student, Thomas G. Siccama, now of the Yale School of Forestry. Johnson and Siccama's research was financed by the U.S. government's ten-year, five-hundred-million-dollar National Acid Precipitation Assessment Program (NAPAP), now concluded.

While agreeing that the red spruce at high elevations were showing loss of foliage and dieback, and while fully aware that a rough scientific consensus had emerged that the tree death could not readily be explained by "current models of usual stand dynamics and forest growth," Johnson and Siccama nevertheless maintained (as did many others at the time) that the pathology did not *necessarily* indicate the involvement of air pollution. In a paper rounding up all the explanations other than air pollution, they cited the infestation of spruce budworm; a series of unusually cold winters following warmish autumns (which subjected new growth to hard freezes); and anomalies in tree-ring studies that showed that a decrease in size of growth rings was not invariably tied to high acidity in rain or cloud water or to soil acidification, since they had found such decreases in areas not subject to acid deposition. Moreover, historical tree-ring data showed that there had been times in the past, before the post–World War II era, when a severe dieback of the spruce had occurred. Johnson and Siccama did not rule out air pollution as a contributing factor, but suggested that there were questions still remaining to be answered in terms of the exact mechanisms by which pollutants were affecting the trees.

As a result of the mountains of statistics accumulated by the many scientists set loose by grants from NAPAP—some of which seemed, on the surface, to contradict the findings of Vogelmann's long-term research on Camel's Hump—the U.S. Forest Service undertook its own effort to determine what was happening in the Northeastern woods. In

1990, Forest Service specialists set up 118 monitoring locations throughout the region, 57 of them in spruce-fir forests, of which 7 were located in Vermont. While they did not measure changes over time, as Vogelmann had done on Camel's Hump, the Forest Service did assess the current "health" of the forest as shown at its monitoring stations, which were intended to represent the New England forest as a whole. According to this research, which looked at needle discoloration, dieback, and at certain indicator herbaceous plant species sensitive to changes in air quality, only 0.2 percent of the red spruce, so devastated on Camel's Hump, showed severe dieback. Ninety-three percent seemed to be healthy. Taking the region as a whole, there's no problem, the government concluded. "The summary of crown ratings data," their report asserted, "indicates no pattern of major decline in any species."

This is the kind of overly generalized, commercial forestry approach that drives Hub Vogelmann and his fellow ecologists nearly to distraction. In the case of the Forest Service's assurances about the Northeast, their research measured gross quantities of *wood* in the form of standing trees on a commodity basis, i.e., after the spruce had died, not the more complex (and significant) issues of long-term biological change. The apparently conflicting findings clearly illustrate the difference between real science and the mere collection of statistics for narrow purposes. "The best of science," writes Harvard biologist E. O. Wilson, "doesn't consist of mathematical models and experiments, as textbooks make it seem. Those come later. It springs fresh from a more primitive mode of thought, wherein the hunter's mind weaves ideas from old facts and fresh metaphors and the scrambled crazy images of things recently seen. To move forward is to concoct new patterns of thought, which in turn dictate the design of the models and experiments." Where Vogelmann was striving to concoct new patterns of thought in the forward quest for knowledge, the debunkers seemed fixed in place, sniping from the rear. As a tool for discovering truth, statistics obviously must serve science. But they are not the same as truth itself.

The truth, as Vogelmann told me there in his Vermont farmhouse—in the closest thing this quiet, unassuming man has to a bellow—"doesn't take a genius to understand. It doesn't take a genius to know that something is happening when seventy-five percent of the spruce die on Camel's Hump." And a lot of other trees, too, for that matter. Since 1965, Vogelmann said, only one species had increased in growth—the white birch. But that was because so many other trees died, letting light into the forest, which in turn encouraged the birch. In any case, the growth spurt did not last. Soon enough they too had gone into decline.

"What you've got," Vogelmann continued, "is seven or eight species—balsam fir, spruce, yellow and white birch, sugar maple, mountain maple—all declining. And there were no diseases. No gypsy moth. No spruce budworm. The obvious agents were missing. At one point, people were looking all over for armillaria fungus as a reason the trees were dying, but the higher up they went in elevation, the less they could find of it, so that there was no correlation. That's why we suggest that something brand new is happening to our ecosystem.

"When we began to publish on the decline of the forest on Camel's Hump, we were approached by NASA to use the area for remote sensing studies, since our ground data were so good. They wanted to see if they could pick up dying and stressed trees with high-altitude photography. And they could. You can see the dying trees on the western slopes but not on the eastern slopes, which tells you something about pollution and prevailing winds. Big pieces of forest were affected. And it showed that with increasing elevation there was more damage, and that the western part of the Northeastern forests were hit harder than the eastern [another effect of prevailing winds carrying airborne pollutants]. The greatest damage is in the Adirondacks, the next greatest in Vermont, and the next New Hampshire. All this stuff adds up. We have a problem, and it is a man-created problem." Finished, for a while anyway, Vogelmann sat down.

At about the time of my visit, the latest findings from Camel's Hump were being analyzed. Studies had been made not only in 1979, comparing forest damage to the 1965 baseline data, but also in 1983, 1986, and 1990. With regard to the 1990 figures, there was, as Vogelmann put it, no doubt about it. The red spruce decline was continuing—though it was statistically leveling off, since most of the spruce were already dead. Where the decline between 1965 and 1979 had taken nearly half the trees, the 1990 figures showed a decline of yet another half. In terms of the basal-area measurement, the most commonly used, the red spruce had declined overall from eight square meters of live trees per hectare in 1965 to about two square meters in 1990. The sugar maple was continuing its decline as well, as was the mountain maple, now virtually extinct on Camel's Hump. The balsam fir, which had not shown much decline prior to 1986, also began to be diminished.

There was, however, an interesting countertrend in the red spruce statistics. While the biomass and basal-area measurements showed continued decline, the density measurements—the gross numbers of trees two centimeters or more in diameter—seemed to show a tiny bit of recovery between 1986 and 1990. The seedlings seemed to be coming back. According to Tim Perkins, one of the authors of the 1990 study, this finding did not suggest, however, yet another instance where the causative chain between acid rain and tree death was shown to be weak or broken. Instead, when fully understood, the apparent contradiction may reveal a new causal factor that was not considered before.

Perkins told me that government-sponsored acid-rain researchers had suggested that the spruce, weakened by acid deposition, were dying from extremes of cold. The implication here would be that, as pollution is reduced and as weather returns to more normal patterns, all would be well with the red spruce after all. But Perkins, Vogelmann, Klein, and the other scientists at the University of Vermont's Forest Decline Program believed that the effects of extreme cold on the trees was more complex and considerably more serious. As Perkins put it to me, "NAPAP says that acid rain reduces cold tolerance of trees. We say that the trees on Camel's Hump are sufficiently cold-tolerant to be able to withstand extremely low temperatures." But, I asked, if that is true, how come most of the trees died over the last twenty-five years, but are now seemingly coming back? It was Hub Vogelmann, replied Perkins, who had come up with an answer to the riddle—a "rapid freezing phenomenon."

The phenomenon obtains on cold winter days that are nevertheless sunny and bright. Warmed by the radiant energy of the sun, just as a skier at Stowe might shed her jacket on a cloudless day on the slopes, so too would the needles of the red spruce "open up," exposing delicate stomata—the pores in the needles used to exchange carbon dioxide for oxygen in the process of photosynthesis—to the newly perceived warmth. In effect, the tree, like the skier, would respond not to the temperature of the air, but to the temperature of its own needles. For them, it is suddenly summer as their deep green coloration soaks up the rays.

What happens, though, when the sun suddenly goes behind a cloud? The skier, who has tied her jacket around her waist, quickly dons it to avoid a chill, and turns her back to the rising wind. Ordinarily, a red spruce would do something of the same nature, quickly retracting its pores so that only the needles' protective waxy coating was presented to the elements. What Vogelmann and his colleagues found, however, was that the red spruce on Camel's Hump were unable to make this transition quickly—at least not quickly enough, on a really cold day, to avoid rapid freezing. The reason was that vital nutrients, calcium and magnesium, had been leached from the trees and the soils by acid deposition, which in turn lowered the metabolism of the trees so that they could not respond quickly enough to a rapid drop in temperature. It was as if the skier, weakened by malnutrition, were unable to pull on the jacket, and would therefore perish.

Thus did the mature red spruce die from the cold (among other causes) on Camel's Hump, while those few seedlings that beat the odds began the long slow process of regeneration, protected through the hardest part of the winter by a shielding blanket of snow. But their safety was only temporary. Once they grew above the level of the snow, they too would be vulnerable to rapid freezing and death. The point of this story is an important one to grasp. In many incidents of forest decline, it is not the mere presence of air pollution that causes the trees to die, but indirect effects as well. In the case of the red spruce of Camel's Hump, air pollution had, over the years, robbed the forest soils of the essential nutrients that could serve to protect the trees—nutrients that are now, for the most part, gone forever.

"Even if you stop pollution altogether," said Tim Perkins bleakly, "the trees will die just as soon as they get big enough not to be protected by a snow cover. Thus, curing the problem may not be so simple, to the extent that the problem is in the soils and not in the air."

All is not well in the Rooftop State—a state defined by the old Appalachian mountains, repeatedly glaciated, worn by eons of erosion from wind and water, clothed by a forest in which there is now a sickness.

State historian and native son Charles T. Morrissey has observed that a sadness has always pervaded Vermont. Despite the attractiveness of the state to retirees, ski bums, and summer people from Boston and New York, an underlying poverty remains. The natives, with their characteristic twang, have for centuries scrabbled a hard living from the fields and woods of this place.

"Woodchucks," the sleek patrons of resorts and the owners of condos and the gentleman farmers call them. Vermonters forgive such boorishness, for they have the mountains, the mountains that Camel's Hump, so faithfully studied over the years, symbolizes. But now what? The mountains are dying, and the agents of their demise are invisible chemicals produced a thousand miles to the west without a by-your-leave or apology. Without, in fact, a willingness even to consider the possibility that the chemicals are importantly implicated, or to accept the right of Vermonters to suppose otherwise. The suggestion is that the dying of their trees is merely local and unimportant.

Hub Vogelmann can tell you two stories about the future of red spruce. One is that maybe the spruce can survive after all. "There are areas where you can find perfectly healthy specimens," he said. "Possibly, they are of a different genotype. Given a long enough period of time, these more resistant trees may be able to take hold. In our greenhouse experiments, some of the plants that were really hammered with pollutants were just as healthy as the control plants being fed clean air. So given time, nature may heal her wounds."

On the other hand, and of course there always is an other hand in such matters, Vogelmann says this: "I just don't know where the point of no return is. My best guess is that the forests will not recover for a long time, no matter what we do. I suspect we may have permanently damaged the soils environment. Given the amount of acidity that has been introduced at high elevations, my guess is that we have permanently altered these soils, reduced the levels of productivity. Maybe for thousands of years."

As a practical matter, that is more years than we are able to reckon—even on the "Spine of Time," as writer Harry Middleton has called the old, worn Appalachians. And down along the spine, from New England to Carolina, time is running out.

3

ON TOP OF MOUNT MITCHELL

. . . and they'll tell you more lies
Than the crossties on the railroad
Or the stars in the skies.
—from "On Top of Old Smoky,"
American folk song

From the red-dirt piedmont of North Carolina, where folks in the days before air conditioning and television sat up past midnight on summer evenings sweltering on their porches, or went to bed wrapped in wet sheets to cope with the unbearably hot climate, where the woods round about are viny and jungly, the fields hard-baked, hard-panned, and gullied out, there rose, in serene relief from these untidy surroundings, Mount Mitchell, like a kind of miracle. I decided to make this mountain my next stop, for at its summit one could stand in the middle of a wonderful, if relict, patch of cool green coniferous forest that you might expect to see in Canada, but certainly not in the southern United States.

In this unlikely boreal zone, whose highest point is 6,684 feet—the highest place east of the Mississippi—the "dominants," as botanists say, were stately red spruce and Fraser fir, standing sentinel over what seemed like a whole continent spread in ranks of smoky-blue mountain ridges stretching westward. The ecosystem had adapted to the harsh circumstances of a cold, windy, and fog-ridden mountaintop climate, and to soils that had mostly washed away eons ago. The evergreens' roots sought anchoring crevices at the rocky summits, and clung precariously to the steep slopes. But they managed, as they had managed for tens of thousands of years. Managed even to be cheerful, for it would smell like Christmas here all year round, owing to the scents of what the old timers call he-balsam (red spruce) and she-balsam (Fraser fir) eddying through the thickets, giving the crisp clean air moving across the Blue Ridge a holy quality, as if one were in some primordial sanctuary.

At least that's the way it used to be. Today, the visitor to Mount Mitchell will find the deep green forest at the summit, and down the slopes from it, dead—a great pileup of fallen tree trunks, now weathered and lifelessly gray, heaped in disarray like giant jackstraws lying across each other, like human bodies after a great holocaust. It looks like a war zone up here, and perhaps it is. Unlike the dying of the trees on Hub Vogelmann's Camel's Hump, which took place over several decades, the laying low of the forest on Mount Mitchell took just a few years.

This was not the first time the spruce-fir forests of Mount Mitchell and its sister peaks of the Blue Ridge had been ravaged, although this time the agent of death was different. The relict population of conifers on these mountains was unmercifully logged off in the early 1900s, for the red spruce are valuable timber trees—straight-grained, strong yet light in weight. The soft wood was easy to cut, too, even before chainsaws, and so millions of trees—firs as well as spruce, though the former were of marginal commercial value—were skidded down the steep slopes until the mountaintops were all but denuded. Such might have been the end of this forest right then and there, for in the southern Appalachians, the spruce and fir are slow to regenerate. As leftovers from the Ice Age, they had been stragglers in the boreal forest's northward march behind the retreating glaciers. Conceivably, they might not have made a comeback at all, to be replaced by the ordinary deciduous trees that grow on the lower slopes. Knowing this, North Carolina conservationists, with the help of President Theodore Roosevelt, persuaded the state government to set Mount Mitchell aside as a park in 1915. They acted in time. The red spruce and Fraser fir began to recolonize the cut-over areas. Then, twenty years later, the National Park Service built the Blue Ridge Parkway, giving millions of visitors easy access to the coniferous forests of the southern Appalachians.

As it turned out, the reprieve was relatively short-lived. Once again the trees have been killed, this time not by the bite of the woodsman's axe, but in substantial part by the silent, invisible chemicals of the industrialized river valleys—the Ohio, the Tennessee—far to the west and south. Such has been the understanding of most, at any rate. Acid rain.

I had long heard about how there was something the matter with the trees on Mount Mitchell from some cousins of mine, who own "Sandy Bottom," a summer place along the Toe River near Celo, North Carolina, where we sometimes have family reunions. You can see the trees up on the high ridges from their front porch. They are dying, they started telling me a dozen years ago. And each ensuing year, as it got worse, they would tell me again, because they knew I was interested in such matters. We stay in touch in this family about important things: births, marriages, deaths—and the death of trees. Then, when I visited Sandy Bottom in the late 1980s, they handed me field glasses and asked me to take a look, which I did. The foreshortened perspective of the binoculars revealed a line of bare dead trunks tipped this way and that like a blasted stockade fence at an abandoned garrison. So I drove up the narrow mountain road to see for myself. To paraphrase Shelley, hell must be a place very much like Mount Mitchell.

My cousins had warned me about this. They had said to be prepared for a shock, since I had last visited many years before the trees started dying. They said the reason the trees were dying was acid rain. Though they had no special knowledge of forest ecology, I was inclined to take them seriously. These are not Gomer Pyle types, these Carolina cousins. Of the three who own shares in the summer place beneath Mount Mitchell, two are noted physicians and the other a circuit court judge. As prominent men of science and the law in North Carolina, they are deeply concerned about the state of the environment, as well as the environment of their state.

But when I got to the top of the mountain, I was astonished to learn that the "official" explanation about the devastation on the summit and upper slopes of Mount Mitchell had nothing to do with acid rain at all. In fact, as I was to learn later that day, the forest was not even dead! An explanatory set of educational posters then displayed at the summit parking lot (they would later be changed, as we shall see) discussed a creature called the balsam woolly adelgid (familiarly the "woolly aphid," although it is not an aphid, but a European import that looks like a tiny tuft of white lint) and drought and hard winters. The official state brochure for the place had not one word about the dead trees, although I was surrounded by them. When I inquired about the effects of acid deposition at the state's visitor center, down the hill from the crest of Mount Mitchell, the obliging ranger gave me a brochure published by the Spruce-Fir Cooperative, a federal program of the U.S. Forest Service and the Environmental Protection Agency to investigate the "decline, reduced growth, [and] death of spruce-fir" all along the Appalachian chain from the Blue Ridge to Vermont and New Hampshire. I looked through it for a summary of findings about Mount Mitchell. While the text told of the decline of coniferous forest in New York and New England, and said that the spruce did not seem to be as healthy as they might be throughout the Great Smoky Mountains of North Carolina and Tennessee, there was no mention of acid deposition or even of any particular problem on Mount Mitchell or nearby areas. Instead, this surprising statement: "At the three intensive [meaning intensively studied, presumably] sites in the Southern Appalachians, standing dead red spruce range from 5 to 13 percent." The brochure added that the "culprit" in the death of Fraser fir on Mount Mitchell was the balsam woolly adelgid.

Five to 13 percent was not what I witnessed at Mount Mitchell. More like the obverse of that—87 to 95 percent. Was the idea that the dead trees were not really "standing" anymore, and so should not be counted as dead? If so, this was a bit of rhetorical dissembling that flew in the face of what any ordinary person visiting Mount Mitchell would surmise to be the truth. The truth was a massive arboreal catastrophe that the statements of the Spruce-Fir Cooperative's brochure belied. According to the abstract of a peer-reviewed scientific article by R. I. Bruck and W. P. Robarge of North Carolina State University, the fact of the matter was this: "Along ridges, and particularly on west-facing aspects, greater than 80% of all mature stands are dead." That statement, at least, comported with what the eye could perceive. "Certain high elevation areas," wrote Bruck and Robarge, "are now completely devoid of any living spruce or fir trees above 10 cm DBH." (DBH means "diameter at breast height." Ten centimeters is about four inches. Typically, mature red spruces are one to two feet in diameter.)

As for the role of the woolly adelgid, the plots selected by Bruck and Robarge for examination (over a four-year period) were not those the insect had already infested, but those where such infestation was absent. But the trees died anyway. Later, Bruck determined that the adelgid was responsible for about a third of the fir-tree death, despite the claims of the Spruce-Fir Cooperative implying that the pest was the sole cause. The adelgid does not attack spruce.

Some time later, in a great deal of puzzlement—and concern, for the complex causes of tree death on Mount Mitchell seemed too important an event to me to be so dismissed—I had the opportunity to visit with Dr. Robert Ian Bruck in his lab at North Carolina State University in Raleigh. It was an important visit for me, not just an interview.

Bruck turned out to be thirty-eight years old, a full professor (remarkable at his age), and a top scientific adviser to the governor of the state. He speaks emphatically, does Robert Bruck, his bald head bobbing atop a thickset frame. He looks like he might be a college wrestling coach instead of a plant pathologist. He has the assertive, husky voice and the confident, forthright manner of an athlete. I told Bruck about the inconsistencies between ordinary perceptions and the odd "finding" of the Spruce-Fir Cooperative. I had also dug up another scientific conclusion, from a report from NAPAP, that dealt with the Mount Mitchell phenomenon. From it, I read him this passage:

> . . . the high rate of red spruce mortality between 1986 and 1987 [on Mount Mitchell] appears to be largely due to ice storm damage which occurred in the 1986–1987 winter. It is difficult to determine what other factors throughout the late 1980s may have played a part in the worsening of crowns because of the large impact of ice damage. The opening of stands due to the death of Fraser fir from the balsam woolly adelgid and pronounced drought are natural factors which may contribute substantially to the condition of red spruce.

"Fraudulent," said Bob Bruck flatly when I finished reading. He wanted me to understand, of course, that the *scientific findings* contained in the description of research activities covered in the main text of this NAPAP report were accurate. It was the official conclusion that was fraudulent because, he said, midlevel government officials had insisted on selectivity in terms of what data to present, and they had required that the politics-driven conclusion at the back of the book gloss over inconvenient findings.

In fact, Bruck had a point. While I found that the main text in several of the NAPAP reports was quite useful in studying the research base on acid rain, it did seem to me that the conclusions of the reports—the material that would be looked at by policymakers, journalists, and others—seemed to be written by someone else, and without reference to the preceding material. I have had just enough experience in government to know how bureaucratic group-write can turn the most clear-cut data into an incomprehensible blob. But there was something more going on here, suggested by Bruck and confirmed by my own textual analysis. I was on the verge of outrage myself when I described the curious disjunction between findings and conclusion to a Washington lawyer, an inside-the-beltway type with long experience in the political vetting of government-agency-sponsored scientific reports. He gave me a pitying look. "Of *course* the government is going to skew the conclusions to meet the needs of their agency's constituencies," he said. So it goes.

Robert Bruck was hardly the first to complain about the NAPAP reports. In 1987, when an interim report was issued, scientists and environmentalists bitterly attacked its conclusions as misrepresenting the facts. According to an account in *The New York Times*, "They contended that it tailored research findings into conclusions that matched the political goals of the Reagan Administration which opposed new controls on air pollution." Three years later, when a draft of the final report was being reviewed, similar criticisms were voiced. In contrast, and perhaps tellingly, the electric power industry was pleased with the conclusions of the final report, as was the forest products industry. Alan A. Lucier, an author of NAPAP Report 16 (there are 27 special reports in all), which I had quoted to Bruck, told a conference at Hilton Head, North Carolina, assembled to discuss the draft, "The data does not support the contention that there is an unusual decline or any sort of decline in the Southern Appalachians." Lucier served NAPAP as an official representing the National Council of the Paper Industry.

Significantly, none of Bruck's many papers were among the four hundred cited in the draft of the final "integrated" report. In NAPAP

16 three of his papers are listed, though they apparently failed to influence the report writers—or at least those who dictated the soothing language of the conclusions, reflecting, presumably, Dr. Lucier's view. But something more than academic pique was going on in Bruck's mind. As it happened, the reason Bruck was so angry just then about governmental fudging with respect to environmental science was that he had just returned the day before our visit from one of the most nightmarish object lessons in government suppression of scientific fact on earth—the Black Triangle of eastern Europe.

The Black Triangle, so named by its inhabitants, is a large industrial area bounded on the west by Dresden (in the former East Germany), on the east by Wroclaw, Poland, and on the south (at the apex of the up-side-down triangle) by Prague, Czechoslovakia. One place Bruck visited was a Czech forest research station at Frydlant, on the Polish border. "We were standing right in the middle of one hundred six square miles of dead Norway spruce," said Bruck. "It had been fumigated to death." He said that huge areas in the Black Triangle were 80- to 100-percent dead—which recalled the statistic that he had determined for Mount Mitchell.

"Here's the big question," he continued. "Where is the threshold? Where is the magic line that once you pass it you have irreversibly damaged an ecosystem? We're talking about soils in eastern Europe so acidified they have a pH of 2.4. That's so low, tree roots just rot when you put 'em in there. There isn't any point in trying to reforest the area."

What especially shocked Bruck, an American scientist used to the freedom to publish findings without government suppression or even (in better days) the kind of gloss provided by the conclusions in the NAPAP report, was not just the career-damaging dangers of scientific forthrightness—dangers that he himself had been affected by—but by the risk of one's physical person—of life, of family, and of future—at the hands of an authoritarian bureaucracy. "The minister of environment in Czechoslovakia told me," said Bruck, "that if he had given me such information in the old days—such as the pH of the soils—he could have been sent to Siberia. He said that if I were caught at the border with the data he had given me, maybe no one would ever see me again. This forest death was top secret, and the world was not to know what they had done to the environment." Apparently, however, the Central Intelligence Agency *had* known. Our intelligence satellites could tell that the forests were dying in the 1970s and 1980s, Bruck said, but had kept the news from the public, because they had believed—with the twisted Cold War logic that is now beginning to sound quaint if not irrational—that such an environmental catastrophe was in the U.S. interest to sustain. The comrades should be permitted to destroy themselves, even at the risk of permanent damage to ecological stability in a sizable part of the planet.

Now, since the collapse of the Communist monolith in eastern Europe and the Soviet Union, the rest of us know. "In one chemical plant," Bruck told me, "six thousand workers are dying a slow chemical death." He paused for a moment in silent recollection. Usually Bruck is a nonstop talker. "Outside the plant," he continued, "where I puked up my lunch from the stench, they showed us a lake, some seventy-four acres in area, eighty feet deep. The lake was white. I took a rock and threw it into the lake and there was no splash. It just sat on top of the white water. Only it wasn't water. This was no lake! It was twenty-two million metric tons of arsenic carbonate sitting on the surface of the ground—from the gasification process that they use to make the hydrocarbons needed for the manufacture of chemicals. Pure arsenic. Think of the groundwater underneath—for miles and miles."

Infant mortality, Bruck learned, was 17 percent—seventeen times worse than the worst state in the U.S. on this score. Various types of cancers, including leukemia and carcinoma of the liver and brain, were 40 percent greater than the U.N.'s World Health Organization standards. Emphysema, chronic bronchitis, and asthma were at twice the levels of U.N. standards. In some areas of the Black Triangle, ten percent of all live births resulted in infants with crippling birth defects. In a diary he prepared partly for his own purposes and partly as a formal report to the U.S. Department of State, which had sponsored the trip, Bruck wrote, "I have had fairly extensive experience in studying environmental problems in many areas of Asia, Central and Western Europe, and all of the North American continent. I believe it is fair for me to state that I have never encountered quite the environmental nightmare that I observed in eastern Europe."

The trees had all died first, of course, giving a warning. But people were constrained—on pain of arrest and banishment, if not death, Bruck told me—not to object. After the trees died, the people began to die. It was a powerful message, and made a powerful impression on young Dr. Robert I. Bruck. There could be no better example of the need for ecologically sustainable development than the devastation of the Black Triangle and of other places in eastern Europe. And there could be no better case for the necessity to tell the scientific *truth.* The destruction of ecosystems was a price the ambitious Communist leaders believed was worth paying to out-industrialize the West. For a brief period it had worked. During the 1950s and part of the 1960s, the Soviet economy grew faster than that of the United States. But upon seeing the result, Bruck, and others who have studied it, have come to realize that the Communists' investment in industrial development failed in the end not only in economic terms, but also by creating an ecological deficit that is all but permanent. In the case of the forests of the Black Triangle, Bruck does not believe that the deficit can be paid down in less than a thousand years.

What of our own ecological balance sheet for the trees? For Robert Bruck, the killing of the eastern European forests struck close to home, not only ecologically but politically—for he saw, in the exclusion of his Mount Mitchell findings from the official reports, a shadow of what had so appalled him in the coverup of the enormous environmental crime he had personally observed in eastern Europe. The causes of tree death in Frydlant were different from those on Mount Mitchell, but the attempt to conceal the truth about it was the same. It is perhaps in the nature of governments of all kinds, democratic or totalitarian, to keep the lid on. But to Bruck, keeping the lid on Mount Mitchell was not then, nor is it now, consonant with our traditions of free, disinterested scientific inquiry, and the right of citizens to know the facts, even though such public knowledge may affect the market price of stock in a forest products company, a proprietary producer of electricity, or an automobile manufacturer.

Let us go on with this for a moment. According to the noted Viennese-born philosopher Karl Popper of Cambridge University, objective knowledge, which is to say *scientific* knowledge, does not just happen. It must be won, and won the hard way. First, says Popper, you must form a concrete hypothesis based on all the data and observations of a phenomenon that are available. Second, you and others must try to prove the hypothesis false by collecting contrary data and observations and by making experiments. At length, if the effort to disprove the hypothesis fails, and you have exhausted all the ways you can think of to carry on any further experiments in order to contradict it, then the hypothesis may be accepted as a *theory*—a theory in the same sense that evolution is a theory. A scientific theory, not just a rhetorical one.

During the late 1970s and early 1980s, available data and observations in Germany, Sweden, Norway, and neighboring countries, and in Canada and the eastern United States, suggested that acid deposition was at least one causal factor in the severe decline of forests along mountain ridges. The assumption was a logical one, since research has shown that air pollution was rendering lakes and ponds lifeless in Scandinavia, Canada, the Adirondacks, and in northern New England since the early 1970s. So a corollary hypothesis could be framed to deal with trees: Just as acid deposition had damaged the waters of lakes and ponds in these areas, so too may it be implicated in the alarming degree of tree death and forest decline in the spruce-fir forests at high elevations in the same areas—in Europe as well as along the Appalachian chain.

In addressing themselves to Popper's requirements, European and Canadian researchers were able, in due course, to negotiate the gauntlet of falsification successfully. That acid deposition was attacking trees, causing them to succumb (although not always as the *proximate* cause) became accepted by virtually all investigators, if not as solid theory, then as the nearest thing to it. "Beyond all reasonable doubt," wrote forest scientists D. L. Godbold and A. Hütterman of the University of Göttingen in a refereed journal in 1986, "atmospheric pollution has been shown to be the cause of the present forest decline in West Germany." Such observations are as frequent in the European literature as they are rare in the papers of U.S. scientists. *Waldsterben*—the "forest death" that, beginning early in the decade of the 1980s, decimated stands of silver fir, Norway spruce, and European beech in the Black Forest of Bavaria, and later throughout Germany—is not verboten to mention. In recent years, the generalized condition has been called *neuartige Waldschäden*, "new types of forest damage."

In America, too, new types of forest damage were identified by scientists at about the same time. Many of them also presumed it to be the result, directly or indirectly, of air pollution. And yet, despite the expenditure of great quantities of scientific time and government money on research, American scientists do not, as a rule—except with tortuous circumlocution—assert a cause-and-effect link between air pollution and tree death or forest decline. Indeed, those few American scientists (like Robert Bruck) who have been as forthright about the forests of the eastern U.S. as Godbold and Hütterman were about those of Germany, have been branded ecological fanatics. For that reason alone, and with the lessons of Frydlant firmly in mind, they may be worth our attention.

Bruck told me that when he was a young assistant professor he was selected (in 1984) to join a team of nine American scientists to take a look at the *Waldsterben* in Germany, long before the nightmare of the Black Triangle became common knowledge. What they saw then was in many ways just as shocking to them as the Black Triangle would be later. Ellis Cowling, associate dean for research at North Carolina State's College of Forest Resources and a leader of the team of which Bruck was a part, later wrote an account of their trip. What they observed, he said, were "scientifically unprecedented changes in the behavior of forests taking place in Germany." For example:

- Simultaneous and rapid decline of forests involving both needle-bearing trees and deciduous hardwoods—a general thinning and change of color.
- The active "casting"—dropping—of apparently healthy green leaves and shoots, which littered the forest floor.
- Leaves and shoots that had grown abnormally, smaller than usual and misshapen, and which were distributed along their stems in unnatural ways.
- In the case of spruce and fir—and perhaps the oddest symptom—the formation of nearly vertical "hanging" branches.
- "Distress" crops of cones and seeds in some species. Such crops occur after a dry spell or insect attack and happen only once. In Germany, the trees had produced distress crops three years in a row, which was unheard of.

Another survey, conducted at the time by European scientists, reported that a third of all West German forests were so affected. Others reported that in some stands, all mature trees were dead. Three years later, over half the trees in Bavarian forests were dead or severely damaged.

With these data in mind, as soon as he returned from Germany, Bruck collared three graduate students and drove them up to Mount Mitchell. His reasoning was simple: If *Waldsterben* had started at the higher altitudes in the spruce-fir forests of Bavaria, why wouldn't the same thing obtain in North Carolina? He had known for some time that red spruce were dying in New England, but "we had the highest-elevation Appalachian spruce-fir forest right here in our own state, and even though it is almost 7,000 feet high, the trees go right to the top, unlike high elevations in New England. I told the students, 'Let's go up there and look around, see what's happening.' "

What they found was a slight amount of damage that year, 1984. It was serious, but nothing that was necessarily unexplainable by the natural cycles of health and disease in such forests. Even so, he and the graduate students took core samples from the trees and soil samples from the earth beneath them and drove back down the mountain. Bruck arranged for one of the graduate students to take the stuff over to the labs for a chemical analysis and then turned to other matters.

"The next day," said Bruck, "I got a call from the lab. They said, 'Get your ass over here, Bruck. You're not going to believe these numbers.' " The numbers were just like the ones coming out of Europe. The soils were full of cadmium, lead, mercury—all indicators of severe air-pollution deposition. Later measurements found levels to be four hundred times greater at the top of Mount Mitchell than at the base. An examination of tree rings revealed that significant growth suppression had started at about 1960.

Bruck and his crew wasted no time getting back up to Mount Mitchell to set out permanent experimental plots so that they could accurately measure the changes taking place. And the changes were rapid. Three years later, said Bruck, "The forest began to fall apart—a complete dysclimax in a very short period of time. About the only kind of dysclimax that might be quicker would be a forest fire." A "climax" forest is one that has naturally attained dynamic equilibrium, having reached, through successional stages over a long period, a state where the dominant species are not replaced or crowded out by others. A "dysclimax" as Bruck put it, would run in just the opposite direction.

The problem on Mount Mitchell, Bruck found, was not so much acid *rain* as acid *fog*—and in the winter rime ice created by accumulations of acid fog frozen in place along the needles, branches, and trunks. The rime ice, Bruck told me, occasionally had a pH as low as 2.1—somewhere between battery acid and lemon juice. Winter and summer, fog can sock in Appalachian peaks like Mount Mitchell for up to seventy days a year.

Clouds are like vacuum cleaners in the sky, Bruck explained. They pick up all the pollutants and oxidize them, combining them with water to create new substances—acidic oxides of sulfur and nitrogen—which then join tropospheric ozone (smog) created by sunlight working on (primarily) automotive exhaust fumes as well as on factory emissions. As the clouds rush over the peaks, the moisture in them condenses *everywhere* on the tree—on the undersides of needles, in the crevices of the branches, deep in the grooves of the bark—wetting the tree with a toxic chemical soup more thoroughly than any rain event could. In fact, the greatest amount of precipitation on Mount Mitchell comes through the agency of those wet, high-elevation fogs—twice as much, on a yearly basis, as through rain, sleet, and snow combined. Bruck said that they found the fog on Mount Mitchell to be between one hundred and one thousand times more acid than the rain water falling on the Piedmont cities below.

These were the *secondary* products of pollution, Bruck emphasized, and much more complex and widespread in their effects than the impacts of industrial pollutants such as sulfur dioxide and sulfuric acid (created by SO_2 combining with water and oxygen and falling as rain) on local areas—such as the forest at Frydlant in the Black Triangle or, nearer at hand, in Ducktown, Tennessee. In the so-called Copper Basin area on the Tennessee-Georgia border, copper smelting since the middle 1800s had turned fifty-six square miles of southern hardwood forest into a desert, many parts of which, even today, are devoid of trees. Our own Frydlant.

But unlike the airborne chemistry and transport of automotive ozone, which has been studied since the late 1950s, only quite recently has the U.S. government understood anything about the transport and effects of nitrogen and sulfur emissions over long distances. Indeed, official ignorance of the transport of secondary pollution products is one of the "causes" of acid rain, and consequently tree death and forest decline over unexpectedly large areas.

"Twenty-five years ago," Bruck explained, "the EPA thought it had discovered a wonderful paradigm: The solution to pollution is dilution." In those days, he said, in the industrial cities of the Midwest and elsewhere, the great problem was *ambient* air pollution—the local emissions from the factory chimneys. The answer: tall stacks. Where heretofore the chimneys on factories might be only a hundred feet tall, the EPA decreed that they should be ten times taller. Some even rose to two thousand feet—literally, as Bruck put it, *injecting* emissions into the stratosphere.

Bruck's description reminded me of a brief period during the late 1960s when I was associated with an environmental management consultant whose main stock in trade was the pollution-dilution-solution paradigm. The head of the firm, a former air-quality commissioner for the City of New York, had been utterly convinced that tall stacks in the Midwest would solve the problem of factory emissions forever, and was making pretty good money telling American industry how tall. I was skeptical. "It's hard to believe that the pollution will just go away," I said.

"Listen, Little," he replied testily, "the amount of sulfur dioxide going into the atmosphere from those stacks is minuscule compared to the *natural* quantities of SO_2 emanating from the dead fish along the coastlines of the world." Well, he was the trained scientist, and I the English major, so I simply muttered something to the effect that what goes up must come down. "Nonsense," he replied. Only it wasn't nonsense, at least not entirely.

"What we found up there," said Bruck, speaking of Mount Mitchell, "was a garbage dump of air pollution from the Midwest. But it was a different kind of pollution. It's not SO_2. You can't even *measure* SO_2 up there. We tried. It's just not there. What's happened is that gases are going out of the stacks, five hundred miles away, and mixing with cloud water and creating sulfate, nitrate, sulfuric acid, nitric acid. That's not the gas that went *up;* those are products of photochemical oxidation that then get dumped *down* on the mountain."

No wonder the trees were dead. In 1988, Bruck was asked by *New York Times* reporter Phil Shabecoff whether he was absolutely sure the cause of the death of trees on Mount Mitchell was air pollution. "Ninety-percent certain," Bruck replied, explaining that the pollution generated from industries in the Ohio and Tennessee valleys, together with ozone from automobiles and other sources, were combining with the natural stresses affecting the trees on Mount Mitchell—high temperatures, drought, and the dreaded woolly adelgid in the case of the Fraser fir. The result was, and is, a catastrophe. And so beautiful, remote Mount Mitchell, the cool peak in the midst of the folded Appalachians, a seemingly pristine place, has the air quality of a Los Angeles suburb. Worse, actually, if you are a tree.

While I was thinking about this, Bruck was still talking. Remarkably, he was talking about what I was thinking about, which was: Why wasn't a 90-percent certainty significant to the overseers of official American science?

"I have given presentations to industry groups," Bruck said, "and I always begin by asking them to accept the truth of the statement, 'Air pollution is bad. I don't say how bad, a hundred dollars bad or a million dollars bad—just bad.' I tell them: 'If we do not accept that as a tenet of our discussion, there is no point in having a discussion and I am out of here.'

"And you see everybody swallowing their olives, and their martinis start coming out of their ears, because a certain segment of corporate society is paid to say exactly the opposite. There's nothing wrong with air pollution, they say. That's the smell of money, they say. But I say, we as a world society are going to have to start dealing with the realities: you cannot use this legal bullshit argument about proving things. What you do is get the best damn mechanistic correlation you possibly can —correlations that make sense.

"I can do experiments in the greenhouse that show that red spruce are harmed by ozone and acid deposition. Then I go up to the mountain with a good atmospheric chemist. And we measure—we measure ozone, we measure acid deposition, and we say, 'My God, the levels up on the mountain even exceed what we were doing in the greenhouse.' Now a greenhouse experiment does not by definition *prove* that something is going on up on the mountain, but boy it sure is good solid evidence.

"Take the example of smoking. If you have a thousand smokers over here and a thousand nonsmokers over there, and if there's a lot of sick people in the first group and healthy people in the second group, you do not need eleven PhDs to tell you that smoking is bad for your health. But it does not *prove,* scientifically, that smoking *caused* the sick people to get sick. You wanna know how to *prove* it? First find five thousand young pregnant women, each carrying identical twins. Then perform simultaneous caesarean sections on all five thousand women (regular birth might stress some of them). Take the babies out and instantaneously—do not contaminate the experiment by letting them take one breath—put half the babies into a chamber receiving nothing but carbon-filtered air for the rest of their natural lives. Put the other ones into a chamber getting nothing but cigarette smoke at a level of concentration that a smoker would receive smoking an average of two packs a day. Observe for one hundred years. Then you will be able to show direct linkages between certain diseases—emphysema, heart disease, cancer—and cigarette smoke versus no cigarette smoke. Now that is a ridiculous experiment, and impossible to do. If I am from the Tobacco Institute, I know that it is impossible, so I smile from ear to ear and say, 'See, I told you so. You can't *prove* it.' Do we in society want to run our lives like that?

"Over the past ten years our government has concluded that 'Environmentalism equals bad economics.' That's exactly what comes out of the science system. Now if I am going to be a good boy and I want to be promoted through the system, and get the grants to do the research, I will sit there and look at you and say, 'Mr. Little, sir, you are not going to get me to say that pollution is killing trees with your tape recorder running. I am a scientist. A scientist does experiments, and no experiment I have ever done *proves* that air pollution is hurting those trees. Thank you and can I go now.' That's the answer we scientists must give to cover our butts. And it is bullshit."

With that, Professor Bruck stopped and clamped his mouth shut for a moment. He looked agitated. His eyes swung to a wall clock in his lab-office, then back to me, then at the clock again. "Jeez, look at the time!" He leapt to his feet and made for the door, pausing just before his bald head disappeared around the corner. "Go back up to Mount Mitchell," he said. "Now, right now. It'll break your heart." And then he was gone. The room fell silent, the tape recorder still turning noiselessly.

There is a difference, of course, between scientific caution and all-too-human timidity. Bruck is suitably cautious, but not at all timid. A good many scientists, like Bruck, believe that the circumlocutions of their colleagues—the inability to get beyond the point of "reasonable doubt"—arise because of timidity, because a finding of *causality,* a clear link between air pollution and forest decline, was politically unacceptable to the executive branch of the government of the United States during the 1980s, and to a large contingent of its legislators even today. These officials have believed, correctly, that economic harm would ensue, at least for the short term, if acid deposition were discovered to be decisively implicated in the death of trees. It would mean that the "cost" of pollution could no longer be externalized by the purveyors of the ubiquitous automobile, or the managers of factories and power plants whose tall stacks send clouds of pollutants eastward on the prevailing winds to come to earth on the needles of Appalachian spruce and fir. It would also mean, to the forest products industry, whose primary assets are standing timber, a possibly disastrous plunge in the valuation of these assets—which would be reflected in the share price of the stock of publicly traded companies. Since a part of executive compensation (usually in the form of stock options) is often tied to stock market performance, it is perhaps unsurprising that the executives of forest products companies would wish to gloss over anything that seems like bad news regarding forest health.

Accordingly, since the federal government was footing the bill for research whose policy outcome the leaders of that government wished to influence, scientists were not asked to find out what was happening to the trees (which would have been the right kind of question), but were asked to provide incontrovertible proof, if they could, that acid rain was in effect the critical problem. Drought, cold, pests—wherever abnormal forest declines were found—would have to be eliminated as the essential causal agents, since their presence would "contaminate" findings that suggested causal effects by acid rain. The concept of a "preponderance of evidence" wouldn't do. As two scientists involved in the study (Arthur Johnson and Thomas Siccama) put it, "Because of the current political environment in which the research is being conducted, rigorous proof . . . is being sought. . . . The data needs for such proof are enormous."

In the United States, even the expenditure of hundreds of millions of dollars could not meet such data needs. After the thousands of studies, the national director of NAPAP's forest research program, the prime contractor that parceled the money out to university scientists like Robert Bruck, concluded as follows: "Available data show that natural stress factors and stand dynamics are important in causing observed changes of forest condition. However, the possibility that air pollutants are also involved cannot be excluded. Generally more knowledge of local weather, disease, and insect occurrences and other influences—either alone or in combination—on tree growth is necessary before changes in forest conditions can be shown to be related to, or independent of, air quality." In other words, not proven.

Such was the outcome of what a Washington lawyer has called the "constituency interest" of the U.S. government. The apparent strategy to avoid reaching a conclusion was to see to it that phase two of Professor Popper's dictum—to find contrary evidence—would be pursued in such a way that it could never be concluded. Minor anomalies or methodological errors in data collection on the mechanisms of tree death were advanced by bureaucrats as decisive disproofs of the hypothesis. Indeed, the debunkers succeeded in shifting the burden of proof so effectively that in the end it became incumbent on acid-deposition scientists to prove a negative—that in no circumstance or situation was the death of trees partially or wholly *not* a function of acid rain. In fact, a wonderful new theory could be formed that could mollify the public—or whatever part of it had not, year by year, seen trees die along an Appalachian ridge. It goes like this:

1. The trees are dying.
2. There's a strong possibility that acid rain (and other forms of air-pollution deposition) is significantly implicated, but the linkage cannot be proven in every single respect.
3. Therefore, the trees are not dying.

I discovered that fallacy first on Mount Mitchell, with the government brochure's assertion that what I was looking at was not a pile of dead trees, but only 5 to 13 percent dead. If I could only believe what I read, rather than the evidence before me, the U.S. government had worked a miracle: they had brought a forest back to life, albeit invisibly, with a single sentence in a brochure. How in the world could that be? I had asked Robert Bruck this question, and his answer—an American *Waldsterben,* with ghastly political overtones suggested by the Black Triangle as a reference point—gave me no comfort, only a sense of dread.

Indeed, there was a dark irony in Bob Bruck's quixotic tilting at the windmills of a politics-driven scientific bureaucracy—a bureaucracy so fearful of hearing any bad news about forests dying from acid deposition that it demanded absurd levels of scientific "proof" to insulate itself from a reality that Bruck's findings on Mount Mitchell made plain. The irony is that Bruck himself was instrumental in creating the component of the National Acid Precipitation Assessment Program that came to consider him a pariah.

After Bruck returned from his first European sojourn and armed himself with personal knowledge of what was happening on top of Mount Mitchell, he journeyed to Washington to convince the Environmental Protection Agency and the U.S. Forest Service that NAPAP ought to include studies of the effects of air pollution on forest resources. This was to become the Forest Response program, which would generate some twenty million dollars a year in research funds. In addition, Bruck encouraged EPA to establish the Mountain Cloud Chemistry Program. Over the next several years, he published scores of papers on his findings on Mount Mitchell and elsewhere.

All seemed to be going well. Bruck and his colleagues had invested some three million dollars on site preparations, facilities, and equipment on Mount Mitchell. Then, after the official reports started to come out, and Bruck found that his work was scarcely mentioned, he returned to Washington, despite the rebuff, in a desperate quest for grant money to continue. "We are just beginning to ask the right questions," he pleaded. Never mind, he was told. "The acid-rain game is over."

One thing is certain. It is over for the mature trees atop Mount Mitchell. The game is over and they lost. I did, in fact, do as Bruck suggested. After a brief visit with one of my cousins, I drove up on the Blue Ridge Parkway, then took the familiar turnoff to the Mount Mitchell summit. It was winter. Down in the Piedmont a cool rain was falling, but up here it was beginning to snow—enough so that the park authorities had blocked off the road partway up. I pulled the car into a maintenance yard near the padlocked barrier, an orange-painted iron pipe that was the only color in a monochrome landscape of black asphalt, dark clouds, driving snow, and the dead gray of the trunks of spruce and fir. It was a sepulchral place, altogether depressing and gloomy.

These days, Mount Mitchell is just barely mentioned in the tourist brochures. A once-popular destination for Blue Ridge vacationers, it is now evidently an embarrassment. The reverse should be the case. Like the vast ranks of gravestones at Gettysburg, or the list of names of Vietnam dead on the black marble wall of the memorial in Washington, the sobering reality of Mount Mitchell's dead trees should be part of every schoolchild's instruction in misbegotten warfare—in this case a war whose weapons are pollutants and corrupted statistics, and whose victims are the trees.

I took some pictures of the place, as if to gather evidence. But to whom should I send them? I wondered; for something more than trees had died here. Dead too, in some measure, was the spirit of independent, disinterested inquiry—although perhaps not entirely. Had I been able to get all the way to the summit that day, I would have seen a new exhibit, this one with text prepared by Bruck himself, and stating (albeit carefully) that air pollution did, in fact, have a role in creating this desolation of trees.

I wished that Bob Bruck and his students could somehow impart their youthful energy and courage and patriotism (in the true and honorable sense of that word) not just to the text of an educational exhibit, but to the struggling seedlings atop Mount Mitchell. Perhaps then my grandchildren, or theirs, might one summer visit here during a family reunion and feel the clean air eddying through the groves of towering he-balsam and she-balsam, air smelling for all the world like Christmas. But now, on this day, there was no fragrance, just an overpowering sense of loss and missed chances.

4

THE CALIFORNIA X-DISEASE

We travel the Milky Way together,
trees and men.
—John Muir

Having inspected the high ridges of the Appalachian chain at both ends—in Vermont and North Carolina—I decided it was time to go home again, to the younger mountains of the far West. I would, of course, revisit the Sierra Nevada, they being the West Coast analogue of the Appalachians, but first I needed to go back to a patch of the Coast Range, the San Gabriels, the mountains of my childhood so deeply etched in memory. Rising like a great wall, the San Gabriels and the adjoining San Bernardino Mountains, which are part of the same range though often referred to independently, separate the Los Angeles basin, the richest agricultural region in the world when I lived there, from the scorching Mojave Desert to the east.

You could walk to the Mojave if you wanted, theoretically anyway—right up and over the mountains, never encountering anyone. All I had to do was scamper out the back of our house, run through an adjoining vineyard, keeping low behind the vine-rows, sneak past a terrific swimming pool occasionally available to neighborhood kids depending on whom the owner was married to at the time, squirm under a chain-link fence, and there I was in the Angeles National Forest, a true wilderness then—and now, too, since portions of it have been so designated by Congress.

Mostly, though, the boys in the neighborhood (and oddly, there were only boys—about six of us) would just hike up the canyons a ways, to where the rancheros had bored the water mines, or we'd scuttle crablike along the hot flanks of the steep, chaparral-covered lower slopes, winding through thickets of yucca and manzanita whose sinewy red branches we called ironwood.

On the occasional long-hike days, when we could get a bigger boy to go with us, we'd strap on our canteens and take a trailless route way up to the top of the first line of mountains, cross the firebreak, skitter down into a box canyon, trudge up again to the next ridge, and there it was—a place so rare, so wonderful, so *green,* it amazed us. For after surmounting that second ridge, we dropped down into an Eden—a mythic place with huge widely spaced pines—I would guess now that they were mainly ponderosas with perhaps Colter pines and some incense cedars mixed in. The cedars smelled like the pencils we had at school, for that was the wood used for them. But it was the ponderosas that were so amazing, with great yellow-plated trunks, almost as wide as we were tall, rising straight and true to the great vault of blue California sky. "Whoo, whoo," we would yell from the dappled forest floor into the cool green treetops where the jays chattered. It was like a hosanna, made in a cathedral that was so dreamlike that I actually saw it in my dreams for many years, one that came back again and again in the way that children's dreams do.

Now I have returned to the San Gabriels. I could never find that very spot again, I am sure. I have little inclination to try, anyway, for it is likely to be gone—as the dream has now gone. Yet, unlike many good places in California, our ponderosa Eden would not have been leveled by a bulldozer, and it is altogether possible that it escaped fire. Its demise would have been through another agency—what used to be (and perhaps still should be) called the California X-disease.

In 1956, some years after my childhood treks into the San Gabriels, a forester in Lake Arrowhead, California, which is surrounded by the San Bernardino National Forest, wrote a memo to his superiors. It is, possibly, the first analysis of a forest decline caused by the long-range transport of compounds created by automotive emissions.

The forester's name is James E. Asher. He still lives in Lake Arrowhead, and, though retired from the Forest Service, continues to work as a consulting forester. In 1956, Asher was a young "timber management assistant," charged with marking dead trees in his ranger district for "sanitation salvage." In the course of carrying out his duty to identify trees not only dead but in the process of dying, he became attuned to the nuances of forest health. And the nuances were troubling. This is how his paper—now a kind of historical document—begins:

> The foliage deterioration, affecting an increasing percentage of the Ponderosa Pine (*Pinus ponderosa*) forest stands within the Arrowhead Ranger District of the San Bernardino National Forest, has been noted with growing concern. This effect, known as the "X Disease" or Needle Dieback, is causing loss of vigor and thus a lessening of annual increments on an alarming number of trees. Though the causative agent is classed as "unknown," mortality is occurring.

What Asher observed, and described as accurately as anyone since, was something called "chlorotic mottling" in the needles of ponderosa, Jeffrey, and to some extent on other conifers. On a ponderosa or Jeffrey (a high-altitude cousin of the ponderosa) pine, the mottling took place on the inner, or oldest, whorls of needles. The first evidence of the disease Asher described as "a faint yellowing in narrow bands along the needles of these whorls," even though the outer, newer whorls remained green and healthy. Then the affected needles would turn completely yellow and drop off, leaving the tree, eventually, with only one or two whorls of needles rather than four, five, or six—a lonely little tuft of needles at the end of a thin bare branch, making the tree look gangly and weak, which it was. Eventually death would come, often brought about by an opportunistic infestation of beetles or fungus in the weakened tree.

Asher suggested various possible causes of the mottling, including a virus. The deadly virus-X influenza had swept through the human population of the country a few years before, being especially virulent in California, so it would doubtless occur to Asher and his colleagues to give the name "X-disease" to the needle dieback syndrome. But Asher knew that a plant virus (analogous to the human one) was not the problem, just as he knew it was probably not some soil deficiency, either—two explanations others had advanced. And it wasn't the drought either, although there was a severe one in those days, just as there has been in more recent years. Drought kills from the top down to the bottom of the tree, and from the outside needles to the inside. The X-disease was killing trees in just the opposite way, Asher noted, from the bottom up and the inside out.

No, to Asher the cause was obvious: "a heavy concentration of air pollutants borne on to the foliage of the ponderosa pine." In other words, some constituent of smog was the culprit, though the mechanisms by which it afflicted the trees remained a mystery.

Smog was, of course, that clever new portmanteau word someone had made up to describe the combination of fog and the characteristic smoky-colored haze that was even then sliding up the sides of the mountains all along the range, from San Fernando to San Bernardino. Another new phrase much discussed in the newpapers in the early 1950s was "the inversion layer," an atmospheric anomaly courtesy of the San Gabriels. Rising steeply from a foothill elevation of two thousand feet to top out at ten thousand, the mountains serve as barrier behind which the polluted air generated in the great megawatt bowl called LA simply piles up. Driven eastward by cool prevailing winds off the surface of the Pacific, the pollution, especially severe (though less brown) during the summer, accumulates because the air above (influenced by the Mojave's hot currents) is warmer than the ocean-cooled polluted air below. And it is a fact of physics that warm air rises, not the reverse. Accordingly, beginning in the late 1940s, even *before* most of the freeways were built in the land of the three-car garage, commuters came home from a workday in the city with red eyes, scratchy throats, chest pains, and headaches. Particulate matter collected in the lungs. The ladies' nylons melted on their legs.

And James Asher's trees were dying.

Given the growing concern in southern California about smog, Asher's paper, together with other investigations of smog effects at lower elevations in the Los Angeles basin, prompted the Forest Service to look into the matter seriously. Much of the work was pioneered by Paul Miller, the now famous forest pathologist who established a rigorous research program to investigate the mechanisms of death-by-smog that Asher called the X-disease. Miller, a quiet-spoken, modest man, told me during my visit to his Riverside, California, office and lab that in his articles and lectures he always gives James Asher credit for the first paper. Miller's own organized testing of Asher's theory that smog was being carried into the mountains by prevailing winds and was somehow killing the ponderosas was first reported in 1963, showing the results of an in situ experiment up in the San Bernardino mountains wherein branch chambers were attached to pine limbs on test ponderosas, and the effects of filtered air, ambient air, and ozone-charged air were compared. The test showed that the filtered-air limbs got better on X-disease trees, and the ozone-charged limbs got worse, indicating that the *x* in the X-disease was smog-generated ozone.

Then, in a 1966 study, Miller and his colleagues sought a typical test area where they could observe smog damage over a period of years. The plot they finally agreed on contained 150 ponderosa pines, 50 of which were relatively healthy, 50 of which had moderate X-disease-type symptoms, and 50 of which were severely afflicted. When they went back for a final look just three years later, nearly half the healthy trees had become moderately affected by air-pollution damage; two-thirds of the trees that had shown moderate damage were now severely afflicted; and among the trees severely afflicted in 1963, two-thirds had died. Taken together, after three years of air pollution, of the 150 trees, only 28 remained healthy, and some 36 had died. To say that this caused some to worry is to put it mildly, for by the mid-sixties the smog had been working on the trees for nearly twenty years. Those that had died in the test plot could be presumed to be relatively resistant; this suggested that previous damage may well have been at an even higher rate.

A later and quite definitive study conducted by Miller between 1973 and 1978 bore this out. Not only had thousands upon thousands of trees died in the mountains, but they were not being replaced. Instead, a whole new kind of forest was taking over—of more resistant conifers. The problem these new trees—incense cedar, white fir, and some others—pose for the regeneration of the original forest (even should the smog suddenly abate) is that the replacement trees are shade-tolerant and shade-making, producing an environment uninviting for ponderosas and Jeffreys, which want open spaces and sun. In many places, Miller told me, "you simply can't walk through the forest anymore, the trees grow so thickly," and he added, "Why, in the old days you could ride at a full gallop through the forest, with its widely spaced ponderosas, and never lose your hat!"

Miller sent me to Lake Arrowhead to take a look for myself. And the trees *did* seem to be thicker and lower on the whole than in the old days when I visited here at my Uncle Don's cabin on the lake. Ordinarily I would have put such an impression down to imagination, except that there were dead trees visible down the slopes, looking toward the smog-shrouded LA basin, and dying ones at the top of Strawberry Peak.

Trucks, planes, and automobiles—especially automobiles, and especially high-compression-engine automobiles—have killed the ponderosa. In the 1940s, when I was a borderline delinquent and owner (well, part-owner) of a hot rod with what was called a "Winfield B" engine, high compression was the holy grail sought after by us youthful scourges of the California highways. Out on Muroc Dry Lake over in the Mojave (with the hard, smooth surface that NASA's shuttle craft now use to land on after a sojourn in space), this vehicle of ours had attained a clock speed of 122 mph. The engine was a modified four-barrel Ford, with the cylinder head shaved to the maximum extent in order to increase compression, while the cylinders themselves were bored out and fitted with larger pistons so that the combustion chambers were correspondingly enlarged. The valves were "port and relieved" in the cylinder block, and a huge, specially designed carburetor sucked air like a ram jet. Individual pipes rather than a standard manifold delivered the exhaust gases into the brilliant southern California sunshine. The result was like riding an ack-ack gun. It was impossible to drive the car slow. And the engine heat was so intense we had to change the oil constantly, and replace blown-out gaskets.

We did not know it, of course, but every time we cruised into Bob's Big Boy in Glendale, going *vroom-vroom,* the heat in that engine was combining the nitrogen in the air with oxygen, creating oxides of nitrogen that would rise from the parking lot at the drive-in (when there was only one Bob's in the whole world) and, along with VOCs (volatile organic compounds) produced by everything from dry-cleaning fumes to the pine-scented trees themselves, would proceed to catalyze in the presence of the hot California sun to make the ozone—O_3—that would kill the trees we had loved as little children.

What we also did not know was that the mass producers of automobiles in Detroit (and Japan and Europe, too) would adopt the hot rodders' techniques for producing greater engine displacement, higher compression, and improved efficiency in delivering as much fuel as possible to the combustion chambers and exhausting the postcombustion gases quickly after each cycle. The result was massively increased horsepower and torque, culminating in the late 1960s and early 1970s with the so-called "muscle cars" that people bragged about in terms of how many "cubes" they had—referring to cubic inches of engine displacement.

And so, what my fellow delinquents and I produced in the 1940s (and that everyone else produced later on) were the gases that would create *tropospheric* ozone, as opposed to the *stratospheric* kind. The troposphere is the column of atmosphere that occupies the first six miles (ten kilometers) or so above the surface of the earth. The stratosphere takes over above six miles and extends to some thirty miles (fifty kilometers) above the surface, after which the atmosphere ends and deep space begins. The stratospheric ozone constitutes about 90 percent of all the ozone in the atmosphere, and, as nearly everyone has now learned, is essential to life on the surface, for if absent it cannot screen out harmful ultraviolet rays that can otherwise stunt the growth of plants and cause blindness and cancer in animals (including humans), among other unpleasant effects. Tropospheric ozone is exactly the same molecule, O_3, and causes the death of trees, and diseases of the lungs in humans, when it is *present* in any quantity. We cannot live without it up there, and we cannot live with it down here.

The immediate question one would ask is whether or not the O_3 produced in the troposphere above LA and other cities on hot summer days can just rise into the stratosphere to replace the ozone that other pollution, mainly from CFCs (chlorofluorocarbons), is depleting. The answer, according to plant pathologists Sagar Krupa of the University of Minnesota and William Manning of the University of Massachusetts, is: Yes, it can, but only a little. According to their study of the matter, some "20 to 30 percent of the decrease in stratospheric O_3 over middle and high latitudes in the northern hemisphere could be compensated for by . . . increasing O_3 in the troposphere." Krupa and Manning were doubtless aware that there must surely be some industry public-relations executive who would seize on this tidbit of science to justify either the current levels of smog, or the current use of chlorofluorocarbons in air conditioners, refrigerators, foam plastics, and aerosol cans (though most manufacturers have mended their ways in this regard), which devour the stratospheric ozone at such a truly frightening rate. Accordingly, the researchers add, dryly, that the consequences of replacing strato-ozone with tropo-ozone "must be considered in the context of vegetation effects." A nightmare sci-fi scenario comes to mind, of a civilization so habituated to a pollution-generating way of life that the only means by which they can save themselves from certain death from ultraviolet rays is to produce great quantities of smog in a last-ditch effort to replenish the stratospheric ozone layer, if only slightly.

In the real world, some scientists argue that tree-killing smog is created in substantial part by the trees themselves, and therefore the whole business is hopeless anyway. One, an atmospheric chemist from Riverside, California (near Los Angeles), said that his research showed that in one day twelve trees can emit as many hydrocarbons (a constituent of smog) as a 1991-model automobile in a thirty-mile run on the freeways. This finding was dismissed by a California state official, who suggested that air-quality standards should emphasize the reduction of nitrogen (another constituent) rather than the volatile organic compounds, such as the hydrocarbons put out by LA trees. In a study of air pollution in Atlanta, Georgia, however, Georgia Tech scientists found that trees were putting as much hydrocarbon into the atmosphere as any other kind of emission source.

Readers may recall that President Ronald Reagan once suggested himself that trees were polluters. He was right, in the arch sense that he meant it, as a means of chiding overanxious environmentalists. On the other hand, many took him seriously. Yet another nightmare comes to mind, wherein the citizens clear-cut all the trees and then die from a surfeit of poison gases and lack of oxygen. The freeways are still, littered with rusting autos and the bones of commuters, but the ozone layer is intact.

During my California days, under the influence of puberty, we did not consider such matters. But then nobody did, for ozone was only something you smelled in an electric storm. As for ultraviolet light, which had a wavelength beyond the visible spectrum (as we learned in physics class), we needed those special rays for our suntans, which were almost as necessary to us as our cars. We worshipped both the sun and high compression, and we were utterly ignorant of what the combination could produce, and its effect on our edenic groves. And most of us remained ignorant, trading hopped-up cars for the tail-finned gas-guzzlers whose effects James Asher and Paul Miller were to record miles away in the cool California forests.

The ozone-producing smog, from automobiles and other sources, eventually drove my family from their hillside home, which now lies *under* the smog blanket rather than safely above it, to a more benign environment. I had long since fled east to college, and by the time James Asher wrote his paper, I was working in New York. But the trees could not pick up and move. They had to stay where they were and cope with the environment we had given them. They could not migrate, for example, to the Sierras, which we had always thought of as the purest of the pure, the pristine place where God's creation was supposed to operate as God intended.

So that's where I went next—to the Sierra Nevada. To visit, first, Trent Proctor, an air resources specialist for the Sierra National Forest, then Dan Duriscoe at Sequoia National Park, and finally John Pronos and John Wenz, experts in tree death working out of the Stanislaus National Forest headquarters in Sonora, California.

Proctor, in his thirties, is from an old California ranching family whose original holdings were in the Sierra foothills east of the San Joaquin Valley near Porterville, where Proctor's Forest Service office is located. Like many other Californians concerned with natural resources and the environmental impacts on them, Proctor reveals a curious combination of optimism and despair. Optimism (which built this state from a semi-desert supporting a thin population of Indians to the home of Hollywood, airplanes, and the richest agricultural economy on earth) in the belief that human ingenuity can always find an answer to any kind of pickle; but despair that *this* pickle—air pollution created by an inversion layer above and a solid line of traffic below—might be beyond getting out of. For the ozone, far from being confined to the Los Angeles area, has been devastating trees in the Sierra Nevada, too. It would seem almost impossible that the little agricultural towns spread throughout this large central California valley with just two major highways—the old U.S. 99 and the new I-5 that has taken its place—

could produce enough smog to hurt trees in the far mountains of the Sierra. But they do, and it does.

Indeed, the San Joaquin Valley is perfectly shaped to trap pollutants in great enough concentrations so that their rise into the eastward mountains is inevitable. According to Thomas Pittenger of the National Park Service, some pollutants are carried in on coastal air that is pumped through breaks in the Coast Range at San Francisco and San Luis Obispo. The rest are generated in the valley itself. Then, filled with polluted air, the valley's air currents make the delivery of ozone to Sequoia and Kings Canyon National Parks and surrounding national forest areas a daily occurrence during the summer months. Pittenger writes: "The Tehachapie Mountains, a barrier to southward flow, cause an eddy to form in the vicinity of Visalia and Fresno, adjacent to the parks. The circulating load of contaminants is carried into [the parks] by rising daytime air currents."

Said Proctor, as we rode up into the mountains in his green Forest Service van, "We have exceeded the carrying capacity of the air here in California."

After an hour's drive, we arrived at a high ridge overlooking the valley. It appeared to me—under a winter sun—pretty much like the view of LA from Strawberry Peak near Lake Arrowhead. Patches of dead trees were visible on the lower slopes, and on our ridge there was a rather perfect specimen, said Proctor, of an ozone-stricken ponderosa which we could examine. I had already learned from Paul Miller that when there's no visible smog in the valleys, the mountain trees are, ironically, at greatest risk—for the lack of visible smog means that the pollutants have risen rather than remained safely close to the ground below. Proctor discussed this, too, when I observed that it was pretty smoggy down there. "In the summer," he said, "the inversion lifts, so in the southern Sierra we see ozone injury in trees up to about seven thousand feet, and in the northern Sierra about five thousand." He told me that the ozone travels up the steep canyons of the western flank on a daily basis. Others have found ozone-caused tree injury at elevations as high as nine thousand feet.

One of the cruel ironies of ozone's effect on vegetation is that trees at low elevations—in the very areas where the pollution is generated—are much less affected than are those in the mountains, where there is little or no generation of pollutants. Proctor explained the paradox:

"Down in the valley," he said, "where the state of California has traditionally done the monitoring, ozone reaches a peak in the afternoon. At night, when there is no sunlight to catalyze the conversion of the nitrous oxides generated by automobiles into ozone, the NO_x actually destroys the ozone molecules present in the air, so that every twenty-four hours, the air in the valley is cleansed. But up here in the mountains we don't have those nitrous oxide generators. So the ozone resides around the clock, with an exposure time much longer up here than on the valley floor. That means that lesser quantities of ozone may have more effect." An additional reason for the greater impact in the evening, Proctor explained, is that during the heat of the day, the stomata of needles close, especially during dry periods, and tend to open again in the afternoon—at the very time the rising ozone is at its highest concentration and can enter the needles.

Once the ozone is inside the cellular structure of the tree, it bleaches—just like Clorox, also an oxidant—the chlorophyll from the needles, so that they lose their ability to photosynthesize, and then drop prematurely. At high elevations a healthy pine will have up to seven or eight whorls, Proctor said. The sickly tree we were examining had only one whorl left on many of its branches. "Eventually, what you end up with, as the tree loses its needles to ozone—and you have other factors playing a role, too—the tree loses its ability to process food, and ultimately it will die."

The "other factors" Proctor was referring to include attacks by the fungus-carrying pine bark beetles, which can wipe out quite large patches of pines. If the immediate causes of most tree death in the Sierra are pests and disease, the initiating cause, in areas afflicted by the gases rising out of the San Joaquin Valley, is ozone. "People just don't realize that urban problems can show up in the wilderness," said Proctor as we climbed back into his van, "but that's what ozone does."

My next stop was Sequoia National Park, to visit Dan Duriscoe, who had recently published a survey of ozone damage. Duriscoe, whose degree is in physical geography, told me about his studies during a walk to one of his favorite spots—Sunset Rock—which overlooks a complex of High Sierra peaks and canyons stretching away into the far distance, beyond sight of highways and cities on the plain many miles to the west. Here in the park, Duriscoe told me, a third of the ponderosa and Jeffrey pines showed ozone damage, including 10 percent with significant injury—a surprisingly large number, considering that his study averaged together vast areas of the interior of the park far from ozone sources with those continuously exposed on its western, San Joaquin Valley side. "In the ten years I've been in this area," Duriscoe said, "last year the mortality of pines and conifers in general has been the most dramatic." Earlier studies in the park have shown that in some of the drainages subject to the air pollution "eddies" that Pittenger described, ozone injury has been found on as many as nine trees out of ten. "The whole point of our ozone research up here," Duriscoe told me, "is to collect evidence to show clearly that air-pollution standards should take upwind impacts on vegetation into account. Under the Clean Air Act, the federal standard is .12 parts per million for ozone, and the state's .09, but that's not sufficient to protect the vegetation in our park. Actually, we should consider a different kind of standard. Instead of a maximum hourly average, we should be concerned with the maximum cumulative dose, since studies have shown that it's the cumulative effects that eventually weaken the tree and lead to its death, rather than a single one-hour air-pollution event." In certain areas of the park, hourly ozone concentrations often exceed national and state minimum standards for "healthy air" during a third of the summer.

In a roundup article on ozone research conducted in the Sierra Nevada, Duriscoe and a colleague, Kenneth Stolte, reported (in 1989) that the number of trees with chlorotic mottle "increased from about 20 percent in 1977 to about 55 percent in 1988 in the Sierra and Sequoia National Forests," and that the "severity of injury has also increased." In a study conducted in Sequoia and Kings Canyon between 1980 and 1982, the Park Service monitored some fifty-four plots of Jeffrey and ponderosa pine and found that 36 percent of them showed the telltale mottle.

Out on Sunset Rock, where we stood looking westward, over the top of the San Joaquin Valley, Duriscoe grew reflective as we discussed these numbers. "Working so much out here alone," he said in the croaky voice people have who do not talk all day long, "I get to know these trees individually. There's a kind of personal camaraderie with 'em. And I kind of object to reducing things to a statistic for a report, although I do it. But really I am thinking more along the lines of tree number eight out here on Sunset Rock. The statistics do not really tell you the story. You have to come here and look at the trees one at a time and get to know them a little bit, and then you might have a feel for it."

After I left Sequoia, I visited Yosemite for a brief look around. There were lots of large patches of dead trees, especially along the road from Wawona to Yosemite West. I recalled that in a 1986 "cruise survey" of Yosemite National Park Duriscoe had reported that some 29 percent of Yosemite's trees showed some mottling of the foliage. Not as great a number as in Sequoia and Kings Canyon (39 percent), but still alarming. Yosemite Valley itself, however, snuggled down beneath the towering ranges all around it, showed signs of drought but probably not air pollution, since it was protected from the ozone-laden "eddies." The local pollution from the astonishing number of cars that cruise the Yosemite Valley floor can make the lodge area of the park a kind of mini-Fresno with high levels of carbon monoxide and particulates. The ozone produced from this traffic is perhaps in concentrations that are by themselves not seriously damaging.

Driving down-mountain due west of Yosemite, I arrived at the headquarters of the Stanislaus National Forest, where I met with John Pronos and John Wenz, plant pathologist and entomologist respectively. Their general reaction to the crisis of the X-disease was a good bit less intense than that of the scientists I had interviewed earlier. A part of this was due, no doubt, to the fact that the Stanislaus and other mid-Sierra forests are at the far end of the ozone gradient, which begins in Los Angeles and peters out at about Yosemite. For these men, the drought was the worrisome thing, and the bugs the drought brought in its wake. In addition, they made it clear that the Forest Service response to environmental issues tended to be commercially pragmatic. Said Pronos, who is well respected in his field, "To an ecologist ozone damage in a National Park might be unacceptable, but if you're a forester interested in growing trees and you can't definitely prove you are losing growth, it doesn't become an issue."

The fact is, however, that research dealing with the issue has shown significant growth reductions in both ponderosa and Jeffrey pines wherever ozone has mottled the needles and reduced the numbers of whorls.

In research conducted by David L. Peterson of the National Park Service, ponderosa pines in areas where ozone injury has been observed have experienced reduced growth since the 1940s. As for Jeffrey pine, Peterson also found that "radial growth of Jeffrey pine had declined at sites in Sequoia and Kings Canyon National Parks where symptoms of zone injury to foliage have been documented."

Most recently, both Pronos and Wenz have been dealing with tree death around Lake Tahoe, where ozone is present, though its effect is uncertain and probably minor. What is certain is that in Tahoe a third to half the trees in certain stands have died. But this is not the only part of the Stanislaus in trouble. Trouble seems to be all over. "Years ago, we did a very large-scale mortality survey in the Sierra Nevada mixed conifer forest," said Pronos, "and we came up with a normal mortality of between 0.1 and 0.3 dead trees per acre. Now we are well beyond 1.0 dead trees per acre—up to a tenfold increase." I recalled that Paul Miller had given me a chart he had made showing a ten-year moving average of precipitation from 1883 to 1990 at Big Bear Dam. Since relative precipitation remains fairly constant throughout the California mountains, Miller's chart indicated more than just a local condition—and the condition appeared to be dire: a steady downward trend in precipitation over the past one hundred years, which, if continued for the next one hundred, would leave California with the rainfall of the Sahara.

This kind of data is why Pronos and Wenz insist on analyses that feature a combination of factors causing forest decline, rather than those that single out one or another and emphasize it in research to the exclusion of others. They are facing what appears to be a drought-and-beetle calamity the likes of which has never before been seen in the state. Said Wenz, "We've never had a drought that has extended quite this long. This is the most tree mortality I have seen."

I was running this alarming statement through my mind in the Forest Service conference room in Sonora when Wenz and Pronos started talking about the trouble with the incense cedar—the shade-loving and relatively resistant tree that has come in to replace the dead ponderosa and Jeffrey pines, which have been cut repeatedly over the years as well as afflicted by ozone, pests, and drought. They told me that the incense cedar were dying—all over the Sierra—and that they didn't know why.

Said Wenz, "The bark beetle in this tree does not kill them, unless they are going to die anyway. Usually incense cedar trees fare well during drought periods, and we expect them to be drought-free."

"But that's not what's happening," said Pronos. "They are dying in very high numbers. It is localized, in patches, but the patches are quite widespread—not just on certain slopes or elevations, or dry soil conditions. There's just no pattern to explain it away. No papers have been written." I thought of James Asher at Lake Arrowhead, looking at trees dying in the 1950s, and wondering what in the world was happening to his forest.

Droughts eventually end, and it is possible that the long siege in California—the longest in four hundred years, some say—may have now concluded, given the more normal rainfall in the early 1990s, including a couple of very high-rainfall seasons. Quite possibly, however, this is merely a respite, and will do little to change the seemingly inexorable century-long downward trend in Paul Miller's ten-year moving-average precipitation chart. Still, in Wenz's view, as soon as the drought is really over, the Sierra Nevada forests will surely recover. But there's a catch. Drought conditions make trees relatively immune to air pollution, for conifers tend to "close down" as a survival strategy in dry times, opening up their delicate stomata when water is present. This physiological attribute may conceal the damage potential of ozone under nondrought conditions. Accordingly, in the postdrought California mountains, ozone damage may increase markedly during the latter part of the 1990s. On the other hand, the state government has legislated rigorous and sophisticated measures to reduce air pollution, limiting the release of VOCs and oxides of nitrogen with laws regulating everything from the use of lighter fluid in backyard barbecues all the way to mandating electric automobiles. That is good news, of course, except that many believe these laws, however draconian their opponents believe them to be, will simply *curb the increase* of pollutants rather than actually reduce total emissions. And it must be remembered, too, that even at the levels of forty years ago, the emissions managed to change the forests around Los Angeles, presumably forever.

For a while, during the Bush administration, it appeared that California might not be permitted, under federal law, to implement its new antipollution measures. The crisis was obviated, at least for a while, by the change in administration in 1992, but the challenges to California's air-pollution hegemony have since taken different forms. The background is this: Since the very first Clean Air Act, passed in 1970, California, which preceded the federal government with comprehensive air-pollution regulations by two years, has been given a "waiver" by the Environmental Protection Agency, which is charged with the implementation of air-pollution legislation. The provision allowed the state to use its own regulations instead of those enacted by the federal government. Until the early 1990s, the waiver was virtually assured; the Environmental Protection Agency would simply grant it as a matter of course, since the EPA saw California as an air-quality laboratory for the rest of the country. This was a not unreasonable policy, for CARB, the California Air Resources Board, has a great deal more money and staff than the EPA, not to mention a political consensus that has given California regulators the kind of operational muscle that the EPA was without through the 1980s and early 1990s.

In recognition of California's leadership, the Clean Air Act amendments of 1990 allowed that other states could join with California and get their own waivers from less stringent federal rules, so long as the states would "opt in" to the California plan entirely. This new provision was quickly taken up by a group of twelve Northeastern states in a coalition led by Thomas Jorling, New York State's Commissioner of Environmental Conservation, who saw it as an opportunity to leapfrog the more timid national regulations in a geographical area—the Eastern urban corridor—very nearly as beset by air pollution as California. Jorling, a national environmental policy leader, had been an instrumental figure as a Capitol Hill aide to Senator Edmund Muskie in establishing national water-pollution abatement standards in 1972. Now the opportunity provided by the "opt in on the waiver" amendment could achieve a major leap ahead in air quality, too.

Then suddenly, for the first time ever, under pressure from large corporations and others, California's waiver was not routinely approved by the EPA, but withheld.

"As a result of other states deciding to opt in, it's becoming more politically problematic for California to get its waivers," the chairman of the California Air Resources Board, Jananne Sharpless, told *New York Times* reporter Matthew Wald in the fall of 1992. The EPA, Wald wrote, had held a routine hearing on California's waiver in the spring of 1992. This was, in itself, somewhat unusual, since many waiver requests are approved without a public hearing. This one not only got a public hearing, but the decision was postponed so that even more comments could be solicited—the burden of which was that California's plan was not feasible, from a technical standpoint, to be adopted by other states. The leaders of the revolt turned out to be Mobil Oil and General Motors, corporations that might be less interested in the technical matters of adapting air-quality programs from state to state than in the economic effects of California's regulations on a substantial fraction of their market. One-half the cars sold in the United States are sold in California and the Eastern states that might "opt in" to the CARB plan.

What the CARB plan proposed—a plan, remember, that many think would only hold the line on pollution, not lower it—was a 40-percent reduction of the smog-forming properties of gasoline by 1996. As for the vehicles themselves, all cars would have to run "60 to 85 percent cleaner than current models"; the plan also mandated that "2 to 10 percent be 'zero polluting' models between 1998 and 2003," Wald reported. "Zero-polluting" means, in effect, electrically powered automobiles, the practicality of which the automobile industry has continuously challenged.

According to *The Wall Street Journal*, the big three automakers sought a trade-off with the Clinton administration in the fall of 1993 whereby they would, as Vice President Gore had urged, form a partnership with government to create "clean cars" in return for relief from the California rules. Instead of waivers for California and other states "opting in," the automakers have proposed national emission standards that are somewhere between EPA and California. The notion had no appeal to Thomas Jorling, who told *Wall Street Journal* reporter Oscar Sims, "It reflects that the energy and focus of the industry is not to move to the car of the 21st century, but rather to oppose the car of the 21st century."

"Politics," as a friend put it to me on hearing the story of this contretemps. "Politics will be the death of trees."

On the subject of politics, it is worth observing here that the U.S. Forest Service, while very much engaged by the politics of air pollution in the East, seems to stand in a more professional—and comfortable—relationship to pollution controversy in California. In the East, the

Forest Service has been routinely accused by environmentalists of being the mouthpiece of the forest products industry—and industry in general—for minimizing the effects of air pollution on trees and forests. By contrast, in California (clear-cutting and other forest management issues aside), regional Forest Service officials tend to be more forthright about pollution damage, and in a mild way are supportive of pollution abatement efforts. According to Trent Proctor, the air resources specialist for the Sequoia National Forest, he and his colleagues attend public hearings on air pollution, "just like any interested citizen," and offer their findings on ozone effects. "We want to let people know what's happening up here," Proctor told me.

None of this would surprise my lawyer friend, who shook his head in disbelief at my naïveté about how much influence the "constituency interests" of any government can have over the outcome of scientific reports. The salient point is this: The major funder of air-pollution research in the Sierra conducted by the Forest Service and others is the California Air Resources Board, not the federal government. CARB, apparently, really does want to reduce air pollution in the state and is lushly supported in this enterprise by an annual six-dollars-per-car "smog-inspection" certificate, plus income from permits provided to polluters. By contrast, much of the air-pollution research in the Appalachians, as described in the previous two chapters, was supported by federal grants (with the exception of Camel's Hump), appropriated by Congress, and subject to high-level political pressure from the appointees of the executive branch as well as members of Congress.

In any discussion of California trees, attention must be paid to the incredible redwoods. And here the impact of ozone is less clear than with the yellow pines—the Jeffreys and the ponderosas—which are so extremely sensitive to O_3 that they can be considered an "indicator species" to determine the presence of this pollutant. The ponderosa is, in fact, almost as good an indicator as Bel-W3, the commonly accepted standard. In early research on the impacts of ozone, botanists discovered that wrapper tobacco grown in Connecticut was hard hit by disease in the early 1950s, and set about to develop a more resistant strain. In the search for a new cultivar, the botanists accidentally produced a supersensitive variety they called Bel-W3. The mistake was not discarded, but soon became the "bioindicator" for ambient O_3. As it happens, the ponderosa pine's susceptibility to ozone damage is very nearly the same as that of Bel-W3. Where the tobacco will show injury with 0.05 parts per million of ozone present in the air for three hours, the ponderosa will show injury with the same level of ozone if exposed for 24 hours.

No one believes that either the giant sequoias of Sequoia National Park or the magnificent coast redwoods at lower altitudes are nearly so sensitive as the yellow pines. And yet redwoods are, like the pines, a tall needle tree, and they have been subject to decades of ambient ozone pollution, the cumulative effects of which are hard to determine.

I am no pantheist, but if I were, I would choose to worship in a grove of redwoods, of either variety. Up at Sequoia National Park, which I often visited as a child, I was just as awed by the trees when I visited Dan Duriscoe as I was in the 1940s. Here are the towering trees (*Sequoia gigantea*) that the National Park Service describes as "Earth's Largest Living Things." The largest of the Sequoia redwoods, the General Sherman tree, is 2,700 years old. It is 275 feet tall. It is 1,385 tons in weight. It is 103 feet in circumference, which means a diameter of nearly 30 feet. "Why that's bigger than a living room in a mansion," my father would exclaim, and I can hear the echoes of him saying it every time I visit a redwood grove. "Why that's bigger than the house you were born in."

The coast redwoods (*Sequoia sempervirens*), a different species, which grows from a few miles south of the San Francisco peninsula northward into southern Oregon, occupy the "fog belt" along the Pacific shore and inland to the crests of the Coast Range. They are not heavy or old or always so stupendous in girth, but they are tall. If the sequoia is the biggest living thing, the coast redwood is the *tallest* living thing. And not just the occasional individual, either, but tallest, period—as a species. According to the National Park Service, the current record holder reaches 368 feet.

Clearly, the remaining redwoods are so precious that we must learn what we can about the effects of ozone upon them. And in this regard, some are worried. In an informal paper written by two visiting German environmentalists, Peter Schütt and Ulla Lang lamented that "every second look at the crowns" of the redwoods along the Redwood Highway, a scenic stretch of U.S. 101 in northern California, "signals missing vigor, illness and dying. Normally the crowns of redwoods are so densely foliated that you are not able to see the sky. It was like this until five years ago. Now most of the needles are missing and remaining needles an abnormal yellowish-green color. Heavily damaged trees are developing many new shoots on the top sides of the branches, which give the trees a strange, larch-like outward shape." (The European larch, a tall, deciduous conifer, has whorl-like needles, and the older branches are thickly studded with spurs of a light green color when they appear in spring.) Schütt and Lang likened what they observed in the coast redwood groves as akin to *Waldsterben,* the forest death they knew well in Germany. "Maybe this kind of development is needed to open the eyes of the public and to show that the 'Waldsterben' is a worldwide event, which will not be rectified by waiting it out or with little technical remedies."

A more scientific approach to examining the possibility of ozone damage to redwoods has been undertaken by Lance Evans and Michael Leonard of the Laboratory of Plant Morphogenesis at Manhattan College in New York. In a 1991 paper, Evans and Leonard point out that, given the demonstrated susceptibility of yellow pines to ozone in the Sequoia and Kings Canyon National Park (they cite Dan Duriscoe's 1986 cruise survey, where he found 39 percent of the trees showing some ozone damage), it would be logical to surmise that the giant sequoia may also be vulnerable. In two experiments, one in 1986 conducted in the Wolverton Ski area of the park, and one in 1987 in the Highland area of the Giant Forest, Evans and Leonard studied leaf tissue samples from fumigated sequoia seedlings in open-top chambers that had been set up by Paul Miller and his associates. In one set of chambers, charcoal-filtered air was pumped in; in a second set, ambient air; in a third, ambient air with ozone levels increased by 50 percent. In the 1986 experiment, after examining the cells of the needles exposed to the various fumigants, Evans and Leonard observed three effects of ozone damage: "plasmolysis" (cell shrinkage), staining, and cell death. Then they compared these reactions to the effects of ozone on yellow-pine needle cells. In both studies, they found that cell death was "always higher for the ambient air + ozone treatment than for the filtered air treatment."

Although the 1987 study did not show a clear correlation of plasmolysis and staining to ozone dose, it duplicated the 1986 findings pertaining to cell death. Evans and Leonard determined that only 1.3 percent of the cells of needles exposed to the filtered air were dead, as compared to 7.8 percent in needles exposed to ambient air, and 8.5 percent in those exposed to artificially increased levels of ozone. In view of this, the researchers concluded that the "morphology" of the needle cells of the sequoia seedlings they studied were "quantitatively similar" to those of yellow pines (i.e., ponderosa and Jeffrey).

According to Dan Duriscoe, the analysis alarmed Paul Miller, who at the time of my visit had just finished checking out the effect of ozone on mature sequoias by means of "branch chambers," much as he had tested the San Gabriel–San Bernardino ponderosas twenty-five years before. Miller's tests of mature trees (located near Sunset Rock) showed no clear relationship of needle damage to ozone levels comparable to that found in seedling cells tested by Evans and Leonard. So hope remains that the great old redwoods will not die or be weakened by ozone to the same degree as ponderosa and Jeffrey pine. In fact, mature sequoias seem to be among the most resistant of trees to ozone, even though first-year seedlings are sensitive. Duriscoe pointed out to me that the potential effect of ozone on seedlings would be mitigated by their proximity to the ground, where studies have shown that ambient ozone levels are lower than they are in the forest canopy.

Still, the findings of Evans and Leonard cannot be discounted. And the observations of the Germans along the Redwood Highway linger in the mind despite their lack of formal scientific analysis.

Back to the San Gabriels for a last look. I decided to take a sentimental journey up to Mount Wilson to view dead trees, before heading off to other Western mountains—namely those in Colorado, the subject of the next chapter.

Mount Wilson was, in my day, the site of the largest telescope in the world, and always thronged with visitors. Now the place is largely abandoned, though a few recreational facilities remain. I stood on a rock wall cracked and crumbling with neglect, and stared down at the smog in the great basin below. My parents used to bring me here often, and we could see for miles, clear to Catalina Island over fifty miles away.

For many of those years, my father had a job with the All Year Club of Southern California, a tourism-promoting and economic development organization that celebrated the glories of our region. One day, just after the end of World War II, he told me: "Son, people are pouring across the border at the rate of a thousand a day! Think of it!" He and the All Year Club had succeeded beyond their wildest dreams.

Before long, however, he came to regret the mad rush to make southern California the postwar growth capital of the United States. But it was done, and now everyone wonders if it can be undone. This had been my Eden, and looking down on the blanket of smog, I reflected on all the tree death I'd seen and had been learning about all over the state, a state that we had decisively trashed. We were so stupid about it, I thought to myself—or perhaps even said aloud into the dead air—so greedy, so absorbed with our automobiles, freeways, and *growth.* The notion struck me then, and it persists, that James Asher's X-disease is not really an affliction of the trees. It is a terrible chronic illness in ourselves.

5

The Fire Next Time

Never does Nature say one thing
and Wisdom another.
—*Juvenal*

At first it was a just vague impression, something working uncomfortably at the edge of consciousness as I drove along the twisty roads and mountain highways of Colorado—my first tour of this part of the Front Range since I left them behind after a two-year schoolboy sojourn that ended here in 1949. I had not been back to visit these particular mountains since, and had no vivid memory of the particulars, of course, forty-odd years ago being not exactly yesterday. Then on the way to Lake City, which is about fifty miles south of Gunnison, I saw a whole mountainside of it. The trees were no longer green. They were brown.

In the days after that, of course, I saw it everywhere—the brown mountainsides—for I began looking for it. Still, everything seemed normal when I arrived at Lake City, a little Victorian village nestled in a remote valley. I spoke to a young Forest Service seasonal worker who was dispensing wilderness advice and handing out trail maps in a storefront ranger station. I told her what I had seen up near Gunnison. "Trees look pretty good here," I ventured.

"Yeah, *now,*" she replied. She was still a girl, at least from the standpoint of my years. But a big backpacker kind of girl, blond and healthy and good-looking with an open honest face.

"But . . ."

"But it's coming. It's all around us. Coming in from the north, especially, and coming from the east and west, too."

"What is *it,* exactly?" I asked.

"Bugs," she said. "A big damn plague of bugs."

She had not yet learned to be a cool Forest Service professional, not to sweat what you can't do anything about and to talk ecology in order to discourage the civilians from asking stupid questions. Instead she told me she was terrified because the mountains were turning brown all around her. She gave me some maps. I could hike all day long around Lake City, she said, and not see any damage at all. Left unspoken was the suggestion that I'd better hurry up.

Back on the other side of the Continental Divide, in Lakewood, I got the ecology explained to me by one of the chief bug experts in the Forest Service's Rocky Mountain Region, R. D. Averill, a forest entomologist who heads up a task force dealing with what "it" was that was changing the colors in the Colorado mountains. R.D. is a Rocky Mountain version of a good ol' boy, an ex-Marine who fought in 'Nam and who now sports cowboy boots, a luxurious mustache, a bolo tie, and a PhD from Michigan State University. He is a second-generation Colorado forester: his ranger dad roamed the mountains with the great ones of a generation ago—such men as the militant wilderness advocate Robert Marshall, who was one of Averill senior's best friends.

Averill told me that there were two bugs doing the damage. First comes the spruce budworm, which doesn't just fancy spruces but quite a lot of different trees, especially Douglas fir. The female budworm moth, said Averill, warming to his subject, "is a real egg factory. She'll lay several egg masses a day, with twenty to forty eggs in each mass, on the tender shoots of a host conifer. When the eggs hatch, about twenty days after they're laid, the young larvae look for a place to spend the winter. So they climb under a bit of bark. Then they wait there until the next spring. When it warms up—about the time the buds are expanding—the larva becomes active and goes into the bud and starts feeding on that cluster."

And then the tree dies?

"Not that simple. After the spruce budworms work for a while, weakening the stand, they're followed by the bark beetle," said Averill.

"In the conventional view, as it's given in the Forest Service literature, the Douglas fir beetle does not build up into large populations. Theoretically it's only a minor component in an outbreak, only lasts a couple of years, not a very threatening type of insect—weak, not an aggressor." R.D. paused to let me catch up with my notes.

"Unfortunately," said Averill, "the beetles we've got in this region haven't read the book, and they don't know how to behave. So in the past ten or twelve years we've experienced much higher losses than we should." R.D. said that the spruce budworm infestations were visible on about 300,000 acres in Colorado, which he felt might understate the severity of infestation, which is concentrated in the lower-elevation areas of the Front Range. One of the interesting things about the spruce budworm, said Averill, is the random way it moves from place to place. When the evening comes the female spruce budworm moth rises up on warm air currents. And if the air is moving somewhere, a whole population, said R.D., "can just migrate out of an area even if it's laid only twenty percent of its eggs. When the air cools down, the moths come down, wherever that happens to be, and then they lay the rest of the eggs."

So. The spruce budworm infests the forest in its immutably random way, the beetles come in after the budworms weaken the trees, and because there is such an infestation of spruce budworms the Douglas fir bark beetles have become killer bugs, boring into host trees by the thousands to carve their galleries and raise their families, in the course of which they choke off the transport of water and nutrients, and import a deadly fungus into the bargain. They are not, it turns out, the mild-mannered fellows they were believed to be. But back to first causes: How come there are so many spruce budworms to begin with?

Although there's a difference of opinion among the experts on how bad the current Colorado budworm-beetle infestation is, they are pretty much agreed on the basic cause, which, not to put too fine a point on it, is *us*—or at least our forebears.

As is often the case. Natural disasters frequently occur because humans have, as George Perkins Marsh put it more than a century ago, "rearranged nature's original balances." In his classic *Man and Nature*, Marsh explained how it was that trees wouldn't grow anymore on the Aegean hillsides, browsed off into hard, dry rockiness by a thousand years of Grecian goats. Paradoxically, the Rockies and other Western mountains have just the opposite problem. The trees are dying because in the last 100 years the hillsides have been growing too many trees.

This dramatic change in the physical geography of the Front Range has been the preoccupation of Dr. Thomas Veblen, chair of the Department of Geography at the University of Colorado, whom I next sought out in order to discuss the rearrangement of nature's original balances in the Rockies. "In the vast majority of cases," Veblen explained to me during a visit to his cluttered office in Boulder, "humans are implicated in one way or another. But when you set out to *prove* that humans are doing something that results in forest decline, it's very, very tricky.

"The major force for change in the Front Range forest is fire suppression," Veblen said. "Under pre–white settlement conditions we had relatively frequent burning of the low-elevation forests—the open-woodland, ponderosa pine forest. But with fire suppression over the last seventy to eighty years, there have been two results. First, an expansion of the forest area into places where the forest did not exist before; and second, at a slightly higher elevation, formerly open stands that have now become very dense stands with a lot of Doug fir in them, which then are susceptible to spruce budworm attack."

Veblen summed it up this way: "In these relatively low-elevation forests we had fire frequencies at twenty- to thirty-year intervals. Now with complete fire suppression we're getting an entirely different kind of stand structure." Meaning that instead of open ponderosa pine woodlands, or meadow, the slopes are now dense with shade-loving firs that are irresistible to spruce budworms. After the budworms weaken the stands (they sometimes kill their hosts after many years of infestation, but not always), the bark beetles move in and finish the job. If there's plenty of moisture about—which has not been the case in the Rockies, now going through what may become the longest drought in memory (more on this later)—the host trees can literally dislodge the bark beetle by concentrating a flow of sap to flush the invader out of the hole he is boring to create a colony. But in dry times, and dry places, the beetle succeeds in penetrating the bark, and in short order —a year or two—the trees die. No water, no flush.

Well, one wants to know, how about adapting the Native American practice of setting ground fires to clear woodlands of brush and tree litter so that it would not serve as the fuel to stoke a dreaded crown fire—fire that reaches to tops of trees and jumps from one to another until an entire forest is consumed? Veblen took the question seriously. "The trouble is that by this time, we've got such an accumulation of fuel we can't even let the natural lightning ignition continue. If we did we'd have very catastrophic fires, whereas previously we had low-intensity surface fires. If we want to reinstitute natural fires into this ecosystem, we'll have to remove fuels mechanically, and that's a very expensive proposition."

Such is the state of affairs throughout the mountain West, where, thanks to man's interference with the forests' natural processes, present-day options are tragically limited. Certainly this was no anticipated outcome when President Thomas Jefferson, eager to move the nation westward, sent Lewis and Clark to scout out the Western territories in 1803. Jefferson thought it might take forty generations to settle this far country. As it turned out, it took about four, and within that time, with the tree cutting and clearing and fire suppression, the white man changed the composition of the forest forever. To demonstrate this historical point, Veblen had sought out old photographs of various spots around the Front Range—most of them prints dating to the turn of the century. Then, with a graduate student, he had found the exact positions from which the old pictures were taken, whereupon he took a picture of his own. In pair after pair of these matched pictures, the mountainsides are sparsely wooded with big trees in the old prints, and lushly forested with smaller trees in Veblen's modern slides.

To be sure, there have always been insect outbreaks along the Front Range and in the other mountains of the West. Tree-ring studies have revealed severe infestations of spruce budworms even in pre-settlement days. So despite the changed composition of the forest, aren't the browning mountains simply part of a natural cycle? A fair number of the dozen or so people I interviewed on this topic believe that this is true—which is a comforting thought, right enough, and one that I was holding on to, myself. But then I ran into Dr. Ann Lynch, a research entomologist at the U.S. Forest Service's Rocky Mountain Forest and Range Experiment Station in Fort Collins, Colorado.

A few years ago, Lynch and a colleague from the University of Arizona, Thomas Swetnam, decided to trace the long-term history of spruce budworm outbreaks in the Rockies of Colorado and northern New Mexico by pulling together all the tree-ring data they could find. Ann Lynch summarized the very elaborate research she and Swetnam conducted this way: "Prior to European settlement," she told me, "you'd have an outbreak in a small area—say in the mountains where the Carson National Forest is now. Then five or ten years later it would be somewhere else. Widely separated and irregular. Then Europeans came in and grazed the area and controlled fire and cut out preferentially the shade-intolerant species. So the forest changed toward the shade-tolerant species, the preferred hosts for spruce budworm." So far, she had only recapped the conventional wisdom.

"But *now,*" she went on, her young voice rising in intensity, "when you have outbreaks they tend to occur over vastly larger regions and all at once." To demonstrate this astonishing finding, she showed me a graph she and Swetnam had prepared. On it were plotted spruce budworm outbreaks in ten locations from the year 1700 to 1980. "See how scattered they are early on?" she said, pointing to the graph. "Then look what happens after European settlement." She explained that the relatively long gaps between outbreaks immediately after 1800 were because of logging operations. But after all the pine has been cut, she said, when all that's left is Douglas fir and white fir, then you begin to see the outbreaks becoming more frequent and more widespread. "Look how the last two outbreaks have hit every stand." And there they were, lined up like phalanxes of Roman troops invading Gaul.

Synchronicity, which is not a comforting thought, is the word Ann Lynch used to describe the coincidence of insect damage in various areas across a broad front at more and more frequent intervals. But it seemed to me to be synchronicity with a vengeance, self-potentiating, with each event becoming ever more frequent and more widespread, more virulent.

"Well, maybe that's as it should be," said Terry Shaw, Lynch's senior colleague and the director of forest pathology work at Fort Collins. "Some ecologists argue that the forest dieback is just what should happen, to restore the original forest composition and area."

Terry Shaw's apocalyptic ecologists may get their wish, but not in the way they would like. A possible, if not probable, outcome in the browning mountains of the West is fire—and not just here and there, either, but widespread conflagrations that, like the bug infestations, may become synchronous and more intense as the mountain trees die. Fire follows bugs as a natural consequence. Ironically, the zealous woodcutters of the West, through compulsive fire suppression, created a forest so attractive to insects that in a time of drought the mountainsides have turned into tinderboxes. The very effort to avoid forest fires has helped, in a later generation, to create them. "A vicious, self-perpetuating cycle has been established," says Timothy Ingalsbee, a seasonal firefighter for the U.S. Forest Service and the National Park Service. "Wildfires are suppressed in order to save trees for logging, and yet the activity, infrastructure, and aftermath of logging causes more wildfires which must be suppressed."

The cycle that Ingalsbee describes is nowhere more apparent than in the Blue Mountain region of northeastern Oregon, which includes, besides the Blues, the adjacent Wallowas and the Seven Devils Mountains. This beautiful, undersung region of the West is sparsely populated and huge—comprising perhaps a fifth of the land area of the state. A hundred years ago, these forests were, like those in many Western mountains, dominated by giant ponderosa pines and Western larch, both disease-resistant and widely spaced so that the occasional harmless groundfires set by lightning, trappers, or Indians could consume accumulations of litter without harming the forest itself. Here, as elsewhere in the West, loggers relentlessly cut the big old-growth trees, so that by the middle of the twentieth century the forests became tightly packed with firs and lodgepole pine, species that were attractive to insects such as the tussock moth, spruce budworm, and pine bark beetle.

The upshot: In 1990, the U.S. Forest Service estimated that within the three national forests of the region, an astonishing 53 percent of the trees were dead or severely defoliated by insects working on trees already weakened by five years of drought. The combination of drought and bugs, here as in the Rockies, has transformed northwestern Oregon into a forest of torches, a kind of worst-case scenario come true. In the cool language of the Forest Service, "There is a growing concern that existing conditions are stretching the ecological limits of the forest." Oregon journalists Johnstone Quinan and Dave Cook, writing in *American Forests* magazine, put the bleak future of the Blues more candidly.

"There is relatively little ponderosa pine left to serve as genetic stock for rebuilding," they report. "And the potential for catastrophic wildfires is very high because of so much dead wood on the forest floor. By some estimates it could take a century to bring these forests back to health."

The Blue Mountain syndrome can be found throughout the West. In the forests north of the Snake River of Idaho, for example, officials have tracked forest fires as a function of insect damage on a five-year running average. The bugs peaked in 1984, and the forest fires three years later, showing a four-fold increase of forest land burned over. As forest conservation expert R. Neil Sampson told me, "They're afraid the whole forest will burn off and never grow back, that the desert will take over north of the Snake, where the forest had once been." The possibility of giant conflagrations throughout the Western mountains —from the coast ranges to the Sierra-Cascades to the Rockies and everywhere in between—worries people like Sampson, the executive vice president of American Forests, the nation's oldest citizen conservation organization, which was founded in 1875 (as the American Forestry Association) to champion the establishment of national forest reserves (the present National Forest system) in order to save them from rapacious lumbermen. Now, Sampson and his colleagues believe that nothing short of a crash program is necessary to save the trees—this time, by cleansing the dying forests of incendiary fuels that have accumulated into great banks, heaps, and windrows of tinder: the deadfalls, slash from previous logging, and the normal litter of dead branches, twigs, needles, and leaves that piles upon itself faster than it can be broken down biologically and returned to the soil. In more places than not throughout the mountain West, such forests are the equivalent of a multimillion-acre garage full of oily rags, ready to explode into massive oxygen-consuming crown-fires with interior temperatures reaching two thousand degrees Fahrenheit, the temperature of molten lava.

Sampson also believes that, in addition to the trucking away of dead and dying trees and litter, the number of living trees must be reduced, so that those remaining can compete successfully for scarce water in time of drought, and to keep the woods open so that mass fires cannot so easily get started. In effect, what Sampson's desperate and implausible-seeming measures suggest is an effort to return to the forest of yesteryear—of 1875—with widely spaced trees in a parklike setting, where the undergrowth is routinely eliminated by natural or purposely set ground fires. The alternative, in Sampson's view, is that "in areas where the ground is covered with large amounts of dead, dry fuel, wildfires will scorch the earth, destroying soil organic matter and even 'firing' soil clays into lifeless brick." The plan, which might partially pay for itself through the sale of timber yielded from the thinning process, would not reconstitute the Western forests as self-sustaining natural systems, however. They would require constant tending in places like the Blue Mountains and the Boise National Forest in Idaho, for the dominant trees are no longer the big yellow pines that for millennia had kept the woods open, beautiful, capable of sustaining forest-cleansing ground fires, and yet resistant to mass fire.

Perversely, most people see the present-day forests, however modified by human intervention, as natural, while at the same time they believe that fire—any fire—is unnatural. This is a misconception that forest ecologists have for years been at pains to correct, but to little avail. As we shall see, the misconception has had a profound effect on forest policy, wherein historically the harvesting of big trees has been encouraged, while fire has been suppressed—in the endless vicious cycle that has changed the composition of the forests of the Western mountains so decisively that their vulnerability to drought and insect infestation, and therefore fire, is a virtually permanent condition.

In 1988, the world was treated to a preview of the widespread fires to come when nearly half of Yellowstone National Park's 2.2 million acres, tucked into the far northwest corner of Wyoming, were burned over. "Everything about the fires seemed exaggerated," wrote historian and forest fire authority Stephen J. Pyne. "Groves of old-growth lodgepole pine and aging spruce fir exploded into flame like toothpicks before a blowtorch. Towering convective clouds rained down a hailstorm of ash, and firebrands even spanned the Grand Canyon of the Yellowstone. Crown fires propagated at rates of up to two miles per hour, velocities unheard of for forest fuels. A smoke pall spread over the region like the prototype of a nuclear winter. Everything burned."

The Yellowstone fire was what might be called Smokey Bear's revenge. For fifty years this admonitory cartoon animal—created by the

U.S. Forest Service and Foote, Cone, and Belding advertising agency in 1944—has inculcated the belief in every schoolchild, every Campfire Girl, every Boy Scout, Girl Scout, Brownie, and Cub in the United States of America, that forest fires are bad, and that they are the fault, usually, of a "careless smoker," of those who do not heed the gruff warning to "drown your campfires," or even, perhaps, of those who are an enemy of democracy. The result has been that any effort to reduce the threat of fire by burning off accumulated fuels in a place like Yellowstone was hamstrung by a popular belief that there was no such thing as a "good" fire. Accordingly, the fuel built upon itself, year after year, decade after decade. While forest fires regularly broke out at Yellowstone, they were, through most of the park's history, hurriedly extinguished, in compliance with the popular horror of forest fire of any kind. Unfortunately, this ursine cartoon animal may have done more to increase the risk of future mass fire in the West than to reduce it, simply by making forest fires unpatriotic.

The original anti–forest fire campaign (sans Smokey), was developed in the early 1940s in response to an astonishing outbreak of wildfire in the early years of World War II, a time during which manpower for firefighting was scarce—since the CCC boys had all been drafted. During the war, the annual burn averaged thirty million acres, an area more than half the size of the entire state of Wyoming. By contrast, even in the fire year of 1988, when mass fires raged not only in Yellowstone but throughout the Rockies, only 7.4 million acres burned in the U.S. —twice as much as in some recent years, but only a quarter of what was burned during a typical war year.

The specific event that led to the invention of Smokey was the 1942 shelling of a Santa Barbara, California, oilfield by a Japanese submarine. The oilfield was close to the Los Padres National Forest, then tinder dry. And the possibility of further shelling was anything but remote in those days. In fact, my uncle, a ham radio operator whose "shack" was perched on a Palos Verdes, California, bluff overlooking a large patch of ocean not far from the naval shipyard at San Pedro, spotted what might have been a small submarine offshore that same year. Excitedly he radioed the sighting to the Coast Guard. Within minutes, jeeps with mounted .50-caliber machine guns appeared on the beach below his house and began firing into the water. A short while later, patrol boats, equipped with depth charges, approached from the flanks. Immediately, a tiny white flag appeared out beyond the breakers, and, herded by the patrol boats, a Japanese two-man sub surfed in to the beach.

Meanwhile, from Oregon and northern California came reports of incendiary balloon bombs sent up by Japanese warships further offshore, to be carried in by the prevailing westerlies and descend on the forests of the Coast Range or even the Sierra-Cascades. The defenseless forests of America, so necessary to the war effort when everything from Liberty Ships to rifle stocks needed wood, had to be saved from the nefarious schemes of the Axis powers, whose assaults on the mainland United States included not only shelling and balloon bombs from the sea, but fifth-column sabotage on land. The advertising sloganeers got busy. "Careless Matches Aid the Axis," they wrote. "Our Carelessness, Their Secret Weapon."

After a few false starts (beginning with a quite ordinary poster campaign which was later improved upon by the introduction of Bambi, courtesy of Walt Disney, for a limited period), the bear himself was conceived in 1943, and finally appeared in 1944. The familiar slogan, "Only You Can Prevent Forest Fires" was not introduced until after the war's end, however. The broadcast voice of the bear, recorded in 1947, was that of a Washington, D.C., radio personality, Jackson Weaver, who spoke the lines into an empty wastepaper basket in order to achieve a properly authoritarian and patriarchal effect. Since then, Smokey Bear has become a symbol of what the U.S. Forest Service hopes is perceived as their faithful stewardship of the nation's forest lands. Indeed, the image of Smokey Bear is guarded so zealously by the foresters that citizen organizations, seeking to use the illustrations of the bear to advance their own views on forest management in opposition to the Forest Service, are told that such a use can lead to fines and imprisonment under a law enacted in 1952 to guard against improper commercial exploitation of the image by trinket makers and retail businesses.

It is inconceivable that congressional intent in safeguarding the Smokey image from commercialization was in any way associated with suppressing opposition to Forest Service policies (as in fact the courts ultimately ruled). Nevertheless, the accreted iconography of Smokey, originated in a flurry of wartime patriotism persuasively expressed in an inspired advertising concept, has become a powerful force that even the Forest Service cannot fully control. Aside from the subversive use of the bear's image by citizen groups, Smokey has turned on his masters in other ways, most significantly in inhibiting a modern "prescribed burning" policy in order to reduce accumulated fuels in national forests.

The Forest Service took a while to reach this concept—of setting fire to patches of flammable woods in order to reduce the risk of a mass fire that might burn out of control. According to Stephen Pyne, it was an anti–prescribed-burning position that brought the new Forest Service to prominence early in this century, when they battled California timber owners, who practiced a form of fire control called "light burning" to keep woodlands clear of underbrush—a practice the Californians had borrowed from the Indians. The fledgling Forest Service, looking for a public-relations angle to gain popular and political support, argued that to allow light burning was to undermine the forest protection message that they, as firefighters, were eager to advance. The new agency was determined to become a powerful force in Western resource management, and was unwilling to be relegated to a minor role in the guarding of the forests.

The service could do little about fires in remote areas, however, and, much as it pained them to do so, they invented a policy called "let burning," to allow back-country fires to burn themselves out in order to conserve scarce manpower for battling flames in more commercially valuable timber stands.

With the advent of the Depression 1930s, however, and the creation of the Civilian Conservation Corps, a large, low-cost manpower pool became almost instantly available that could be trained in firefighting. Subsequently, the Forest Service virtually took over the CCC in much of the West. The cheap labor was short-lived, however. With the onset of World War II, the ranks were severely depleted, and the forest work camps were closed. Once again, fires raged unchecked.

The overriding concern with "mass fire," says Pyne, began with World War II as a matter of national defense, as discussed earlier. But after the war, public fears of forest fires were not allowed to subside; Smokey Bear's anti-fire message was continued in postwar campaigns, and played on a new set of anxieties related to atomic attack, once the Soviet Union had succeeded in developing their own nuclear bomb in 1949. The bomb was, says Stephen Pyne, "the quintessential incendiary weapon."

By the late 1940s, with manpower problems significantly eased after the boys at arms returned home, and with the public squarely in favor of an all-out fire-suppression effort, the Forest Service could once again mount a comprehensive assault on forest fire, even in the remotest places. The policy now was to put small fires out—every single one of them—before they became big fires, a patriotic duty easily justified after several years of Smokey Bear propaganda. This message was significantly enhanced by public-relations campaigns featuring romantic images of eremitic rangers scanning the horizon from their fire towers for any wisp of smoke, of valiant smoke jumpers—former paratroops—hitting the silk to get at remote blazes as quickly as possible, of the dropping of chemical suppressants from C-102 Flying Boxcars by ex-bombardiers, and of the sooty-faced crews of fire-line troops, former GIs who were trucked into the back country over the fire roads that were beginning to lace all the national forests, carved into the mountainsides by war-surplus D-8 bulldozers. Patriotic stuff, every bit of it.

By the mid-1970s, twenty-five years after the introduction of Smokey Bear and new mechanized firefighting techniques, the number of forest fires was cut in half and the number of acres burned reduced to one-eighth of the wartime average.

There were two problems. First, the cost of these activities began to escalate out of sight. In the ten-year period between 1965 and 1975, the price tag for fire suppression and "presuppression" activities increased tenfold. Moreover, during the greening-of-America 1960s and 1970s, an environmental sensibility had steadily gained currency which held that "natural" fires had their place, especially in wilderness areas, despite the implied message from Smokey Bear that all fires were anathema. To save money and to mimic, in a sense, the role of natural fire in a forest, the Forest Service finally embarked on controlled or "prescribed" burning to reduce the risk of mass fires raging over millions of acres of forest. By letting some naturally caused (lightning) fires burn, and by setting others, they could help forests return to a more mass-fire-resistant natural composition that would include burned-over spots mixed with newly regenerating areas mixed with more mature (and flammable) stands of timber—as opposed to vast areas of older trees with great accumulations of deadfall and litter, leading to the kind of fire that throws firebrands a half mile and can bake the earth to brick.

The trouble was, neither a return to a "let burn" policy, which had been experimented with in the early days, nor the use of prescribed burns in areas with high levels of fuel accumulation, could truly approximate the effects of pre-Columbian "natural" fires. That was because, as we have seen, the forests had been made *unnatural* by a century of rapacious logging and fire suppression, which had changed their composition and therefore their vulnerability to insect attack. As a consequence of these factors, plus the years of drought, the forests had become more vulnerable to fire than ever before.

At length, criticism of the Smokey Bear campaign began to mount. Wrote one expert, Eldon G. Bowman, in *American Forests* magazine in 1968, "When the forty-niners poured over the Sierra Nevada into California, those that kept diaries spoke almost to a man of the wide-spaced columns of mature trees that grew on the lower western slope in gigantic magnificence. The ground was a grass parkland, in spring-time carpeted with wildflowers. Deer and bears were abundant. Today much of the west slope is a doghair thicket of young pines, white fir, incense cedar, and mature brush—a direct function of overprotection from natural ground fires." Bowman laid the blame for the policy of overprotection on success of the Smokey Bear campaign in shaping "public opinion and expectations" regarding fire suppression.

Smokey Bear's managers and apologists in Washington have taken considerable umbrage at the increasing criticism that the bear's advertising campaign distorted forest management policy, making it difficult for the Forest Service to move toward a more ecologically oriented fire-control approach. The bear's defenders point out that the campaign is directed at children and concerns itself only with human-caused fires, not natural fires or prescribed burns. Smokey's official "biographer," Ellen Earnhardt Morrison, is outraged at the idea that the bear has been accused of having "brainwashed" people into thinking that all fires should be prevented. "To a bear who has been a hero for a whole generation," she writes, "such criticism must come as a shock. What has happened in the last decade to make anyone question his motives? Why is he suddenly the object of scorn?"

Given the perspective provided by the Yellowstone fires, to insist that the Smokey Bear campaign did not thwart the development of an ecologically sensitive fire policy seems disingenuous to many experts. In fact, Smokey all but precluded a "natural fire" policy for wilderness areas. But given the accumulation of fuels in an aging forest of closely spaced, afflicted trees, the only way that such a policy would presently be possible would be through a massive effort physically to clear the tinder and extra trees out of the forests, which Thomas Veblen of the University of Colorado told me was nearly impossible, but which Neil Sampson of American Forests now advocates. Absent such a massive effort, natural forest fires will always have to be monitored carefully, lest they become "mass" fires. Moreover, even prescribed burning may not be possible in many areas, due to the accumulation of fuel. According to Stephen Pyne, "Wildland fire is not a precision instrument. It is not some kind of Bunsen Burner that can be turned on and off at will. Starting in the mid-1970s, most of America's disastrous wildland fires resulted from breakdowns in prescribed burning. At the other end of their shovels, firefighters found something that resembled smoking existentialism."

The big issue raised by the 1988 Yellowstone fires—whether such fires were "natural," and whether letting natural fires burn themselves out would be ecologically sound—seems entirely academic. The fact is that in vast areas of the West, the forest composition has so decisively been altered by human intervention—converted to "doghair thickets" through logging and fire suppression over the years—that any argument today about whether a given forest fire is "natural," or whether "natural" fires should be allowed to "let burn," ignores the point that the forest itself is *unnatural,* and will probably remain that way until it passes through another cycle of glaciation. For the time being, humankind will, somehow, have to cope with the fire-prone forest it has created. The perverse irony is that today, when Smokey is under attack from so many quarters, we need him more than ever.

There is a further bit of bad news for the Western forests, that even more than overharvesting, fire suppression, insects, and drought, has dire ecological implications: global warming.

Nestled up against the Flatiron mountains, those dramatically tilted redrock slabs that provide a backdrop for the city of Boulder, Colorado, is the headquarters of the National Center for Atmospheric Research (NCAR—referred to as "En-car" by Boulderites and others concerned with its doings). Here Stephen H. Schneider, a climatologist, leads a group of researchers trying to figure out what is liable to happen to the earth's climate given the escalating levels of CO_2 and other greenhouse gases. Schneider, a competent and oft-published writer on the research findings in his field, has produced the definitive book on the subject, the plainly titled *Global Warming*, now in paperback. Here is what he says on page 304: "It is well known that the 25 percent increase in CO_2 documented since the industrial revolution, and the introduction of manmade chemicals such as chlorofluorocarbons (as responsible for stratospheric ozone depletion) since the 1950s should have trapped about two extra watts of radiant energy over every square meter of earth. That much has been accepted by most climatological specialists. Less well accepted, however, is how to translate those two watts of heat into 'X' degrees of surface temperature change, since this involves assumptions about how that heat will be distributed."

If the distribution of the heat is still a puzzle (in general the greatest amount of temperature change is expected to occur in the middle of continents and of oceans, where weather extremes are unmediated), a consensus about what *x* should stand for on a world-wide basis has pretty much been established: a gain of 3° Celsius (5.4°F), give or take a degree and a half over the next century. This is the conservative estimate; some fear that temperatures will rise 5°C within *fifty* years. Either figure has serious implications for forest health in the American West. What has surprised Schneider, along with many other scientists who have studied the issue of global warming, is how many citizens fail to grasp that such a change is widely accepted within the scientific community—which has patiently explained in book after book and article after article how increasing levels of CO_2 and other "greenhouse gases" in the atmosphere trap heat on or near the earth's surface.

The rate of CO_2 increase is estimated at approximately three gigatons (a gigaton is equal to one billion metric tons) per year, an imbalance caused not only by industrial-age emissions of CO_2 into the atmosphere, mainly from the burning of fossil fuels, but also by the reduction of terrestrial greenery—mainly forests. Over the past millennia, the world's forests have served as carbon "sinks," via oxygen-producing photosynthesis which could keep increasing CO_2 in check. Were it not for their destruction over the past thousand years (only about half the original forests remain on the planet), the trees would ordinarily be able to maintain a rough balance between carbon sequestered in vegetation as cellulose and carbon in the air as CO_2.

A substantial part of the blame for public confusion about whether or not temperatures will rise from a surfeit of CO_2, says Schneider, should be attributed to the press. A professional criticism that is supposed to make a journalist's bowels seize up in fear, is that his or her work is not "balanced"—especially in presentations of competing expert opinion. In journalistic accounts, for every view that something is the matter environmentally, there must be an opposing view that all is well, that the "alarmists" should be ignored. Conventional editorial wisdom holds that such balanced reporting produces truth. But in environmental writing, such a notion can be dangerously wrong and lead to something that is quite the opposite of truth.

What reporters forget, says Schneider, is that scientists do not discuss what they agree on very much, only what they don't agree on. Questioning is the essence of the scientific method. And this often gives the impression that the experts are squabbling over an important concept when, in fact, there may be a well-formed consensus about it. The squabbling is over the details. "The public policy process," he writes, "is subverted in confusing debate that inadequately represents the true nature of informed opinion."

This was certainly the case when James Hansen, who opened up the public debate, published a 1981 article in *Science* stating that the globe was heating up, and later testified to that effect before Congress in 1986 and 1987—the latter in widely reported hearings. As director of NASA's Goddard Institute for Space Studies, Hansen had to submit his testimony for vetting by the Reagan administration's Office of Management and Budget. "OMB marked up my testimony so badly they completely distorted what I wanted to say," Hansen recollects. Accordingly, he abandoned the OMB's politically approved script and testified as a private citizen. Ever since, the argument over global warming has raged —fueled, it would appear, more by politics than by scientific differences. And reporters have added to the cacophony by confusing politics with science, assuming in a simpleminded way that any radical, politics-driven scientist with a good press release—but who may well be a couple of cans short of a six-pack—has a scientific opinion every bit as valid (for "balance") as that of a more moderate and reputable scientist representing a research consensus.

For Schneider, the best of all possible media worlds would obtain if writers would kindly "back off the concept of 'balance' in favor of the concept of 'perspective.' If an issue is complicated, it simply is not enough to play off 'all sides,' particularly if the opinion of the majority of the experts—the people who created the consensus—is left out."

Leaving out the consensus is, of course, exactly what has happened in the journalism on global warming. Differing views were (and still are) "balanced" against one another, suggesting scientific doubt and continuing disputation when in fact an extremely broad international agreement exists that over the next century the planet's climate really will warm up at an unprecedented rate—ten times faster than ever before.

Schneider suggests that a good way to put scientific disagreement into perspective is for writers to express a range of opinion in "probabilistic" terms. A comparison of scientists' assessments of probability—the likelihood of something happening—can communicate differences accurately, as opposed to a story written "as a misleading debate among feuding scientists, or occasionally as a travesty perpetrated by polemicists and ideologues." Schneider himself tried out a journalistic probability question by asking the handful of fellow scientists known to be extremely skeptical about global warming to express their views on the probability that global temperatures would rise a minimum of two degrees Celsius in the twenty-first century. He found that the differences tended to wash out. For the most part, the skeptics put the likelihood of such warming at 60 percent or greater, as opposed to the 90 to 95 percent probability held by the great majority of scientists—not anywhere near the level of disagreement typically reported in the press.

Still, the details count—especially the details pertaining to forests and trees, for it is the trees that serve to restore equilibrium in the global carbon budget, which is now going into deficit at such an astonishing rate. The carbon balance issue is, by and large, raised mainly in terms of the devastation of tropical forests, where more than twenty-five million acres of rainforest are cut over every year and the slash is set afire, a dual-impact process that at once reduces the capability of the forest to absorb CO_2 because of the clear-cutting, and at the same time massively increases CO_2 release because of the burning. But the same thing is happening right here in the browning mountains of the western United States. Though our circumstances may be different from those of Brazil, we too have clear-cut the forest, and we too have our "burning season." On a worldwide basis, a study conducted by Ronald P. Neilson of Oregon State University revealed, the current rate of burning, here and elsewhere, together with the decomposition of dead vegetation, would increase the carbon dioxide discharged into the atmosphere by 43 percent annually.

In Fort Collins, Colorado, where I had gone to interview experts in bugs—Ann Lynch and Terry Shaw, who told me of the synchronicity of the infestations that were responsible for the browning I had observed—I also met one of the first U.S. scientists to call attention (during a 1979 lecture series sponsored by the American Geophysical Union) to increasing levels of atmospheric carbon dioxide. He is Douglas G. Fox, chief meteorologist at the Forest Service's Rocky Mountain Forest and Range Experiment Station, a physicist (PhD, Princeton) whose breadth of scholarship includes not only the dynamics of carbon balance, but philosophy, theology, and literature as well. His wife is a seminarian, he told me, in the process of becoming a Methodist minister. His daughter, a poet. In our interview, Fox showed himself to have the essayist's ability to glide seamlessly from topic to topic. He could speak of computer modeling, Wordsworth, acronymic government programs, Teilhard de Chardin, and the Almighty all in one sentence. "Forests may be God's strategy," he said by way of introducing one of his more reflective disquisitions, "in the way they mediate climate change."

Fox went on to explain that there is more carbon dioxide exchange between terrestrial (i.e., land-based) ecosystems than there is between the ocean and the atmosphere. "This is remarkable," he said, "when you consider that the terrestrial ecosystems are only twenty percent of the surface of the earth. The rest is ocean." The reason for the effectiveness of that crucial 20 percent is trees, which if everything is working properly on a global basis can take up excess carbon dioxide which, acting as a fertilizer, then causes the trees (and other plants) to put on additional "wood," which fixes more carbon and in turn increases the rate of photosynthesis in a self-regulating cycle until all is back to normal. Thus do the forests of the world carry out God's strategy.

The strategy, like many other divine balancing acts in nature, is elastic, able to tolerate shifts in environmental conditions. But only to a point. What happens when the forests are massively destroyed, as they are being destroyed in the tropics and potentially in temperate regions as well? What happens when there is an increase in CO_2 that is too massive and too sudden for the balancing act to bring everything back to normal? "We now have a dramatic input of human-generated CO_2 into the atmosphere in an extremely short time," said Fox. "So short that there cannot be an ecological adaptation fast enough to accommodate it."

In fact, the capacity of forests to increase in order to restore carbon balances has been called into question. Fox said that a colleague, Robin Tauche, a plant ecologist at the University of Nevada at Reno, had examined isotopes of carbon to determine increases in the rate of growth of trees because of increases of CO_2. Unlike the fertilizing effect of fluctuations of "natural" CO_2, Tauche found that when it comes to humanly induced carbon, different isotopes are involved that *do not* cause plant growth. Thus does the elastic in God's strategy finally snap.

"You can kill off a forest pretty easily at a sensitive point in its life," Fox said. "The mortality of the forests is, then, a stochastic [random] variable associated with other stochastic variables. What really concerns me at this point is not so much that the climate is changing, but how that change is going to lead to a change in the disturbance phenomenon. Such as fire."

Ordinarily, during the long sine-waves of natural global warming and cooling, trees can "migrate" to more northerly or southerly ranges, or to higher or lower elevations, in order to accommodate to hotter or cooler weather. Such migrations occur seasonally with birds and animals. With trees, which cannot move, the process is one in which new trees grow in new territory made available by more benign weather conditions, as old ones die where the climate has become inhospitable. Thus forests, over many hundreds or thousands of years, can relocate to accommodate a long-term change in weather as a warbler does with the coming of spring. According to a roundup paper on global warming by Fox and his Fort Collins colleague, Robert C. Musselman, "Each 1°C warming can move the range of plant distribution 100 to 160 km [60 to 100 miles] northward. . . . Past records of treeline elevation suggest about a 100m [333-foot] shift for each 1° change in temperature."

For some trees, faced with such changes—at three degrees Celsius, the latitudinal shift might be as much as three hundred miles, at five degrees, five hundred miles—the rapid warming over the next fifty to one hundred years will mean that trees will weaken and be more susceptible to drought and adventitious insect attack and disease, and because of a changed environment may no longer be able to regenerate. Accordingly, though a species may not necessarily be extinguished because of warming throughout its range, "northern" trees in a southerly part of their range will simply die, adding more fuel to an already fuel-ridden forest. As NCAR's Stephen Schneider puts it, "During the transition to a climate that would force redistribution of forest species, trees that were no longer suitable for the new climate might begin to die. If the climate change included a summer that was substantially drier and hotter than normal, as climatic models suggest is quite plausible in the United States, then the dying trees subject to that kind of heat stress would be much more vulnerable to fire."

For my final interview in Colorado—actually there were two visits, one in summer and another in December—I arranged to meet (on the day before Christmas) with Professor Jeffrey Minton, of the Department of Environmental, Population, and Organismic Biology at the University of Colorado in Boulder ("Our students call it 'orgasmic biology,' " Minton told me).

An enthusiastic researcher and teacher, Minton specializes in evolutionary biology, a field that will surely become increasingly important as the congeries of forces discussed in this chapter put the forests of the mountain West at risk. Minton is a fellow with a long view. "I get genotypes from trees and try to find what causes long life, what environmental factors are driving evolutionary changes on a microgeographic scale," he said. I showed him my picture of the dying trees north of Lake City. "Normal business," he said. "The spruce budworm has been killing trees for twenty-five million years—you can find it in the petrified forest in Arizona." He reassured me that tree-killing bugs have a survival strategy of their own, which is not to kill off the host. He said that this sort of survival strategy seemed to be operating in the case of the American chestnut, where the parasites are becoming less virulent and evolving toward a more symbiotic relationship with their host.

All of this was, I will confess, something of a relief, at least partly, until Minton started talking about how the frogs and toads are disappearing from Rocky Mountain areas. "Peepers, boreal toads, all are shrinking fast," said Minton. "Very clearly, here is a support group for the tree. You can't help but wonder what is causing all this." He paused for a moment. "Did anybody notice that twenty and thirty years before the forests got hit, the frogs and toads disappeared?"

Nature's braid has many strands. But which are the crucial ones to our posterity? Finding out is one of the evolutionary biologist's tasks. We are, apparently, in a post-crisis situation in the mountain West. The forest is different from the one encountered by those pioneers encouraged to go westering by the example of Jefferson's intrepid explorers Lewis and Clark at the beginning of the last century, finally to settle in the valleys of the Rockies and other mountain masses. Who knew then that it was not "God's strategy" simply to cut down every big tree in sight? Who could ever suspect that they would not just grow back? Who knew that it was not a similarly moral act to suppress ground fires? Fewer fires, more trees to build America and to guard it from its enemies. And if the bugs infested the forest, was that not a natural occurrence? Also a part of God's strategy?

The mystical Douglas Fox spoke to me of the assertion of the "Gaia hypothesis" that the world will always maintain itself in equilibrium, that whatever humans do will be finally overcome by a natural rebalancing so that the earth may continue on its cosmic course. I have no doubt that this view is correct. It's just that the process of natural rebalancing may not be altogether healthy for the species that caused the imbalance in the first place. By contrast, Teilhard de Chardin, Fox said, assumed that man had a responsibility to take care of the world; and I believe that, too.

Meanwhile, the climate warms, changing at a rate ten or, as some say, maybe even a hundred times faster than normal. The CO_2 load in the atmosphere increases at a rate 143 percent of normal, year after year. The trees cannot adapt, and then at some point the true nightmare begins, of such tree death and fire that nothing will ever grow back on the fused slopes of the Western mountains, the great ranges transformed to mere piles of dirt and rock interspersed by desert shrubs, like the browsed-off slopes facing the Aegean Sea, ruined for the millennia by mercenary Greeks. The forests are half gone already around the world. And with the remaining trees being eliminated by an array of forces entrained by *us*, the question, as voiced by Robert Bruck back in North Carolina, becomes starkly simple: Where is the threshold? If there are not enough forests left to absorb—according to God's strategy—the excess CO_2 we create on a global basis, what then? As I write this (in the summer of 1994), twenty-six mass fires are raging throughout the Sierra-Cascades and the Rockies. In one of them, near Glenwood Springs, Colorado, thirteen firefighters have lost their lives.

The words of the young Forest Service girl at the storefront office in Lake City echo in my mind. "Terrified," she had said. She was no ecologist, of course. But as the great conservationist Aldo Leopold warned, the ecologist "may become as callous as an undertaker to the mysteries at which he officiates." So perhaps hers is the right word for it after all, in these dying, tinder-dry unnatural forests of the American West. *Terrified.*

6

Path of the Gypsy Rover

The fault, dear Brutus, is not
in our stars, But in ourselves . . .
—William Shakespeare,
Julius Caesar, *I:2*

For a good many citizens, a discussion of spruce budworms and pine bark beetles in Western mountains has to do with such large issues of resource management and global ecological balances that the implications are hard to apprehend in personal terms. For the majority of us—especially those living in metropolitan suburbs of the Middle West, the Northeast, and parts of the South—these are abstractions, dealing with unfamiliar creatures, unfamiliar trees, and unfamiliar controversies. But there is one tree-scourge that people in these populous parts of the country know all too well. An unwelcome migrant, it came to these shores a century and a quarter ago, in 1869.

Let me put the event in context. In 1869, Texas rivers rose an incredible forty-seven feet after three days of rain, inundating whole towns and killing thousands. In Kansas, renegade Indians raided presumably peaceful and secure white settlements along the Republican River. In Illinois, the Mississippi River paddlewheel steamer *Stonewall* caught fire off Cairo, killing two hundred passengers and crew. In New York, Jay Gould and Jim Fisk cornered the gold market, setting off a ruinous financial panic. And in suburban Medford, Massachusetts, Etienne Leopold Trouvelot of 27 Myrtle Street, a Harvard professor of astronomy recently arrived from France, whose hobby it was to crossbreed silk-producing caterpillars, misplaced some gypsy-moth eggs he had brought from his homeland.

The last of these events, compared to the others, sounds trivial, but as anyone who has seen a gypsy-moth ravaged woods now knows, only the minor mishap at 27 Myrtle Street turned out to be permanently disastrous. And it is a disaster that keeps unfolding, as the progeny of those tiny specks, *Lymantria dispar,* spread inexorably through the weakening forests of the New World—with the rates of diffusion and degrees of destruction increasing as the mortality of gypsy-moth defoliated trees is potentiated by other human-caused environmental stresses.

The full-grown gypsy-moth larva, with whom a significant percentage of the American population has now become intimately acquainted, is a fuzzy, two-inch-long eating machine with a double row of red and blue dots lining its back, interspersed with whitish stripes (mnemonic: the tricolor of France) on a black background. Threadlike caterpillars emerge in spring from egg masses deposited the previous year by the flightless female (a creamy-white moth), which lays eggs in hidden places, fifty to a thousand in a clutch. The male, which is brownish, does fly—in a zigzag pattern, sniffing out females who emit a pheromone as an attractant—and will mate with many females during his summer of life.

After delivery, the female moth covers her eggs—a flattish irregularly shaped mass from the size of a thumbprint up to that of a big toe—with buff-colored hairs from her abdomen, helping protect her future progeny through the cold winter. Then she dies. The egg masses can survive temperatures as low as twenty below zero Fahrenheit.

Eastern deciduous oaks of virtually all kinds, and the aspens (quaking and big-tooth) are the preferred meal of the gypsy-moth larvae—although they will also feed on birch, willow, crabapple, and Norway maple to the point of total defoliation. More resistant are white pine and blue spruce, plus hickory, service berry, alder, basswood, ironwood, beech, elm, sweetgum, poplar, and birch. These trees are eaten but not defoliated. Trees that the caterpillars tend to avoid include ash, locust, tulip tree, spruce, hemlock, fir, sycamore, and black gum. If hungry enough, however, the larvae have been known to eat practically anything.

The gypsy-moth larvae eat from the top down and the outside in on a favored tree, going first for the tender leaves, of which one caterpillar can consume several a day. As soon as the larvae emerge from the eggs they head upward toward the light. Then, after attaining elevation, they launch themselves into space, rappelling down a silken thread of their own making. The idea is for the wind to catch them and swing them over to another tree—"ballooning"—so that the defoliation can continue with the least interruption. The defoliation on preferred tree species is complete, with trees utterly denuded in the space of a week. Great patches of woods can, at the height of summer, have no more leaves than in midwinter. When the caterpillars stop eating to pupate, first-year defoliated trees will put out another flush of leaves, but this depletes their energy so severely that they often cannot survive a cold winter. After two or three years of defoliation, not even the hardiest tree can survive.

As Northeasterners have learned (for they have had the longest experience with the pest), at the peak of a gypsy-moth season the larvae will balloon by the thousands when frightened, covering a passerby's head and face with squirming bodies attached to a vast intertwined network of threads. Even without causing a mass descent, a woods walker knows when there is an infestation from the sheer noise of thousands of caterpillars defecating "frass," the droppings which rattle on the dry leaves below in an unmistakable pitter-pat that for all the world sounds like a summer rain, even though the sun may be out and the day clear. It is not a comforting sound.

Finally, in midsummer, the caterpillars pupate, creating a dark brown shell. A couple of weeks later the moths emerge to begin the cycle all over again.

In Monsieur Trouvelot's Medford neighborhood, the cycle repeated itself for nearly twenty years before government scientists began to pay attention to homeowners' reports that something dreadful seemed to be happening to the trees. Finally, one spring, J. P. Dill's yard (among others) was utterly overrun with gypsy-moth larvae. "There was not a place on the outside of the house where you could put your hand without touching caterpillars," he said. "We always tapped the screen doors when we opened them, and the monstrous great creatures would fall down, but in a minute or two would crawl up the side of the house again. The caterpillars spun down from the trees by the hundreds, even then they were of a large size [and] were so thick on the trees that they were stuck together like cold macaroni."

And so, after two decades of marshaling forces, did the gypsy moths' march begin. Nobody knew it then (and even now many have not yet gotten the message), but the moth was unstoppable. J. P. Dill's experience has occurred year after year in ever-widening circles. By 1891, two years after appearing en masse in Medford, the gypsy moth had moved into adjacent Boston suburbs as far north as Beverly, though not yet into Boston proper. Ten years after that, caterpillars had reached the Rhode Island line. The New Hampshire border was crossed in 1903, Connecticut fell in 1906, Vermont in 1912; by the early 1920s, gypsy moths had reached southward to the New York City suburbs and northward to the Canadian border.

As infestation progressed throughout New England over the fifty-year period following M. Trouvelot's awful accident, various control measures were attempted, with just enough success to keep a growing legion of entomologists gainfully employed. During the relatively localized outbreaks in the 1880s, the affected Massachusetts towns mounted an effort to control the gypsy moth by destroying the egg masses by hand, one at a time. That this approach was rear-guard and scarcely adequate soon became clear. In 1891, Charles V. Riley, head of the U.S. Agriculture Department's new Division of Entomology, recommended to the Massachusetts Gypsy Moth Commission that the only way to deal with the pest was not local handpicking of the moths' ova, like some sort of hapless Easter egg hunt, but a massive eradication campaign using Paris green, an arsenic compound, in heavily infested areas.

Riley was persuasive. He pointed out that so far the gypsy moth was relatively confined, and that it did not seem to spread quickly, since it had taken more than twenty years to infest a few Boston suburbs. A budget of $100,000 would do it, said the government man. Only it didn't do it. The spraying equipment, meant for tidy orchards, was hard to manage in the rough terrain of New England woodlots. Worse, the Paris green was killing the trees as well as the gypsy moths. After two years, the Gypsy Moth Commission decided to go back to a version of their original plan. They hired large crews to search out and destroy the egg masses during the winter, and in summer to do spraying where they could, augmented by traps and sticky bands—a regimen used by millions of suburban homeowners to this day.

In those optimistic times, the commission thought that if they just kept at it they could eventually eradicate the gypsy moth. They returned to the state legislature year after year seeking increasing levels of financial support for the work. Mercifully (or so it would seem), the infestations began to diminish, and as they did, the legislature became less and less interested in providing the appropriations so urgently requested by the scientists. They did not know it, but the gypsy moth was not being vanquished by their appropriations. *Lymantria dispar* was in one of its mysterious periods of population decline (about which more later). Thus the legislature fell into the trap of a post-hoc fallacy and in 1900 abolished the commission, suggesting that gypsy-moth control was henceforth a matter for landowners to tend to on an individual basis.

With a perversity that the pest has become known for, the gypsy moth came roaring back a couple of years later. A new craze took over—a full-court press with biological controls, beyond the ladybug level begun by Charles Riley. If the gypsy moth was only a minor pest in Europe and Asia, then all that would be needed would be to import the insects that preyed on it in the old country. In 1905, Leland O. Howard, Riley's successor at what was then called the Bureau of Entomology, with an optimism bordering on hubris (which seems to be the norm for control-oriented entomologists), said that it would take only a couple of years for the predators to bring the gypsy-moth population down to manageable levels. The trouble was that the imported parasites, unable to adapt, quickly died out, simply vanished (although one fungus did survive, as we shall see), or had no discernible effect. Meanwhile, the caterpillars were routinely defoliating large areas of New England while World War I came and went.

By 1922, the gypsy moth finally reached the Hudson River, which was then declared to be an entomological Maginot Line. Wherever a local population was found in New Jersey, it would be quickly exterminated, at whatever cost, with every weapon known in the control arsenal, from the one-by-one destruction of egg masses to repeated arsenic sprayings. The strategy was to hold off any further advance, in the hope that a new pesticide would be found that would be more effective than the arsenic-based compounds.

They got their weapon as soon as World War II was over. It was DDT.

DDT—dichloro-diphenyl-trichloro-ethane—was synthesized in 1874, just five years after M. Trouvelot's fateful carelessness, but it was not until 1939 that the compound's miraculous bug-killing properties came to light, winning a Nobel Prize for its discoverer, Paul Müller of Switzerland. As Rachel Carson points out in her still-powerful book *Silent Spring,* DDT was first used during wartime in powder form to dust lice-infested soldiers, refugees, and prisoners of war. Since there were no physiological reactions on the part of the dustees, it was generally assumed that the compound was safe as well as effective. But the army scientists had jumped to the wrong conclusion. Unlike other chlorinated hydrocarbons, Carson's book revealed, "DDT *in powder form* is not readily absorbed through the skin. Dissolved in oil, as it usually is, DDT is definitely toxic. If swallowed, it is absorbed slowly through the digestive tract; it may also be absorbed through the lungs. Once it has entered the body, it is stored largely in organs rich in fatty substances (because DDT itself is fat-soluble)." She also pointed out how DDT persists and therefore is concentrated as it progresses from organism to organism in its journey through the food chain. DDT-sprayed alfalfa (in her example) is converted into a meal to feed chickens, whereupon it concentrates in the eggs the chickens lay, and thus moves to the human breakfast table where concentration continues in the bodies of children. Alternatively, a nursing mother can concentrate DDT in breast milk and pass it along to her baby, who perhaps already has a fairly large amount stored in its tiny body from transfers through the placenta during the fetal stage.

It is not as though large segments of the population were not aware of the characteristics of DDT, even before Carson's book. As she points out, the Food and Drug Administration suggested in 1950 that "the potential hazard of DDT has been underestimated." The effect on wildlife was identified even earlier, in 1946, when ornithologist Richard H. Pough of the National Audubon Society warned of extreme toxic effects in a story carried in *The New Yorker*—the magazine that would, sixteen years later, serialize *Silent Spring.*

The relation of DDT to the march of the gypsy moth through the Northeastern woods and beyond is both close and tangled; the irony is that while industrial forestry thought that DDT would finally vanquish the gypsy moth, the reverse happened. The gypsy moth, in effect, vanquished DDT. At first, the ever-expanding use of DDT, despite warnings here and there about its dangers, seemed ineluctable. The miraculous new compound was used with abandon on all manner of crops and pests during the late 1940s and into the 1950s. Any concerns expressed by citizens and scientists about DDT were politically ineffective and easily dismissed by the chemical industry and its allies in the U.S. government as the fears of a bunch of alarmist birdwatchers hindering the great postwar technological advances then under way in industrial agriculture and forestry.

Then the "economic entomologists," as they are called—the government and industry scientists concerned with pest control—made an astounding public-relations error, not to mention a scientific one. They decided, in the spirit of Charles Riley who seventy-five years before had promised eradication, that this time, through the use of DDT, they could really do it. Where Riley had sprayed a limited area of eastern Massachusetts by crudely pumping Paris green through the nozzles of orchard equipment, this time the control entomologists would spray millions of acres all along the gypsy moths' advancing front by means of aircraft flying low over town parks, farm woodlots, suburban gardens—anywhere there might be a tree harboring an egg mass, a larva, or the moth itself. The trouble was that the advancing front was not located in a remote forest, but in the suburbs of New York City, among other places, including populous and well-heeled communities on Long Island and in Westchester County.

The gypsy-moth carpet-bombing campaign targeted one million acres in 1956, after which the USDA announced that the next year three million acres would be treated. With this news, Robert Cushman Murphy of the American Museum of Natural History in New York sued to prevent the spraying on Long Island. The case, which went to the Supreme Court, was lost, and the sprayers blithely prepared to inundate the New York suburbs, ignoring the pleas of dairy farmers, beekeepers, shellfishermen, and the parents (like me at the time) of infant children. "Please do not spray *us*," we all said.

They sprayed anyway, and indiscriminately. As Rachel Carson reported, "The gypsy moth programs were marked by many acts of irresponsibility. Because the spray planes were paid by the gallon rather than by the acre there was no effort to be conservative and many properties were sprayed not once but several times." The outrage that I felt then is strongly recollected as I write this, for I objected to the spraying, too, knowing that my children would play on the poisoned grass outside our garden apartment, run through bushes with DDT-covered leaves, pick toxic flowers along the woods path that led to the railroad station, play with sprayed toys, put all manner of objects coated with this persistent pesticide into their mouths.

Bland reassurances came from the officials in charge of the spraying, who said there was nothing to worry about. But none of us was mollified. Citizen meetings were held by the National Audubon Society and others. Significantly, the meetings I attended were not attended by mere nature lovers or little old ladies in tennis shoes, but by people who worked on radio programs, who were television newscasters, who wrote for or edited magazines and newspapers. Among the folks whom the economic entomologists had dive-bombed were what some latter-day politicians have called "the media elite." And they were sore as a boil, and righteously so. On Long Island, which along with Westchester County had been utterly drenched, the gypsy moth staged an astonishing "flareback" in 1958, almost as if the DDT was nourishing the progeny of the previous year's moth population rather than destroying it.

Even though the spraying programs were greatly curtailed after the 1957 debacle, citizen outrage intensified. Apologists for DDT, lushly financed by industry and government, did their best to discredit the opponents, but we had resources of our own. The writers for *Time* and *Newsweek* and *The New York Times*, the producers of TV documentaries and radio shows, did not just cover our meetings, they were participants—suburban homeowners with small children of their own. Then, once *Silent Spring* came out in 1962, what had been an inchoate movement coalesced, and DDT was attacked in the media on a broad front, not just for its terrible failure to control gypsy moths in the Northeast while putting humans, wildlife, farms, and fisheries at risk. The upshot: A decade later, this compound and some other persistent pesticides were banished. The reasons for the ban were multiple, and certainly there are other pesticides today that should also be proscribed. But at least DDT is gone, and the gypsy moth started it all—perhaps the only good thing this dreadful creature has ever done for humankind in America.

By the 1960s, the gypsy moth had become firmly established in the New York suburbs, having defoliated trees there with the same intensity it had shown in New England; and it had crossed the Hudson's entomological barrier as easily as the Germans rolled over the real Maginot Line. By the 1970s, it had moved resolutely beyond New Jersey westward to Pennsylvania and, just as the entomologists had feared, by the 1980s was marching southward along a broad front down the Appalachians and spreading across the piedmont regions. Today the gypsy moth routinely defoliates woodlands in Maryland and Virginia and all points north nearly to the Canadian border, where it is stopped by twenty-below-zero winter freezes that the egg masses cannot survive.

While the Northeast and the Middle Atlantic states constitute the largest area where the gypsy moth lives and dines, the place that has forest scientists most concerned at present is in central and northern Michigan. Here the moth, though it was discovered in Michigan in the 1950s (and was targeted by the 1957 aerial spraying campaign), has since the late 1980s gone on a rampage, opening up a vast new territory to invade and conquer—in effect a Middle Western second front. The crucial datum is this: the rate of gypsy-moth spread is now much more rapid than before. Many have tried to assign a miles-per-year figure to the moth's advance—with some entomologists suggesting that in the southerly and westerly expansion, beginning at 27 Myrtle Street, the leading edge is moving at the rate of somewhere between five and twenty miles a year—but there seems to be no statistical consensus. One reason for the imprecision is the maddeningly random way gypsy-moth populations explode and then seemingly subside, which makes it nearly impossible for scientists to develop a predictive model. I have read in various scientific articles that this cycle averages three years, or that it averages seven years, or that it averages twelve years. The confusion among the experts is yet another victory for the gypsy moth, this time a psychological one, after a century-long string of them.

Recently, researchers from West Virginia University and the U.S. Forest Service Experiment Station at Morgantown, West Virginia, addressed themselves to this problem with something of a reverse twist.

Using data developed under the Domestic Plant Quarantine Act, which annually identifies "infested" areas in order to control inadvertent dispersal of gypsy-moth egg masses on plant material, the West Virginians found that when they applied a modern rate-of-spread predictive model, taken from Quarantine Act statistics of 1966 to 1986, to the period from 1900 to 1950, the "spread model" based on 1966-to-1986 data "greatly over-estimated the rate of spread from 1900–1950." That is, the rate in recent years is now so much higher it cannot be applied as a predictive model historically. This may be a backward way of proving it, but the method does tend to confirm what seems to be an alarmingly rapid advance of the gypsy moth into vast new territories in recent years. These researchers believe that the rate of spread (their data indicate twelve miles a year) would be much less, were it not for gypsy-moth egg masses being moved from place to place at an increasing rate on recreational vehicles, nursery stock, and in the holds of ships.

Up in Michigan, now the locus of much entomological attention in view of the recent gypsy-moth population explosion, the woods have been hit before. The devastation was not by bugs, but by humans.

To Longfellow, pre-Columbian Michigan was the mystical "dark and gloomy forest" that once rose behind the shores of Gitchee Gumee, "the shining Big-Sea-Water." But Hiawatha was displaced by a more powerful legendary figure, Paul Bunyan, a lumberjack twelve feet eleven inches tall and weighing 888 pounds, who could topple thirty-one trees with a single swipe of his ax.

The figure of Paul Bunyan, the giant tree-feller of the North Woods, may, some scholars believe, have misty origins in Irish folk tales. But the legend as we know it did not arise from campfire songs and stories of preliterate Bronze Age Celts, but from the typewriters of turn-of-the-century American journalists and public-relations men. The first Bunyan story, "The Round River Drive," was written by James MacGillivray and published by the *Oscoda Press*, a small-town northern Michigan newspaper, on August 10, 1906. "The unsigned tale," writes historian Mary Jane Hennigar, "was undoubtedly first published merely to amuse the lumberjacks and company owners with a story they had probably heard in the camps. Although Bunyan tales may have been printed before 1906 in other local newspapers in the timber regions, this is the earliest one to come to light."

"We'd placed our camp on the rivers' bank," MacGillivray's text begins, "we didn't know it was Round River then and we put in over a hundred million feet, the whole blamed cut coming off one forty. You see that forty was built like one of them 'Gypsum' pyramids, and the timber grew clear to the peak on all four sides." In a later version of the story, somewhat revised for a general audience and appearing in the *Detroit News Tribune* on July 24, 1910, MacGillivray explains, tellingly, "You see, back in those days the government didn't care nothin' about the timber and all you had to do was hunt up a good tract on some runnin' stream—cut her and float her down."

The playful notion of "The Round River Drive" is that, having logged off the forty-acre "Gypsum" (Egyptian) pyramid, Paul Bunyan's crew floated the logs down the river, "makin' about a mile a day" on the drive, when they came upon a logged-off "hill forty" much like their own. And then another, and another. At length they figured it out: "It was Round River." They had been passing their own camp again and again.

After 1910, Bunyan stories appeared more and more often in print. A verse version of "The Round River Drive," by Douglas Malloch, was published in *The American Lumberman* magazine in 1914, and in that same year, William B. Laughead, an advertising copywriter with the Red River Lumber Company, produced a booklet for customers with embellishments to the Bunyan story, including, for the first time, Babe the Blue Ox. The company, headquartered in Westwood, California, had holdings throughout the Great Lakes states, and is credited with giving the Paul Bunyan legend national prominence—leading one academic folklorist to label the whole business "fakelore."

Unfaked, however, was what happened to the woods, which in turn may well have something to do with the gypsy moth.

"When the timber crew descended on an area, events moved swiftly," writes Michigan author John Eastman of the rapacious logging of the late nineteenth century. "Lumbering was an attack operation, as thoroughly strategic and disciplined as a military siege. The forest, suddenly noisy as a factory, swarmed with men in a hurry." By such means did the commercial sawyers level the bulk of the pineries in just fifteen years, between 1875 and 1890. "The white and red pine forest began on an east-west line from Saginaw to Lake Michigan and extended virtually unbroken to the Straits of Mackinac and above," says Eastman.

The loggers not only cleared the pines north of the Saginaw line, they left a layer of slash—the tops and branches of the great logs—sometimes accumulating to a depth of three feet, discarded in the rush to send the timber down the rivers and into the mills. As a result, what the loggers did not destroy, fire did, as what Eastman describes as a holocaust swept through northern Michigan.

Some of the old pine stumps survived, remarkably, and are the only reminder of what the forest of Longfellow's Nokomis must have been like; for the pines never grew back. Though some red pines are grown commercially, and a few remnant stands of white pine remain, the original forest was never to arise again, for the pines could not regenerate from the stumps. "No living person will ever experience the Michigan pine forest as it was in the nineteenth century," says Eastman.

The old forest was much on the mind of a state official with whom I was chatting as we toured a gypsy-moth ravaged oak-and-aspen woodland in Roscommon, a county that lies about knuckle-high on the handprint that a map of lower Michigan resembles. "It's not the same forest," he said. "Not the *natural* forest, the forest that used to be here, which was pine, now cut over and gone. The soil is not quite right for the replacement trees. That is one reason why the gypsy moths have done so much damage."

Paul Bunyan, meet *Lymantria dispar.*

The gypsy-moth tour was arranged for the benefit of local officials and state legislators by Cora Gorsuch, a former school teacher turned forest entomologist now with the Michigan State University Cooperative Extension Service. Her assignment was to coordinate the Michigan Gypsy Moth Education Program. Gorsuch is an open-faced, pleasant woman reminiscent of the kind of popular classroom teacher that finds most of the world interesting and agreeable. "Actually, I like insects," she said. "They're cute." But then she added, "Not the gypsy moth—at least not in the massive numbers we've been seeing lately. That is scary."

Gorsuch went on to tell me that the gypsy moth, which had heretofore been confined to an area around Bay City (although the moth was first discovered in Lansing in 1954), had begun spreading up through the hardwood groves and former pineries beginning in the mid-1980s, moving northward just as the Paul Bunyan lumbermen had done a century before. At the outset, gypsy-moth defoliation had been negligible, she said, not too worrisome—with defoliation occurring on no more than 100 or 150 square miles. But then, starting in 1989, the defoliated area in northern Michigan suddenly quintupled, and the tree death was extensive in a half dozen counties. Upwards of thirty counties in all were hit in the next several years, all but a few of them north of the "Saginaw line" that once marked the beginning of pine country. (Geographical note for non-Midwesterners: "northern Michigan" is the phrase used by Michiganders to describe the northern part of the hand-shaped lower peninsula. There is a section of the state—the Upper Peninsula—that is north of northern Michigan, separated from the lower peninsula by the Mackinac Strait, but that doesn't count as part of northern Michigan.)

"The trees can stand two or three years of defoliation," said Gorsuch, "unless they are already weak." As it turned out, the oaks and aspens of northern Michigan—the forest that had risen between the stumps of the felled pines—had been weakened during the 1980s by several years of drought followed by widespread flooding of the rivers and creeks that had swept the soil away in some wooded areas and deposited a thick layer of silt in others, to the detriment of the trees in both cases.

With the massed gypsy-moth attack that began in late 1989, vacationers owning cottages in the woods returned in the spring to find the roads dangerously slicked by the green guts of caterpillars mashed by traffic, and the outer walls and roofs of the summer places shrouded with masses of heavy-bodied larvae. "I have seen cabins so completely covered by gypsy-moth caterpillars," said Gorsuch, "that I couldn't tell what color the siding was painted." The recollection of the thick, squirming layer of hairy larvae made even bug-lover Gorsuch shift uncomfortably in her office chair as she told me of it.

As the gypsy moths increased their devastation of northern Michigan, so did the demands of residents, vacationers, and commercial forest owners that authorities do something to put a stop to it. But the Cooperative Extension Service at Michigan State University, the experts at the University of Michigan, and others knowledgeable about the ways of the gypsy moth, were not about to let state and local government agencies be stampeded into a massive aerial spraying attack, as had happened in 1957 and again in 1964 when a concerted—and failed—effort at eradication took place in and around Bay City. Significantly, Cora Gorsuch's job title named her coordinator not of a gypsy-moth control program, but of an *education* program, which meant that the challenge was to figure out how *not* to spray, or at least to keep spraying at a minimum.

But she and the others were not having an easy job of it. According to Ron Priest of the Michigan Department of Agriculture, also a participant in the gypsy-moth tour I attended in Roscommon County, "We decided against excessive spraying because it is not practical to spray the entire state—ecologically or economically." Still, the U.S. Forest Service, even though it does not believe the gypsy moth to be an economic problem, offers to pay half the cost of spraying private forest land if the counties pick up the other half, in a program administered by the Michigan Department of Agriculture. Since many second-home landowners, private and commercial forest owners, and others are clamoring to be sprayed, and since there are many aerial applicators eager for their business, considerable pressure is put on the counties to avail themselves of the Forest Service–MDA program. Such is the shape of gypsy-moth politics in Michigan. When Stuart Gage, a Michigan State University entomologist, told the Roscommon tour group that "You can't hammer this thing into the ground with chemicals," a representative from the U.S. Forest Service rose to state that in view of the potential for the gypsy moth to spread to other states of the upper Middle West, Michigan had a "moral obligation" to do a "lot more spraying." Tom Ellis, who like Cora Gorsuch is also on the gypsy-moth education team from Michigan State, replied that since the state borders on two-thirds of all the fresh water in the United States, it has another kind of moral obligation—having to do with whether or not Michigan's rivers and streams, which empty into four of the five Great Lakes, should be laced with pesticides. "We have to keep environmental issues uppermost," he said.

In the case of Michigan, the environmental concerns have prevailed; the state's preference is neither to eradicate the gypsy moth nor even to control it much, but to let it control itself. The limited spraying program uses Bt (short for *Bacillus thuringiensis*), a benign (to humans and most other life forms) biological agent whose active ingredient is a bacterium that exists in nature and causes the gypsy moth to lose its appetite. Other pesticides are legal, but frowned upon. Carbaryl (sold under the name Sevin), a pesticide greatly touted as nonpersistent replacement for DDT, is so toxic to bees that its use is discouraged in Michigan (and many other states, as well). Diflubenzuron (Dimilin), a replacement for Sevin, is better, not so harmful to bees, but does affect crustaceans and therefore may not be used over open water. The potential for disrupting aquatic ecosystems is what concerned Gage, who feared that Dimilin, being much more effective than Bt, would be widely used in aerial spraying. The problem with Bt is that, while efficacious, it must be sprayed on the larvae at exactly the right stage of development, or it won't work. The crucial moment is when the larvae are still tiny, about a half inch long—the first instar, which lasts between seven and ten days. The scenario that Gage and other scientists worry about is that the gypsy moth might develop resistance to Bt if the pesticide is used too much. "Then we are in real trouble," he said, "because then people will demand that the government use harder pesticides." In contrast to the U.S. Forest Service's official view, Gage recommended that "We treat Bt very carefully."

The general antipathy on the part of scientists like Gage toward the mass spraying of chemicals as a means of control is not necessarily based on any refined environmental sensibility, but on an awareness, after nearly a half century of trying, of the miserable fact that mass spraying doesn't work. These days, gypsy moth experts are more interested in the various ways the moths control themselves. One of these is the apparently self-generating gypsy-moth "wilt." Although observed since 1911, it was not until 1947 that the cause of the wilt—in which limp, oozy gypsy-moth cadavers hang by their middles from leaves, twigs, and branches—was found to be a virus, now familiarly referred to as NPV (nucleopolyhedrosis virus).

In Michigan, Cora Gorsuch told me, NPV had already created a gypsy-moth population crash. Just prior to my visit, scientists had identified a 1,200-acre area where the populations had totally collapsed. "When that happens," she said, "the virus in the gypsy moths causes a kind of ooze in the trees which smells terrible," and she directed me to a place where I could sample the odor at first hand. I did not need to, for I had smelled it in my own Maryland backyard. Later, I discussed the matter with a USDA lab technician on a gypsy-moth project, who said she could hardly keep her food down when working with the stuff.

It is comforting to know that the gypsy moth carries within it the possibility of self-limitation. The trouble is, for NPV to kick in decisively requires just the right set of climatic circumstances—dark and cloudy days, since the virulence of NPV is greatly reduced by ultraviolet radiation. And it requires extremely high densities of full-grown caterpillars, which makes the idea of the moth regulating itself a kind of entomological catch-22. NPV can function well naturally, but only where the forest is subject to catastrophic defoliation. A possibility exists that artificially applied NPV can be effective under certain circumstances. In 1978, the U.S. Forest Service created a concoction of various strains of the virus in solution, called "Gypchek," which may be applied to infested areas. More recently, a quite fast-acting strain was isolated by U.S. Department of Agriculture scientists, and dyed red to screen it from harmful ultra-violet rays. This formulation may be able to induce epizootics—the term biologists use to describe the simultaneous death of a large number of individuals within a species—prior to defoliation, since unlike Gypchek it can infect the larvae at an early stage of their development, before the caterpillars become such voracious leaf-eaters.

A more recent discovery pertaining to the natural regulation of gypsy moth populations is *Entomophaga maimaiga*, a fungus that like NPV can also cause epizootics. And here at last is a bit of poetic justice in the century-long beating U.S. trees and forests have been taking at the hands of the alien gypsy moth. "Good news," trilled Joan Lee Faust, the *New York Times* garden writer in the spring of 1989. "Gypsy moth caterpillars met their match this year—a fungus. Homeowners and foresters, who found dead caterpillars adhering to the trunks of trees, have seen the evidence of this kill and can thank the wet spring for their good fortune."

The discovery came about when field workers at Lockwood Farm, a facility operated by the Connecticut Agriculture Experiment Station in New Haven, observed what they thought was an outbreak of NPV. But something was different about the way the gypsy moths died. Instead of the larvae corpses hanging by their middles in an inverted V from leaves and twigs, as is typical of NPV, the dead caterpillars at Lockwood Farm were attached to the trunk, head down. Moreover, the epizootic, which occurred in June, was unusually early for NPV, since it struck prior to the massive buildup of mature caterpillars that is necessary for the virus to take hold. Puzzled, entomologist Theodore Andreadis, a staff member at the New Haven experiment station, collected samples and, back at his lab, discovered that the cause of death was not NPV at all, but a fungus that he could not identify. Immediately, he sent some of the collected material to the Boyce Thompson Institute for Plant Research at Cornell University for examination.

According to Ann E. Hajek, a researcher on the team asked to get to the bottom of the mystery, the Boyce Thompson scientists confirmed that the dead gypsy moths Andreadis sent them had indeed been killed by an unusual fungus. More unusual still, reports from gypsy-moth watchers throughout New England flooded in, describing epizootics similar to the one found at Lockwood Farm. "Caterpillars from all over the Northeast were sent to our laboratory for dissection," Hajek writes in *Natural History*, "and to our great surprise, biochemical analysis of enzymes and DNA fragments of fungus isolated from cadavers revealed that the pathogen was the same as that known to cause epizootics in Japanese populations." The reason for the surprise was that *Entomophaga* (Greek for "insect eater") *maimaiga* (Japanese for gypsy moth) had been collected by government biologists in 1909—during the surge of interest in biological controls after the failures of arsenic spraying and the handpicking of egg masses. The Japanese fungus had been propagated in a Massachusetts laboratory by those early entomologists, and released in the Boston suburbs in 1910 and 1911. But nothing had happened, and so the experiment was forgotten until the mystery fungus was identified by scientists at the Boyce Thompson Institute eighty years later.

The following spring, Hajek introduced the fungus, which eats the gypsy moth from the inside out, into some Boyce Thompson test plots by spreading fungus-laden material around the bases of some oak trees she expected to be defoliated during the summer. On some others, she placed a number of fungus-infected caterpillars directly on the bark. She waited one month. The kill rate was a satisfying 85 percent.

The question is: Why does the fungus work now, when it did not before? One answer, suggests Hajek, may be that some of the epizootics of the past that were attributed to NPV were actually caused by the Japanese fungus. Others speculate that it took nearly a century for the fungus to adapt to a new environment and to reach sufficient diffusion to create an epizootic. Whatever the case, the fungus is with us now, and left to its own devices will make its way quite naturally into the areas the gypsy moth has infested. Still, Michigan's Cora Gorsuch was interested in the fungus, but wary. "There's a problem," she said. And indeed, with the gypsy moth nothing is easy. "*Entomophaga maimaiga*," she continued, "takes nearly one-hundred-percent humidity to cause an epizootic. And how often is that going to happen at just the right time?" The point was confirmed by Ralph E. Webb, a U.S. Department of Agriculture entomologist headquartered at Beltsville, Maryland. "In a dry year," Webb told *Science News*, "the fungus would fall flat on its face." And so a moment of hope came and went. The gypsy-moth war would go on for a while longer.

When you listen to people like Cora Gorsuch, Tom Ellis, Ron Priest, and Stuart Gage talk of their research in forums that they give in Michigan every year, you have to realize that these sorts of meetings take place in county seats everywhere in all the states (thirty-one) to which the gypsy moth has traveled so far. Thousands of Americans are briefed, thousands of brochures are printed and distributed about Bt and burlap bands and sticky tape to trap the caterpillars as they climb the oaks and maples. A mighty enterprise.

After looking through the footnotes and bibliographies of even twenty or thirty scientific papers, as I have done in the course of my study, you realize that in any one year many hundreds are written. A comprehensive gypsy-moth bibliographic database would tax the memory bank of a mainframe computer, never mind the brain of a scientist wishing to be au courant in his or her field. Indeed, there are probably more American scientists—in government, university, and corporate laboratories and field stations—devoting a substantial part of their careers to this one insect than to any other single species save *Homo sapiens* itself.

Moreover, when you consider the spraying—from planes or tank trucks or backyard hose attachments—that has gone on to combat the gypsy moth, you realize that the sheer tonnage of pesticides used must be awesome. And when you think about the money spent, by governments and private landowners and backyard gardeners, and by chemical companies to produce, advertise, and distribute their products intended to kill this one creature of God's creation, you realize that over the last one hundred years the aggregate dollar amount devoted to *Lymantria dispar* is absolutely staggering.

The restless shade of poor M. Trouvelot must be in agonies of remorse.

And the story is nowhere near its conclusion. So far, some sixty million acres of Eastern and Midwestern forest have been defoliated over the years. The worst single year was 1981, when twelve million acres were defoliated. Now the possibility arises that such devastation may become commonplace, perhaps even minimal.

Attentive readers will recall that in my description of the gypsy moth I mentioned that the female moth does not fly. This small blessing is what has kept the critters' "leading edge" advance down to fifteen or twenty miles per year—despite the propensity of egg masses to hitchhike on plants, camping equipment, and such. Moreover, while known to feed on a variety of trees and plants, the gypsy moth larvae nevertheless have their favorites—oaks and several other deciduous broadleaf species—which leaves a large number of trees largely free from attack.

Now, even these small comforts must be questioned. In May of 1991, inspectors from Agriculture Canada who were examining the holds of Russian grain ships recently arrived from Siberia at the port of Vancouver, British Columbia, noticed familiar orangeish patches on bulkheads and in other places in the ship's holds. The patches were, the inspectors realized, the egg masses of gypsy moths, and they deduced correctly that they were of the Asian strain of *Lymantria dispar,* which has infested the forests of the Asian part of Russia. The Canadian officials destroyed all the egg masses they could, but found that some of them had hatched. The tiny larvae were already ballooning with their silken threads and, carried aloft by onshore breezes, were floating toward the forests of North America.

The so-called Asian strain, dubbed the AGM, is a variant of the species that arrived here from Europe in 1869, which itself had originated in Asia. AGMs look very much like our own gypsy moths, albeit a bit larger. What distinguishes them more than size is that they do not share the two characteristics that have kept the progeny of M. Trouvelot from doing even worse damage. First, the Asian female moth does not just move a few feet and lay its eggs, but can fly a fair distance, like the male. As a U.S. Forest Service entomologist told Ann Gibbons of *Science* magazine, "The Asian female zips right along with a payload of 600 to 700 eggs and will fly in to lay its eggs just like a stealth bomber." And second, unlike our own gypsy moth, the AGM is not picky about what it eats—some five hundred different tree and plant species are known to be on its preferred list, including conifers such as the commercially valuable Douglas fir, larch, and spruce, on which it can and does feed voraciously when these trees are within flying range. Said Mike Schwisow of the Washington State Department of Agriculture of this new complication, "The Asian gypsy moth . . . has the potential to be the most [seriously damaging] exotic insect ever to enter the U.S."

A further difference between M. Trouvelot's escapees and the AGMs coming into the Pacific Northwest is that the new moths have evidently been introduced in several places at once. During 1991, AGMs were found not only around the Seattle-Vancouver area, but also near Portland, Oregon. Even further south, an egg mass was found on a Russian ship docked at the port of Sacramento, California. Moreover, Russian ships suspected of carrying AGM egg masses, according to one report, had already called at ports in the Great Lakes waterways and up the Mississippi River.

Given the airworthiness of the female AGM, the strain's eclectic diet, and the large number of places where ballooning larvae may have wafted ashore from Russian ships, the possibility of eradication, or even significant control, is probably slim. According to Denver Burns of the U.S. Forest Service's Northeastern Forest Experiment Station, "The U.S. Department of Agriculture has plans to go forward with pest control efforts, but the Forest Service is not sure that normal pest control strategies will work." Even so, the USDA beefed up its gypsy-moth war chest by $15 million in 1992 for the sole purpose of battling the AGM yet another time via Bt (*Bacillus thuringiensis*) applied through aerial spraying—in the wan hope of reducing future damage in Washington and Oregon.

The mobility of the female AGM, and the wide dispersal of egg masses as a result, presents a strategic conundrum to economic entomologists used to slow movement in the gypsy moth's territorial advance. The battle so far has been concentrated along the front lines, with special attention paid to control efforts concentrated in uninfested forests adjacent to the leading edge. Now the front lines will be harder to locate, and will be moving more rapidly—perhaps to the next order of magnitude: instead of 12 or 20 miles a year, 120 or 200. Even worse, according to *Science* magazine, "entomologists fear that newcomers will mate with the moths that are already here to produce a horde of hybrids in which both males and females can get around." The hybridizing scenario would suggest that all the forests of the continent may suddenly be at risk.

After I took Cora Gorsuch's official gypsy-moth tour in Roscommon County, Michigan, I asked her to direct me to some other places where the gypsy moth attack had been especially severe—even though we had seen hundreds of dead and dying oaks in Roscommon and endured the dry showers of frass. She suggested an area in Gratiot County between Merrill and Breckinridge, two small towns on Michigan Highway 46, an east-west two-lane that serves as the "Saginaw line," the southern boundary of the pine country that once stretched away to the north, beckoning Paul Bunyan-inspired loggers to "hunt up good tracts on some runnin' stream—cut her and float her down," in the words of James MacGillivray.

The dirt roads in this part of north-central Michigan tend to be straight and unpopulated, though here and there narrow tracks lead to cabins. After a few miles of off-highway exploring, I was beginning to wonder just where exactly the area was that Cora had wanted me to see. The woods were bright and sunny, the trees greening up nicely. But of course, that was just it! I was visiting here in midsummer, not in spring. The forest had already been defoliated and the oaks and aspens were expending precious energy sending out a second flush of leaves. When winter came, some of them would not have enough stored energy to survive, and they would die. Others would die the year after that. A few might hang on for three years. This was a gypsy-moth spring—not a spring of renewal, but of death.

Cora Gorsuch said that after a while the composition of the forest would change—from oak to red maple, since the oaks did not seem to be regenerating. And so in Michigan yet another forest would rise north of the Saginaw line. The first one—with the great pines—no living person can now remember. The second would perhaps be forgotten, too, after sufficient generations of people have come and gone. And throughout all these years, and perhaps beyond, the gypsy moth will be studied and sprayed, studied and sprayed, and people will curse M. Trouvelot and (as of 1991) the Russians.

Were it not for all this foreign trade, goes the conventional wisdom, we would not have a gypsy-moth problem. And (more conventional wisdom) were it not for all these people from the East being careless about exporting egg masses on their campers (the Midwesterners say), the gypsy moth might have been confined to New England where it belongs. Now the camper-carried egg masses from the West will be passing camper-carried egg masses from the East on the interstates.

To blame foreigners, whether they are people or pests, is always comforting. Glib analysis about how many ships ply the seas these days suggests that the blame for devastation can be laid against destructive immigrants—like the bomb-throwing Bolsheviki—who have come among us because we have not guarded our borders and our ports. And yet the gypsy moth has been around for millions of years, and the seas have been plied for at least four hundred, to these very shores. Are we to believe that no four-masted schooner sailing from Le Havre to Boston ever had a gypsy-moth egg mass laid in its hold? Or that a brigantine out of Vladivostok never carried the ancestors of the AGM now terrifying the experts in the Pacific Northwest? Even the Dutch elm disease and the chestnut blight are relatively modern. Why did they not appear earlier, along with, say, the Norway rat and the earwig, both of which apparently arrived in the New World simultaneously with the Europeans?

My question is, could the swath of devastation that the gypsy moth leaves in its wake as it moves westward and southward out of New England, and now eastward out of the Pacific Northwest, have *entirely* to do with the degrees of difference in the numbers of ships docking at U.S. ports and the number of campers traveling the interstates? Or does it have something to do with the condition of the forests that imported pests may find to their liking? There may have been a change in shipping in the last one hundred years, but there's been an even greater one in the composition and the ecological diversity and resilience of our American forests. It is well to remember—as the cooperative extension agent did up in Michigan—that the forest now being attacked is not the same one that was there before. It is also well to remember that New England, where the gypsy moth got its start, had also been utterly cut over, nearly a hundred years before the pines of Michigan were eliminated.

That the gypsy moth found a toehold in America may not be a random, adventitious event having to do with changes in merchant shipping on the high seas. And the path of the gypsy rover may have little to do with egg masses being transported on vacationers' camping equipment. Indeed, *Lymantria dispar* seems to be intent on tracking the path of earlier devastations—those of the settlers and the lumbermen who cleared the continent and thereby changed the forest: New England first, then the Appalachians and the piedmont, then the North Woods of the Great Lakes states, then the coniferous forests of the Northwest, and finally the bottomland hardwoods of the South, where the gypsy moth is headed next.

Indeed, perhaps poor M. Trouvelot should not be blamed at all—and his troubled spirit allowed to be at peace. For the path of the gypsy rover, among other exotic destroyers of America's trees, did not necessarily begin at 27 Myrtle Street or in the hold of a Russian ship, but in changes in the forests themselves, forests whose ecological integrity we vanquished by our own hand.

7

A History Only of Departed Things

This is the forest primeval. The murmuring
pines and the hemlocks,
Bearded with moss, and in garments green,
indistinct in the twilight,
Stand like Druids of eld, with voices
sad and prophetic . . .
—*Henry Wadsworth Longfellow,*
Evangeline

What were they like, then, these forests that have so greatly changed since the Europeans arrived? And the crucial corrolary question: To what extent have the changes precluded the kind of healthy forest ecosystems that the white man (and the red) originally confronted? Forests beget trees; we know that. We are less sure that the reverse is true. When we destroy forests, we can, as we have seen, destroy not only the trees that had occupied the landscape, but possibly future trees as well. The replacements trees, set out in rows, all the same size and species, are less able to resist the drought and bitter cold, the adventitious pests and diseases, because they grow only in simplified *stands,* not in the vigorous, complex ecosystems that evolved naturally over eons.

Indeed, the primitive forest met by the early British, Dutch, and French colonists was filled with trees of mythic proportions and biblical age. White pines reached two hundred feet in height. Great stands of hemlocks, more permanent than Gothic cathedrals, were common, not rare and kept secret as they are today. Black walnut trunks were five and six feet through the middle, with the slabs milled from them used for tabletops and dropleafs. Chestnuts spread two hundred feet from branchtip to branchtip. The graceful arching trunks of elms sheltered the nurslings with dappled shade. Marvelous flowering species—magnolias, crabapples, loblolly bays, basswoods—perfumed Southern woodlands each spring. Such was the forest that stretched from the barrier islands on which the first British colonists landed four hundred years ago—a hundred years after Columbus's triumph of persistence over sense—to the prairies of the Middle West. It was said that a squirrel could travel from the Atlantic shore to the Mississippi River without once dropping to the ground.

The great Eastern forest was where many of the Siberian immigrants—our Native Americans—settled as well, in their great migrations twelve thousand to fourteen thousand years ago. As the glaciers receded, and the forest returned, the region ultimately comprised four-fifths of the forested land in what we now call the lower forty-eight (with the remaining one-fifth in the Rockies, the Sierra-Cascades, the coast ranges, and other Western mountains). In the northern latitudes, between Maine and Minnesota, an unbroken coniferous woodland prevailed, giving way to hardwoods as it moved to lower latitudes—beeches, maples, oaks, chestnuts, elms, hickories, basswood, locusts, magnolias, live oaks, tupelo—in a largely unblemished blanket of green from the Great Lakes to Louisiana. The effect of the earliest migrants on the forest was observable, but probably ecologically insignificant. George Perkins Marsh, the father of natural resource conservation, wrote of the Indians' "oak openings," in which fires were deliberately set to create pastures to which game animals would be attracted. But the openings were distanced from one another, and appeared to have no lasting impact.

Unlike the aborigines, who lived on the edges of forests along the shores of bays and rivers, and who made forays into the forest for timber and game, the colonists required that the forests be cleared—a form of redemption, according to British geographer Michael Williams. The very size of the forest, he writes, "astonished and frustrated the New World pioneers." Because it was "impersonal and lonely in its endlessness," clearing the forest, in Williams's view, "was likened to a battle or struggle between the individual and the immense obstacle that had to be overcome to create a new life and a new society."

Indeed, in 1646 or thereabouts, William Bradford, the Puritan leader, wrote in his *History of Plymouth Plantation* of the first landing at Cape Cod, wherein even the glorious colors of a New England autumn—

today the subject of tourist brochures—were found to be fearsome and hateful:

> What could they see but a hideous and desolate wilderness, full of wild beasts and wild men—and what multitudes there might be of them they knew not. Neither could they, as it were, go up to the top of Pisgah to view from this wilderness a more godly country to feed their hopes; for which way so ever they turned their eyes (save upward to the heavens) they could have little solace or content in respect of any outward objects. For summer being done, all things stand upon them with a weatherbeaten face, and the whole country, full of woods and thickets, represented a wild and savage hue.

There was, however, a contrary strain in the early settlers' apprehension of America's forested wilderness. By 1791 William Bartram, son of the Quaker botanist John Bartram, wrote as follows in his exhaustively titled *Travels Through North & South Carolina, Georgia, East and West Florida, the Cherokee Country, the Extensive Territories of the Muscogulges or Creek Confederacy, and the Country of the Choctaws; Containing an Account of the Soil and Natural Productions of Those Regions, Together with Observations on the Manners of the Indians*:

> Proceeding on our return to town, continued through part of this high forest skirting on the meadows; began to ascend the hills of a ridge which we were under the necessity of crossing; and having gained its summit, enjoyed a most enchanting view; a vast expanse of green meadows and strawberry fields; a meandering river gliding through, saluting in its various turnings the swelling, green, turfy knolls, embellished with parterres of flowers and fruitful strawberry beds; flocks of turkeys strolling about them; herds of deer prancing in the meads or bounding over the hills; companies of young, innocent Cherokee virgins, some busy gathering the rich fragrant fruit, others having already filled their baskets, lay reclined under the shade of floriferous and fragrant native bowers of Magnolia, Azalea Philadelphus, perfumed Calycanthus, sweet Yellow Jassamine and cerulean Glycene frutescens. . . .

So entranced were the English Romantic poets with Bartram's description that the New World forest images worked their way into what is now some of the most familiar poetry of the period, including Samuel Taylor Coleridge's "Rime of the Ancient Mariner" and "Kubla Khan," and William Wordsworth's "She Was a Phantom of Delight" and "Ruth." Coleridge and Robert Southey, who was later to become British poet laureate, proposed to establish in these woodlands a utopian community, which they described as a "pantisocracy," to be sited on the banks of the Susquehanna. According to literary critic Alfred Kazin, the community was to "consist of educated men and women who should withdraw from the world to some suitable spot . . . for high intellectual converse."

Wrote Wordsworth:

. . . Paradise, and groves
Elysian, Fortunate Fields—like those of old
Sought in the Atlantic Main—why should they be
A history only of departed things,
Or a mere fiction of what never was?
For the discerning intellect of Man,
When wedded to this goodly universe
In love and holy passion, shall find these
A simple produce of the common day.

But such was not to be. The groves elysian departed from the New World as decisively as they had from the old. As historian T. H. Watkins points out in a discussion of the American wilderness, "the European community suddenly was confronted by that common mythic past it had rejected. . . . The tragedy, of course, is that . . . the choices they made were almost invariably those which continued the [Europeans'] long alienation from the wilderness that had nurtured their beginnings."

European population in the New World was thin during the colonial period, and the new arrivals clung to the Atlantic shore—except for the handful of Spanish missionaries that moved up the Rio Grande and into California del Norte and what became the American Southwest, the conquistadores who made forays through Florida and into adjoining territory, and French trappers plying the Mississippi. But these were not true settlers, as the colonists were. The colonists were mainly British and Dutch, and for two centuries they scarcely budged from the tidewater lands and the Eastern piedmont. Westward expansion did not begin in earnest until the beginning of the nineteenth century, when the Allegheny frontier was finally crossed. But once begun, the power of "westering" was extraordinary. Indeed, the period ended, according to Frederick Jackson Turner, hardly more than three generations later, when, in 1893, the great historian declared the frontier closed. There was no place left where people (meaning Europeans) weren't. They lived everywhere. And everywhere they lived they cleared the forest. Scarcely a scrap of land from Cape Cod to Ohio, and from the Upper Peninsula of Michigan to the mouth of the Mississippi, had not been cut over or high-graded at least once. At the peak of this frenetic time, says forest historian John Perlin, the changes in the landscape were astonishing—even before the chainsaw had been invented. Perlin writes: "The amount of forests lost due to pasturage and felling trees to clear land for cultivation, for lumber, and for fuel [accelerated] from 1,600 square miles per year in 1835 to 7,000 square miles twenty years later. As the pace of deforestation picked up, the area of land covered by dense forest declined considerably. In 1850, 25 percent of the land area of the United States was densely forested; twenty years later, this figure had dropped to 15 percent."

Trees grow back in most places, of course, but as we are learning, they do not re-create the same forest as before—either by man's design or nature's intractability. Trees may be a "renewable resource" in a commercial sense, but forests are not. By the early 1800s, Vermont, originally the "breadbasket" of the colonies, was so stripped of trees that only twenty percent of its land was left wooded, where nearly one hundred percent of Vermont had been clothed in trees since the retreat of the glaciers. What has grown back? "A forest of sticks," as Hubert Volgelmann, the University of Vermont botanist and forest ecologist described it to me. In Michigan, as I reported in the preceding chapter, the great pines felled in the late nineteenth century never grew back, but were replaced by the oaks and aspens on which the gypsy moths now so voraciously feed. In the South, great hardwood forests were cut—some not even harvested, but simply burned over—in order to plant pines that would grow to merchantable size in twenty or forty years. Nowadays, from North Carolina to Arkansas, pine plantations dominate the rural landscape—though they do not always grow as rapidly as the plantation owners had hoped.

Moreover, ecological research strongly implies that the life history of replacement trees will be materially different from that of their giant predecessors, even when no effort is made to change the species mix for commercial purposes. If the evolved, biologically rich ecosystem that created the original forest is once destroyed, by clear-cutting for example, it may well be destroyed forever.

In some disquieting research conducted in the southern Appalachians, David Cameron Duffy and Albert J. Meier, of the University of Georgia's Institute of Ecology, make this very point. Although previous studies of the effects of clear-cutting had dealt with the regeneration of trees and the return of animal species to reforested areas, the Georgia ecologists believed that a more reliable measure of the possibility of regeneration might be found in a study of the herbaceous layer, which of all forest organisms is the most sensitive to massive disturbances such as clear-cutting—the shrubs and other plants that are sheltered by forest trees. Given sites in which they could compare undisturbed "original" forest with adjacent cut-over areas of varying ages since the time of cutting, Duffy and Meier hoped—in a clear-cut southern woodland, where plants grow rapidly in the moist, warm climate—to be able to determine if a true recovery was taking place, and if so how quickly.

Accordingly, they scoured the mountains for sites where old growth and regenerating second growth could be found side by side—a "primary" forest site, where little or no cutting had ever taken place, next to a "secondary" site that had been clear-cut. They identified nine such areas—in North Carolina, Tennessee, Georgia, and Kentucky—representing different elevations, slopes, latitudes, soil types, and geologies. The characteristic trees in these nine paired areas were yellow poplar (tulip tree), hemlock, three kinds of oak (white, black, and basket), white basswood, white ash, sweet buckeye, and eastern ironwood—an assortment typical of the woodlands of the southern Appalachian mountains.

Duffy and Meier measured the rate of revegetation in terms of "species richness" as well as "total herbaceous cover" to show the degree of recovery each clear-cut secondary site was making in comparison to its paired primary site, where there had been no disturbance. They hoped to be able to establish some sort of standard rate of recovery, since the time that had elapsed since clear-cutting ranged from ten years to eighty-seven in the paired sites they had selected, and since of all clear-cut forests in the United States, the warm Southern woodlands could be expected to recover the most rapidly. In this assumption the researchers were disappointed. Even in areas with the longest period since the clear-cutting, the number of species and the extent of "cover" was minimal—only half the species had returned compared to the undisturbed control sites, and only a third of the cover. Worse, there was no trend showing that the degree of recovery increased with age. In fact, Duffy and Meier found that just the reverse was happening—the longer the period, the *lower* the rate of recovery in both species richness and cover!

Even the least disturbing conclusion to draw about this contrary finding is not particularly comforting: that eighty-seven years, nearly a century, is too short a time span to measure the rate of recovery, and therefore the fact that the number of plant species and the total area of vegetative cover were less well along on sites with the longer period since clear-cutting was simply anomalous. Another possible explanation that came to mind as Duffy and Meier contemplated their data was that the "type and severity of initial disturbance" on the secondary sites where recovery was low might have been greater than on the other sites. The researchers did not comment upon the likelihood that some sort of sampling error could have skewed the findings, although their care in designing the research approach would seem to rule this out.

Another possibility was that the means by which forest succession takes place naturally is so decisively interrupted by clear-cutting that a much longer time is required for the emergence of plant species and overall vegetative cover than had been assumed by forestry experts. In a natural forest, Duffy and Meier explain, trees have all the time in the world to become old and large, and eventually to fall and decay. When they do fall, the upended root structures create a "pit and mound" microtopography, with patches of bare earth where plants can grow readily, protected by the natural berms and mulched and fertilized by the decaying deadfall. By contrast, in a clear-cut forest, there are no pits and mounds, and comparatively little decaying matter to nurture the growth of recolonizing plants. Thus, while trees will grow in previously cut-over areas, the biodiversity is lost, and as a practical matter lost forever, since species richness and cover will take longer to become reestablished than the normal 40-to-150-year logging cycle would permit. The question remains as to how many logging cycles may be possible before the forest ecosystem, with its myriad plants and animals so decisively limited in their diversity, no longer functions even for commercial purposes—a mere forest of sticks, good only for pulp and chips and charcoal, and finally so dwarfed that it has limited value even for that.

But Duffy and Meier's grim analysis is not yet done. There is yet another explanation for the failure of species to grow back in the cut-over forests of the Southeast. And that is that climatically it may no longer be possible for them to do so. "The original Appalachian forest," they write, "may have become established under cooler and moister conditions than occur at present. In addition, conditions during future climate change, even several centuries into the future, might become sufficiently unfavorable to prevent complete secondary success following present-day clear cutting." In other words, given the likelihood of global warming, the great old forests can never return to their original state, even if we quit logging them altogether. Accordingly, what small patches of old growth we have now remaining are all that we will ever have. And the new growth is at risk.

After the Eastern forests had been leveled, we looked westward for the timber needed to build the growing cities, swelling with immigrants come to work in mines and factories. The two-man saws ripped through the huge pines and spruces and firs and redwoods, and to make sure we could saw them all, we effectively suppressed natural forest fires. As we have seen, the suppression worked too well in the intermountain West, for the composition of the forest changed: the widely spaced big trees were replaced by densely growing smaller ones that were, unfortunately, less resistant to pests, so that now the great accumulation of dead trees and litter, now tinder-dry in many places from a protracted drought, constitutes a fire threat greater than any of the ad men who invented Smokey Bear could have conceived. The question arises: Are we doomed, through some irreversible cultural overlay, or even, perhaps, some deep-seated genetic characteristic, to continue unceasingly to lay waste the forests, again and again, with the replacement forest each time a little bit less well adapted to its environment?

Today, just 5 percent remains—5 percent of the original wooded land that stretched from the Atlantic to the Mississippi and from the Great Lakes to the Gulf of Mexico, and that grew throughout the Western mountains beyond the Great Plains and most magnificently of all in Pacific Northwest rainforests.

This tiny remnant of our nation's original forest, this 5-percent forest of old growth, would if consolidated make a square patch of trees just forty-seven miles on a side. In the Pacific Northwest, it is generally agreed that an "old-growth forest" is any sizable, self-sustaining system of coniferous trees ranging from 250 to more than 1,000 years old, with the larger trees having wind-damaged tops and thick growth of lichens and mosses, and with a forest floor crisscrossed with undisturbed, centuries-old deadfall, providing the shelter, moisture, and nutriment for the permanent regeneration of the ecosystem. These old-growth remnants are located in the so-called Westside—the forest stretching from the crest of the Sierra-Cascades westward across the Coast Ranges to the Pacific shore in northern California, Oregon, and Washington. In no other place in our contiguous states can one still find substantial tracts of merchantable, uncut timber, however few and scattered these may now be.

What grows on these tracts are huge, magnificent conifers in stands that environmentalists now call, collectively, the Ancient Forest. However fragmented it may be, the Ancient Forest is, ecologically and in every other way, the most impressive coniferous forest remaining in the United States, or anywhere for that matter. According to two renowned forest ecologists, Jerry Franklin and C. T. Dyrness of the University of Washington, these remnant stands are all that is left of "the classic coniferous forest of the world."

The Ancient Forest is, in fact, relatively young in geological terms, a temperate-zone, coniferous rain forest that arose after the last Ice Age some eleven thousand years ago. It ran virtually uninterrupted from Glacier Bay, at the top of the panhandle of Alaska, some 2,000 miles south nearly to San Francisco Bay. The lumberjacks arrived just prior to the Civil War, cutting Sitka spruce for ships of the line, and redwoods and Douglas fir to build the new metropolises of the Northwest—San Francisco, Portland, Seattle. Just as they leveled the forests of the East, the South, and the upper Middle West, the loggers, arriving by train and boat in greater and greater numbers in search of jobs, leveled most of the low-elevation trees along the rivers that tumbled steeply into the Pacific. By the end of the century, with the exception of the Alaskan panhandle, most of the coastal and riverine forest had been felled, and along with it, the most magnificent of the trees—giant Sitka spruce, Western hemlock, Douglas fir, and most of the coastal redwoods in northern California and southern Oregon. What survived the onslaught was in the mountains, harder to get at and to transport to merchant ships in the harbors, on steep land that still belonged to the U.S. government because the trees there were smaller and had less commercial value.

Remarkably, large tracts of these big trees remained relatively undisturbed—some twenty million acres of them—until the end of World War II, when two-thirds of the Ancient Forest on public land was still unlogged, since nearly all the cutting was taking place on privately owned land. Then, the government of the United States, with the U.S. Forest Service playing the role of an eager apparatchik, allowed the forest products industry to take the high-elevation Ancient Forest apart, tree by tree, stand by stand, until today less than one acre in ten of the original public forest on the Northwest still survives. The federal government obligingly constructed logging roads into the wildernesses at public expense to accommodate the trucks and men and machinery. The government's estimated "stumpage" value—how much the felled trees were estimated to be worth on the market—was put so low that even the most inept mill owner could scarcely fail to make a profit on the timber sales conducted by the Forest Service. Local governments, too, cooperated, glad to have their economy boomed for them. Of course, the Forest Service insisted that the loggers be careful to leave a "beauty strip" of uncut timber flanking the public highways—a kind of Potemkin forest—so that the tourists traveling through would be deceived as they drove along the mountain roads. "My goodness," they would say, "what a lot of trees!"—unaware that only a few score yards beyond the strip lay devastation dramatic enough to make even the most jaded observer heartsick. Today, the clear-cut patches run so closely together across the great, folded landscapes of the Westside that from the window of an airplane high above it seems as if some terrible skin disease had infected the surface below.

In the end, the loggers, encouraged by the government, destroyed in less than forty years all but a trace of possibly the most uncommon coniferous forest in the world. Uncommon because such coniferous forests—the true coniferous forests of the arctic north, adapted to the cold—were, virtually everyplace else, replaced by angiosperms, the flowering trees, as the glaciers retreated at the end of the last Ice Age. In the Eastern forests, for example, hardwoods now dominate the forest at this southerly a latitude, save for a tiny fringe of spruce and fir on the topmost ridges of the Appalachians. But in the Pacific Northwest, the conifers stayed put, even at sea level, the result of a strange, fortuitous climate that had permitted a prehistoric forest to live among us, at least for a while. The winters here are suitably wet and cold and often snowy (although the lowlands of the Olympic Peninsula of Washington have fewer freezing nights than a good many of the cotton fields in the deep South), but the summers are hot and dry, too dry in the dark green forests to support deciduous trees, which need sunlight and plenty of moisture for growth while they are in leaf. (The winter rains don't help—even though they average 133 inches a year in some places.) And so the conifers, which photosynthesize all year long, not just during the spring and summer, prevail—in a climate so improbably perfect for them that they can live to great age and become giants. Writes ecologist Elliott Norse, author of the definitive book on the plight of the Ancient Forest, "A nearly ideal coincidence of climatic factors between the crest of the Cascades and the Pacific Ocean has yielded [a forest] so big, so lush, and diversified that it is difficult not to use superlatives."

The quintessential forest tree of the Westside is Douglas fir—commercially the most valuable of all the conifers on a volume basis and therefore planted exclusively in even-aged stands in the vast private Western land holdings of corporations such as Weyerhauser, which bills itself as "the tree-growing company." But plantation trees are only a tenth as valuable to loggers as the five-hundred-year-old pre-Columbian monsters, which can grow to a diameter of sixteen feet and rise to a height of well over three hundred.

This is not to say that other trees of the Westside are of ordinary size. In fact, says Norse, there are thirteen different conifer species in the forest that are taller than the tallest of all Eastern trees, the Eastern white pine, which (in the old days) would often grow to two hundred feet, but not much more. The Sitka spruce, for example, a lowland species along the northern Pacific coast, can reach three hundred feet and, says Norse, "add a foot of girth per decade." The tallest Western species is the coast redwood, which I described in an earlier chapter. This magnificent tree, with pre-logging-era specimens soaring as high as four hundred feet, is restricted to the southerly part of the coastal forest and now so decimated by excessive logging that the meager remnant of the once-monumental redwood forest—much of it now in parks and reserves—is something of a separate case.

Although popular accounts of the dramatic old-growth rain forests of the Westside deal often with the incredible size of the trees, even more remarkable are the unique ecological characteristics. Indeed, a single Douglas fir is a kind of microecosystem all by itself, with as many as 1,500 invertebrate species taking a living from it. Such a tree, with up to sixty million needles whose surface area totals more than an acre, also serves as a water source for its ecosystem—the needles "comb" the heavy fogs so effectively that 20 percent of the precipitation in the typical old-growth forest derives from its "needle-shed." What is more, such a tree's ecological utility is just beginning when it reaches old age, for then its trunk and branches become covered with mosses, giving shelter to all manner of creatures. Within the tree are stored upwards of two thousand gallons of water, a reserve against dry times. The soils covering the roots of the tree contain what scientists believe may be the highest levels of terrestrial biodiversity on the planet. When, at length, the top of the tree dies and is broken off in a storm, an aging tree provides perfect perches and nesting sites for eagles, hawks, and other birds of prey, including the spotted owl.

To a large degree, the Douglas fir, as well as other forest giants of the Westside, truly comes into its own, ecologically speaking, after it dies, for in the Ancient Forest it is the dead trees that create the living forest. Fallen trees are needed for forest regeneration as "nurse logs," without which, according to Elliott Norse, neither Western hemlock nor Sitka spruce could regenerate effectively. The reason for this is that the forest floor is covered with an impenetrable mat of moss—so impenetrable that a seed falling upon it has no access to the soil nutrients beneath. The fallen tree solves that problem by offering deep crevices and other openings along its length to give seedling roots purchase and nourishment. Norse makes the point that this service is available only for a limited period, since the fallen logs will, in time, become covered with mosses, too. Therefore, a continuous supply of newly fallen ancients is needed to maintain the long-term health and balanced composition of the forest.

How old are the old trees of the Ancient Forest? According to the loggers, they are too old at a couple of hundred years, or even less, which is to say when they reach physical maturity. In human terms, this would be somewhere in the teens. After that, say the loggers, the trees are "overmature." When trees stop growing vigorously they are essentially dead, they say, making a dead forest. They should be cut and replaced with seedling trees capable of growth—an interesting idea that resonates in revealing ways when the analogy is drawn with human communities. Novelist and essayist Brenda Peterson, a resident of the forests of Washington State, evocatively drew it this way:

> If my granddaddy were one of those old Douglas firs I saw being trucked out of the forest, could he really be equalled by a tiny sapling? Old trees like old people survive the ravages of middle age competition for light, or limelight; they give back to their generations more oxygen, more stories; they are tall and farsighted enough to see the future because they are so firmly rooted in the past. Old growth trees or persons are nurturers; the young saplings planted to replace them need nurturing.

The grandfather Douglas firs live to a thousand years or more, but remain nurturers long after that. First, as "snags," the standing dead trees that characterize a natural old-growth forest. The snags, the largest of which can remain standing for 125 years or more, furnish a home and food for certain creatures of the forest that could not readily survive without them. The beetles that infest them supply food for woodpeckers and bears who tear open the soft, rotted wood to get at the delicacies within. Birds and rodents live in the cavities. The spotted owl nests in the broken tops. But the grandfather's nurturing is not over yet. After a snag falls, it then provides the nursery for seedling trees as I have described, as well as general nutriment for the forest soil. The bole—the trunk and remaining bark—retains moisture in the ecosystem, and clarifies streams that tumble over the downed logs by creating "plunge pools" necessary to salmon and trout. Clearly, the life of the forest depends on its fallen trees. If one defines the age of a living tree to include its entire life-giving period, some old trees live for two thousand years—and have their most nurturing effect during the final centuries, when they provide a seedbed so that other trees can take their place.

Once while visiting Britain for a summer, mainly to hike the remoter footpaths of William Wordsworth's Lake District in the north of England, I became acquainted with an elderly man who had been a merchant seaman. I cannot recall his name, only that he came from Crewe, a Midlands city not far from the lakes. The man from Crewe had a shaky memory, so he always asked me when we met out walking, "You say you're from the States? Well, have ye seen *Oregon*?" And he would fling out his arm, gesturing at the treeless fells of the north of England. "Not like this," he would say. "Nae, not like this at all.

"In *O-re-gon*," said the man from Crewe, emphasizing every syllable in a kind of incantatory way, "in Oregon they have *trees*, giant trees, *huge* trees. Have ye seen 'em? By Jesus, I'll never forget those trees. Coos Bay, that's where we went. By Jesus, I'll never forget Coos Bay and the trees of *Oregon*." Of course I did not tell him that they were almost gone, the trees that so astonished him, almost all gone, and that it had happened within his lifetime: at the time he was born, scarcely 1 percent of the upland Ancient Forest had been logged. What had taken a thousand years in England—the razing of the natural forests—had required less than the span of a single lifetime in Oregon.

The remaining patches of Ancient Forest constitute about 10 percent of the original big-tree coniferous forest of the Westside, and these patches are what the loggers wish to cut, and what the Endangered Species Act has barred them (so far) from cutting, since to topple the forest would extinguish the spotted owl and the marbled murrelet, two species (among others) that require old-growth habitat for survival. But the murrelet and the owl are merely emblematic of the effects of clear-cutting the remaining Ancient Forest of the Westside. Beyond the risks to a few species of wildlife is the ecological certainty of irrevocable biotic change that will affect the future of all species of the region because clear-cutting so decisively modifies the operation of the ecosystem itself. As Peter Raven, director of the Missouri Botanical Garden, has put it, "By treating 500- to 1,000-year-old forests as if they were a renewable resource, we are acting out a fiction, and thereby making a grave mistake. . . . Once they have been removed from a particular area, the ancient forests . . . will never appear again, given the nature of human activities in the contemporary world and their consequences." In clear-cutting such forests, then, we not only kill the trees that are cut, but we annihilate the *possibility* of such trees for all time. No manifestation of the anthropomorphic causes of tree death could be more permanently fatal than this.

The mechanisms of what some call "ecocide" in the Ancient Forest are too many and too profound really to be fully knowable by ecologists. But a few have been identified. Chris Maser, for example, a wildlife ecologist, and a colleague, James M. Trappe, discovered how clear-cutting severed a crucial linkage between certain rodents and forest regeneration, where, as Maser puts it, "a fecal pellet is more than a package of waste products, it is a pill of symbiosis dispensed through the forest."

As Maser and Trappe discovered, deer mice, the flying squirrel, the Western redbacked vole, and the creeping vole, all native to the Westside forest, love to feed on truffles, which are, as any gourmet will tell you, the underground "fruit" of a fungus, just as its mushroom (such as the famed chanterelle, also a denizen of the old-growth forest of the Pacific Northwest) is an above-ground fruiting body. Now, another favorite food of these rodents is the seed of the Douglas fir, which falls in great quantity after a fire. As the rodents scurry about eating Douglas fir seed, their droppings are distributed widely in the burned area of a forest. And within the droppings are the spores of the fungus, ingested during truffle-eating time.

After the spores enter the forest soil, and as the seeds overlooked by the rodents begin sending out rootlets, the newly imported nonreproductive tissue of the truffle fungus, the mycelia, creates a mantle around the tiny roots, producing the symbiotic effect that is called a "mycorrhiza" (discussed briefly in Chapter 2), which means, literally, "fungus-root." As the fungus wraps itself firmly around the roots of the seedling Douglas fir, the fungal cells even penetrate the outer layer of root cells. The effect produces a sponge-like surface on the new roots, permitting them to absorb water and nutrients more rapidly and efficiently than they could manage on their own. In fact, say Maser and Trappe, many woody plants, including the Douglas fir, require mycorrhizal fungi for survival.

Clear-cutting radically interrupts this delicate interaction which helps to regenerate burned-over areas and to maintain stocks of healthy trees. The growth of the truffle-producing fungi is suppressed in cut-over areas because of environmental changes that, by removing old and rotting wood, reduce opportunities for fungus growth, as well as reducing the opportunity for dissemination by means of the voles, mice, and other rodents. Research conducted by ecologist Jerry Franklin found that "once the host species is killed through the cutting process, many fungi disappear if they do not quickly encounter another host." Observes old-growth authority David Kelly, "It is these fungi that are adept at conserving moisture on the steep slopes where ground water runs off rapidly and where foresters have a hard time growing new trees." Moreover, the rodents do not move into clear-cut areas the way they do into naturally burned areas, for the abundant seed-fall that follows a fire is absent. And natural fires are perforce suppressed. Thus, where the truffle-rodent-mycorrhiza connection is broken, the forest ecosystem is changed. And the connection is broken almost everywhere.

A hardy perennial in the weedy garden tended by the propagandists for clear-cutting is the notion that those who are concerned about biodiversity—involving rodents, truffles, or anything else—should relax. Clear-cutting, its apologists explain, creates "edge," and as everyone knows, edge—the place where two habitats join, forest *and* meadow—must be twice as rich in species. In a quite narrow sense they are right. The clear-cuts produce "edge forbs," the herbaceous plants needful of sunlight which serve as fodder for deer and elk. In turn, the nearby uncut patches of forest provide the shy animals protection. However agreeable this conjunction may be to game animals (and therefore to those who wish to hunt them), the edge effect does not justify clear-cutting in terms of the trees that remain—which are put at mortal risk from wind, water, weather, and the very animals attracted to them which tend to overbrowse, often severely, during the hard winters.

To begin with, even a natural forest fails to shelter itself from the harsh winds of winter and especially spring, when the ground is softened by rain and trees can more easily be uprooted. In clear-cut areas, the likelihood of a "blowdown"—where vast areas of forest are completely flattened—is vastly increased. Research conducted after two disastrous mountain storms in Oregon has shown that 48 percent of the forest blowdowns were adjacent to clear-cuts in one case, and 81 percent in the other. Such storms produce a kind of domino effect in which edge trees, receiving the full brunt of the wind, not only fail to protect their leeward neighbors, but cause them to fall upon one another. The forest trees are no more able to withstand these dual vectors of lateral pressure than a prairie wheatfield can withstand a tornado.

The risk of blowdowns in forested areas is perhaps the most dramatic effect of clear-cutting on the remaining trees, but not the only one. Landslides of unprotected soils on clear-cuts located on steep land are frequent after rains, and sometimes kill trees on forested land below by suffocating roots under debris. Moreover, the forest roads built to get the timber out erode as well, often bringing whole mountainsides down with them and destroying everything in their path. Other effects include marked changes in temperature—where the land lies bare and baking beneath the summer sun or unprotected from winter cold—creating microclimates that, subtly or not so subtly, change the composition of plant and animal species within the uncut remainder forest. "The climate in a clearcut," writes Elliot Norse, "is more severe than that of the ancient forest it replaces: hotter, colder, drier, windier, and with greater snow depth. Summer winds from clearcuts penetrate nearby forests, making them hotter and drier. This harms species that need cool, moist conditions, and makes the forest fragments more vulnerable to fire."

Thus does the highly touted "edge effect" turn out not to be an ecological advantage, but the agent of environmental catastrophe in clear-cut areas. Typically, cut-over patches of twenty-five to forty acres are interspersed in forested areas; ideally, these patches are located at sufficient distances from one another to preclude damage from the elements to the remaining forested areas. But the ideal in the Westside forest has long since been abandoned, so that now the place looks like the lacy pattern of biscuit dough that lies uselessly on the drainboard after all the biscuit rounds have been cut out and sent to the oven. In Jerry Franklin's view, the pattern of chained, interlocking clear-cuts, so evident in photographs taken from low-flying aircraft, produces an arrangement of residual trees in patches so small that even their interiors are totally unlike those of natural forests, "since temperature, humidity, and wind are modified for a distance equivalent to two or three tree-heights from the boundaries" of the clear-cuts that abut them on every side. In a phrase, then, the original forest has literally been "edged" to death. Writes Elliott Norse, "Because of edge effects, we really lose about 60 acres of old-growth for every 25-acre patch that is clearcut."

"Residual tree death," this phenomenon might be called—when for every tree cut, two others die. But there are other, longer-term consequences of removing huge trees from the ancient forests of the Westside and replacing them with seedlings to begin a new "rotation," as the foresters call it. One of the consequences has to do with the extirpation of species that the spotted owl dispute has suggested. But not just one or two species are involved. In fact, according to Chris Maser, in an intensively managed "young-growth" forest where all the snags and fallen logs have been removed, you can anticipate that 29 percent of the wildlife species will be removed with them.

Another effect has to do with C—carbon—the carbon that is beneficially locked up (the term of art is "sequestered") in an undisturbed big-tree forest. The sequestration is beneficial because without it the C, sooner or later, is converted to CO_2, and in sufficient quantity to make a difference in atmospheric carbon levels. For most Americans the "carbon-balance" issue has to do mainly with the destruction of the rain forests of Brazil and other tropical regions around the globe. And yet the rain forest of the Pacific Northwest sequesters better than twice as much carbon on a per-acre basis than either the Amazon or the Congo basin—a matter of 350 metric tons in an old-growth Douglas fir–Western hemlock forest, compared to 168 metric tons in the tropics. An astonishing amount of the carbon is in the form of fallen logs, estimated to account on the average for one-fifth of the carbon stored, and in some places a great deal more. In some areas, especially where streams flow over the down wood, thus reducing the rate of oxidation, the fallen logs can total as many as 265 tons per acre.

In the process of lumbering, the majority of the great tonnage of carbon, in standing trees as well as down wood, is relatively quickly oxidized, reducing the capacity of the forest to sequester carbon to a very small fraction of its original potential. In areas slated for cutting, most of the down wood and snags are removed and chipped for fuel, and the branches of felled timber (slash) are burned after logging and thus immediately oxidized. Right there, half of the forest's carbon has been converted to CO_2 in one stroke. As for the rest, about half the "boles"—the useful timber—winds up as chips used for fuel or as pulp used for paper, both of which are quickly converted to CO_2 after leaving the forest. The roots, which remain in place, constitute about 20 percent of the biomass, and will oxidize eventually. As for the wood that is actually turned into structural timber or plywood, even that survives only fifty years on the average, before becoming landfill—a useful life span that is roughly 10 percent of the age of the tree whence the lumber came. Concludes Elliott Norse, whose calculations I have been citing, timber operations "release a huge pulse of CO_2 in the few years after logging," which in no way is fully rectified by replanting cut-over areas. The amount of carbon stored in any young-tree forest is a tiny fraction of that found in old-growth standing timber, snags, and down wood. The effect then is to add, in some small but actual amount, to the atmospheric CO_2, and therefore to increase, in some small but actual amount, the impacts of global warming, which as we have seen may be potentially catastrophic for the forests of the western United States by increasing the likelihood of pest infestations, tree death, and uncontrollable wildfires in the dry, lifeless stands. Writes Norse, "If climatic change increases tree mortality from pests and fires, the disparity in C storage between vulnerable young tree plantations and resistant ancient forests will only increase."

It would appear that the current president of the United States, William Clinton, has believed for quite some time (and perhaps does so even yet) that the issue out there in that far corner of America, the dark green and rainy place where only a few voters live but much noise is made, is simply that some people want to cut trees for money and others want them to remain standing for posterity. And the spotted owl is the cat's-paw. Wrong. The issue has to do with mycorrhizal fungus, with edge effect, with global carbon balances, and with the death of trees cut and the death of trees not cut and the premature death of the weaker and weaker trees to follow that will be grown in a place that was once a forest. Not a problem. Surely, there must be a policy approach, thought the president of the United States, to have it both ways. Save the owl, save the loggers. Win-win. The Ancient Forest has news for him: It is too late. Lose-lose. Despite the noble effort by a consortium of conservation organizations to offer legal protection to remaining old-growth forests in the Northwest, resulting in a compromise that no one seems to be satisfied with, on a regional ecological scale the primeval big-tree forest of the Northwest is, or soon will be (excepting scattered remains), gone. The compromise plan is the so-called Option 9, designed to meet the requirement of a federal district court to afford protection to the spotted owl by protecting some, but not all, of the remaining old growth. As forest policy analyst Jeffrey St. Clair describes the compromise between the environmentalists and the Clinton administration, it is a "confusing landscape of scientific double-talk and ecological ironies, a protean realm where clearcuts inhabit 'old-growth reserves,' species are 'saved' by being brought to the brink of extinction, and ancient forests are logged off for their own protection. Another case of good science gone wrong, traduced once again by politics as usual."

In Canada, the big trees have a few more years, although old-growth logging is more rapacious there than in our own country. No help from that quarter. And with the felling of the original coniferous forests, so has the lumberjack business been felled. Paul Bunyan's crew started in the Northeast, and they cut that all down. Went to the upper Great Lakes, cut that all down. Went to the Pacific Northwest, and cut that all down—except for some patches of it here and there. Where to now? The taiga of Siberia? Maybe so, only another group of loggers is coming around the other way.

As for the owl, hanging on by a thread in the one acre in ten that is left of its original range, the prognosis is dim. And what of the other species, as yet undiscovered and perhaps not so media-worthy, that have already been extirpated or soon will be—the lowly fungi no longer welcome in a dried-out forest, the tiny freshwater fish whose plunge pools have been eliminated, the invertebrates that no longer busily create the linkages in turning death into life on the forest floor?

In the television documentaries about the cutting of the old growth of the Pacific Northwest, the obligatory sequence shows the rattling chainsaw biting deeply into the wide trunk of a centuries-old Douglas fir, the wood seemingly soft as flesh as the saw glides deeper and deeper. At length the great tree leans, then with a groan rising to an unworldly shriek, plummets to earth, its twenty-six tons half burying itself in the forest duff. "The death of a giant," intones a voice-over. And so it is.

But there is another scene, scarcely ever shown, even on public television. It is of the logging trucks, the sixteen-gear Kenworths coming down the twisting mountain roads at fifty miles an hour, one after another, each trailer carrying three great logs, or sometimes just one huge bole, thicker than a man is tall, a tree that was putting on wood before Columbus was born. This scene, the cortège of logging trucks coming off the mountain, depicts the death not of a single tree, but of an entire ancient forest, therefore severing the ecological *possibility* that such a forest could rise ever again.

"Have ye seen the trees of *O-re-gon*?" asks the man from Crewe on Wordsworth's paths. Yes, we tell him. Yes, we have seen them.

8

Lucy's Woods

The question is not what you
look at, but what you see.
—Henry David Thoreau,
Journals, *November 16, 1850*

This is about a visit I made to Rock Creek, West Virginia, and the events that followed, which are still unfolding even as I write. Rock Creek is a hollow—a "holler," properly speaking—a steep branching system of coves running to a creek that is a tributary to the Coal River, which itself runs northward through this compressed region of wooded steeps and deeply folded valleys of the Appalachian plateau.

The Coal River Valley lies west of Beckley, West Virginia, a smallish city, yet with an interstate and motels and cardboard hamburgers and all manner of whatnots of automotive America-on-the-move. But once you get into the valley, served by Route 3, a twisty two-lane state highway, you are in a different world. The mountains rise abruptly from the wedged defiles, separating the hollows where the dwellings are clustered. Once you see this country, you realize that the hollows, so decisively walled off from one another by the mountains, are geopolitical entities, not just neighborhoods. And that thought provides some of the reasons why this region suffers not only from poverty, but also from political powerlessness. The people are physically divided and therefore economically conquerable—and for nearly all their history, they have been decisively conquered by fewer than a half dozen giant natural resource corporations that own whatever of value grows on the land and whatever of economic value lies under the land, namely coal.

In Appalachia as a whole, some 80 percent of the surface land and almost all subsurface mineral rights are owned by companies such as the Westvaco Corporation, the pulp and paper titan with offices in New York City, or by the Peabody Coal Company, with offices in Saint Louis. Here in the hollows the people live by the sufferance of such distant corporations, who are quick to promise employment, but equally quick to lay off the miners and loggers when times are bad.

"The shrewder, money-minded people control the destinies of those whose values are of a higher order," says my friend Holler John Flynn, a writer born and bred in West Virginia and a lover of its woods and people. "It's forever been that way and forever will be—until the final lump of coal comes out of these valleys and the final tree is cut." For these reasons, despite the astonishing natural beauty of the landscape, it is surprisingly easy to be sociological in West Virginia, to relate the gloom of poverty to the looming mountains.

But my mission here was not sociological; it was ecological. I had learned from one of North America's great forest ecologists, Professor Orie L. Loucks, Ohio Eminent Scholar of Ecosystem Studies (at Ohio's Miami University), that Rock Creek Hollow was representative of the mixed mesophytic forest, and that the mixed mesophytic was in trouble. Loucks patiently explained the scientific name for this forest, taking me backward through the etymology: *phytic* means "plant"; *meso* means, roughly, a "middling" or in botany-speak "mesic" kind of growing environment, which is the best kind (not too wet or too dry, nor too cold or too hot); and *mixed,* in this instance, means that there are a large number of big, dominant trees making up the "canopy"—the highest interlacing of branches—in the mixed mesophytic forest. Here then was a mix of trees, with many dominants, not the usual two or three as in other forests, so it could not be called simply "oak-hickory" or "maple-beech-birch," for example.

Fact: The mixed mesophytic forest is the oldest forest in North America. Fact: It contains our largest relatively unbroken block of deciduous woodland. There's only one other forest like it in the world, said Loucks—in south-central China.

The mixed mesophytic turns out to be a huge place, taking in parts of Ohio, Pennsylvania, most of West Virginia, a touch of Maryland and of Virginia, eastern Kentucky, east-central Tennessee, and a county or two in northern Alabama. Almost as big as New England. And in the forest live some eighty species of trees. The forest canopy alone can consist of three dozen different tree species—basswoods, magnolias, some of them rare species, many kinds of oak and hickory, a "forgotten" subspecies of locust, the nearly extinct red mulberry, and beech, maples, tulip poplar, buckeye, sweetgum. Unglaciated during the ages of ice and uninundated by the seas across one hundred million years of geological time, this is the "mother forest" of eastern North America, the forest that has provided the germ plasm resources from which all other forests have subsequently risen. "With its large number of dominant trees, particularly the broadleaf species such as magnolias and basswoods, it has very much the feeling of a tropical rain forest," says evolutionary biologist Charles Werth of Texas Tech University. Says biologist Stewart Ware of the College of William and Mary, "Many of the trees have relatives in the tropics, and certainly it is the most diverse hardwood forest in North America." The mixed mesophytic is, in short, our rain forest, our Brazil, though the United Nations has not yet singled it out for the focus of international ecological concern. It should.

When I asked what was the matter with the mixed mesophytic, Loucks did not answer. "Just go there," he said. "Then we'll talk." He gave me the phone number of John Flynn, now the writer friend whom I call Holler John, and that was how I got to Rock Creek, West Virginia, to see the "forest of the hollows," the quintessential woodland of Appalachia.

Flynn in turn took me to see Joe Aliff, and Joe took me to the woods—his own small patch of twenty-five acres or so of mountainside and ridge. He told me to climb onto the back carrying rack of his four-wheel ORV, powered by a Japanese motorcycle engine that he was impatiently revving after having carefully packed a dark-bearded cheek with a substantial wad of Red Man. "Are you set?" Aliff yelled. And without waiting for an answer he opened the throttle and up we rode, through a high pasture and into the late-fall woods of West Virginia along a rough fire road he had built himself, switching back and forth along the steep slope to make the grade.

And so did I find myself on a low ridge overlooking Rock Creek Hollow, in the company of a leading citizen and lifelong resident. He was hunkered down, Joe Aliff, poignantly hacking at the swollen base of a red oak tree with a bowie knife that glinted clean and sharp in the dull woods. The base of the tree, like others around it, was bulbous with extra cambium in a last-ditch attempt at life, a valiant effort to make up for rotted roots which no longer functioned.

"He's dead," said Aliff, rising slowly and a bit awkwardly to his feet. John Flynn told me that Aliff had been in a coal mine accident some years before—a cave-in—and was in constant pain. "He just don't know he dead," Joe Aliff went on, referring to the tree we had inspected. His was a Welsh coal miner's voice, high and husky, every word spoken distinctly, carefully chosen as if the time above ground were too precious to waste on misunderstandings. He described the trees exactly to me, confident of their species and of his estimate of their condition.

To Joe Aliff, these trees had individuality. They were like ailing friends met at the post office, or greatly missed because they had passed away. He turned, pointing with his knife-tip to a nearby tree. "Here's a white oak dead." Then another, prone on the downslope nearby. "He went down this year." The tree still held its leaves. "See that hickory over there, that's laying on the ground?" The knife-tip swung to another quarter. "Once they hit the ground they go away fast because they're rotten inside. Dead on the inside, even though they still have leaves." The knife-tip moved again. "See that red oak over there? He'll pull water another year or two then he'll be gone. They either snap off in the middle or just fall over of their own weight. They just turn over, like an old tooth, like a mushroom."

And in ten years, or five, or only two, depending on the species and the rot inside, the fallen trees will simply disappear into the earth, as if swallowed up by the dark anthracite seams that run under these mountains, run beneath the seabed of the Atlantic, to the sad, treeless valleys of coal-pitted Wales.

As Joe Aliff went through his litany of death, his own sadness came into me. His forest was dying. "The last few years it has really started hitting the red oak," said Joe. "I first saw it in the locust on the dry ridges, about twenty years ago. Then I started watching it in the hickory. In the last five years the hickory and the red oak are going away really quick. It's picking up pace. There stands a dead hickory; and there's another. Every time you walk out you find another one. Why I could take you to places where you can't keep a trail open for the four-wheeler. You got to take a chainsaw to keep cutting it out. Makes me feel real bad. My family don't even want to discuss it. They don't even want to see this. That's how bad it's going down."

And so we walked back and forth along the ridge, kicking the leaves, Joe answering my questions politely until we both knew there was nothing more to say. Abruptly he returned to his ORV, kicked it over, and waited for me to climb aboard. The engine sputtered, roared. I took my seat on the carrying rack, facing rearward again, and we jounced down the fire road and into the pasture, the woods receding behind until at length, in the distant view, they looked like woods again, instead of death.

Nobody knows much about tree death in this forest region. In fact, nobody knows much about this forest region, period. And that is a pity. I have come to think of it as "Lucy's woods," after the remarkable botanist and forest ecologist E. (for Emma) Lucy Braun, who studied it all of her life, and named it, too, in 1916 when she was a brilliant twenty-seven-year-old professor at the University of Cincinnati, whose faculty she had joined six years before. The "mixed mesophytic," she called it.

To botanists of a certain age in America, the doughty Lucy Braun is a much-admired figure. "She was a gentle, unassuming type person," according to William Nearing, a botany professor at Connecticut College who told me that he had taken field trips with Braun during the 1950s and 1960s. (She died in 1971, at age 82.) "But she gave as good as she got." Nearing explained that field botany had not been a calling that was hospitable to women; there were as few female scientists in the 1950s and 1960s as in the prewar decades. "She was a short, petite woman," Nearing said. "But she held her own. She was an individualist, with a good deal of personal courage." Clearly it took personal courage for her—usually in company of sister Annette, also petite—to brave the backwoods of eastern Kentucky (the part of the mixed mesophytic she loved the most) and surrounding areas in West Virginia and Tennessee where she took her exhaustive botanic censuses, beginning in 1934. That was the year Lucy Braun bought her first motorcar, which meant that she and Annette (neither was married; the sisters were inseparable) could range far afield each summer. Prior to that time, they would take the Cincinnati, Georgetown & Portsmouth traction line to the edge of the mixed mesophytic forest region, then hire a horse and buggy and get as far into the countryside as possible.

Once equipped with an automobile, the sisters were able to move further into what were then still primeval woods of Appalachia, populated by Hatfields and McCoys of uncertain disposition. According to one account, the sisters quickly learned "moonshine manners," gave the copper stills a wide berth, and never failed to ask permission to conduct their studies on private property. According to Hal De Selm, a professor of ecology at the University of Tennessee, the sisters were respectful of local custom. When De Selm was a graduate student bent on doing his fieldwork in Kentucky, Lucy Braun advised him with a twinkle in her eye, "Better not plan on doing any research on Sunday in the mountains. That's the Lord's day." Soon, word of the tiny women scientists spread through the woods of Kentucky and beyond, so that they were met with warm welcomes every summer by the mountain people as their car approached, jouncing along the dirt roads of the region.

By the time she was ready to send her classic 1950 book, *Deciduous Forests of Eastern North America*, off to the publishers, Braun had traveled some 65,000 miles through the mixed mesophytic forest in her little car and in those that replaced it. She had studied many areas, but none so carefully as the magnificently diverse, big-tree mixed mesophytic, her beloved woods, to which she felt a nearly maternal attachment—Lucy's woods. When, during the 1950s, she learned that the American Museum of Natural History was planning a Hall of Forests, she traveled to New York to make a case for the mixed mesophytic of eastern Kentucky to be depicted as the best way to teach people about the origins of the Eastern deciduous forest and complex biological associations. However, according to Richard H. Pough, the museum's curator of conservation who had been charged with the responsibility of putting this permanent exhibit together, "the powers that be in the museum wanted a forest better known to most museum visitors." So the woodlands of the Great Smoky National Park were chosen as a model for the dioramas. "It was almost as good," said Pough when I asked him about the incident.

"A pity," said Orie Loucks when I told him of this. "The mixed mesophytic is the treasure trove of broadleaved diversity of North America."

That this is not the exemplary deciduous forest displayed in our greatest natural history museum reveals a pattern of ignorance about the mixed mesophytic that persists to this very day. Loucks would soon tell me why, but for now insisted that I get hold of Lucy Braun's book, which I did. But it wasn't easy, for the book has been in and out of print for forty years. It is now out of print, and yet her eighty-two-page chapter on the mixed mesophytic is still the definitive source of information about this astonishing forest region that covers "all of the Cumberland Mountains, the southern part of the Allegheny Mountains, all but the northwest area of the Unglaciated Allegheny Plateau, and all but the southernmost ends of the Cumberland Plateau," she writes. And within this vast geography grows "the most complex and the oldest association" of all deciduous forests. "From it, and from its ancestral progenitor, the mixed Tertiary forest as a whole, all other climaxes of the deciduous forest have arisen." Braun adds that the mixed mesophytic forest is reminiscent of "luxuriant tropical selva," in that it contains so many dominants. "Most northern forests," she explains, "have few dominants," adding that where conditions for forest development are optimal, the rain abundant, the weather warm, nature produces a *mix* of dominant trees. "It is a recognized fact," she says in her careful scholarly prose, "that the tendency toward dominance by few species increases with the distance from equatorial regions."

But here, the trees of the forest canopy are many and various—many of them topping one hundred feet in a tropical profusion of intermingled leaves and branches. In her surveys of the forest region, Braun paid special attention to the three dozen canopy or near-canopy trees that grew in a typical mixed mesophytic area, although the composition of the forest tended to change from one place to another, with greater or lesser numbers of different species. Almost everywhere, however, was the elegant American beech (*Fagus grandifolia*), with its smooth, tidy Oxford gray bark and luminous yellow leaves in autumn; and the towering tulip poplars (*Liriodendron tulipifera*), their giant trunks as straight as doric columns in a Grecian temple. There were four basswoods (*Tilia heterophylla, T. heterophylla* var. *Michauxii, T. floridan, T. neglecta*) that perfume the forest in spring. The soft-wooded basswoods are good for whittling, and produce a fiber of the inner bark that Native Americans wove into cordage as strong as Asian jute, made from a tree in the same family. And there were three kinds of sugar maple (*Acer saccharum, A. saccharum* var. *nigrum, A. saccharum* var. *Rugellii*), as well as the sweet buckeye (*Aesculus octandra*), a ninety-footer with a shiny, and poisonous, brown seed—whose paste is still used by bookbinders because it resists insects.

The blighted American chestnut (*Castanea dentata*) was widespread in the forest in the early days of Lucy Braun's explorations—with up to 50 percent coverage in places—but is now gone from the canopy it once dominated. The chestnut is not forgotten by the mountain folk, however, who admire the way shoots still come up from the old stumps, hanging on despite adversity. Oaks have moved in to take the chestnut's place—especially the red oak (*Quercus borealis* var. *maxima*) and the white oak (*Q. alba*) that dominate the south-facing slopes. These are the oaks that Joe Aliff has found dying on his ridge.

Some of the canopy trees of the mixed mesophytic forest are rare—the red mulberry, for example. No relation to the white and black mulberries of residential streets, which are exotics from Asia, our own *Morus rubrus*, uncommon in Braun's day, may perhaps now be extinct in the mixed mesophytic forest. In the Northeast, the red mulberry is a shrub, but in the southern Appalachians it could grow to seventy feet, with a diameter of four feet. With wide-spreading branches, the mulberry was eminently climbable by the boys and girls of the hollows, to whom the fruit, the size of a baby's thumb, was a summer miracle of mouth-filling sweetness.

Other trees are downright mysterious, such as the yellow locust. If you ask the average botany professor about this tree, he or she will tell you there is no such thing. "You mean black locust. People who call it yellow locust are wrong. It is the black locust they are describing." (I know this, because I have asked such a question of botanists at the University of Maryland.) But the people in the Southern mountain hollows who know their woods insist that they are not the same—there are two very different kinds of locusts here. The ordinary black locust (*Robinia pseudoacacia*) is a tree that grows typically to forty or fifty feet in this region (and occasionally to seventy or eighty)—a smallish, gnarly-looking tree with wide, complex branching, beginning low on the trunk. Its forked branches make the tree subject to borers, and therefore the tree has a short life span of fifty to seventy-five years, and rots away rather quickly after being cut. It is definitely not part of the dramatic big-tree canopy; and its dense wood is not commercially valuable. Nowadays, the tree is used mainly to provide a quick vegetative cover on the scarred landscapes left after strip mining.

The yellow locust is another matter entirely. This tree, called "yellow" because its wood is a lighter color than that of the black locust (which is brown), has the same sprays of compound leaves as the black, and the same leguminous seed pods, like the pods of field peas or fava beans. But there the similarities end. The yellow locust rises as tall and straight as the mast of a sailing ship in the forest, its first branches not beginning on the stout trunk until fifty or sixty feet from the ground. Its crown is narrow, not broad like the black locust's, and the top of the tree is at or above the canopy—often at 150 feet or higher. Also, unlike the black locust, the yellow is long-lived—borers do not trouble it—and the wood, used by mountain people as structural timber for bridges and buildings as well as for fenceposts, is virtually indestructible. John Flynn told me that the deep-pit coal miners of Appalachia have to be sure *not* to use yellow locust for shoring timbers for their "rooms"—the scores of lateral diggings off a main tunnel in what is called "room and pillar" mining. The reason for avoiding yellow locust for shoring, Flynn told me, is that engineers want the shoring timbers to rot and collapse relatively quickly and irregularly after the seam has been mined out in a given area, in order to restore supporting earth to the small rooms so that the structural integrity of the honeycombed mountain is maintained and the possibility of massive subsidence of surface areas avoided. The miners found that, with yellow locust, the rooms were too permanent to permit actively mined areas to restabilize. Thus, knowing the difference between a black locust and a yellow one could be a matter of public safety for the huddled communities above the diggings.

The mystery of the yellow locust as a tree distinct from the black arises not because the mountain people are confused, but because the yellow was more or less "lost" in the literature of academic botany for over forty years. It is perhaps no wonder that young botanists and foresters deny its existence. Recently, a sampling of this lost literature was collected by John Flynn, who, following up a vague reference in Donald Culross Peattie's 1950 book *A Natural History of Trees*, scoured the U.S. Department of Agriculture Library at Beltsville, Maryland (with the enthusiastic help of the librarian on duty), for early articles on the yellow locust. Reading through a packet of a half dozen papers from the 1930s and 1940s, he found that the tall, straight tree presumed nonexistent in the Appalachian forest had, for generations, been alive and well in Long Island, New York, where it was called the "shipmast" locust, and had been planted, under the encouragement of the Soil Conservation Service, to reduce erosion and enrich the soil. The tree was identified in 1936 as a separate botanical variety by Oran Raber (*Robinia pseudoacacia* var. *rectissima*).

The trouble with *rectissima* was that it was shy-bearing, and would not propagate from seeds, only from cuttings. Why this might have been so can be explained by the story of S. B. Detwiler, of the Soil Conservation Service, a government man with an uncommon amount of historical curiosity. In his article, "The History of Shipmast Locust," appearing in the *Journal of Forestry* in 1937, Detwiler reports that the yellow locust had been brought to Long Island in 1636 by John Sands, "a seafaring man" (after whom Sands Point is named), whose ship suffered a broken boom that was replaced by a yellow locust fetched from the forests of Virginia. After the repairs, Sands balled up a live specimen of this useful Southern tree to bring home. Cuttings were propagated, and the tree proved to be even more useful to Long Island farmers than to boatwrights. Landowners were planting whole woodlots of the tree—"for each child, ten acres of locust" was one farmer's rule.

Detwiler reports, however, that the tree's original range was not coastal Virginia at all. Whether or not Sands got his tree inland (perhaps from West Virginia, which prior to 1863 was part of the Old Dominion) or from a coastal Colonial planting is not known. "Extensive scouting for the original source of shipmast locust in the lower Chesapeake Bay region failed to locate any such trees," writes Detwiler. The mystery of its origin remained unsolved until 1948, when Henry Hopp, of the Bureau of Plant Research, "discovered" some stands of "a form of black locust" in Randolph County, West Virginia, with trees so tall and straight that it must, he thought, be the ancestral form of the familiar shipmast locust of Long Island. Peattie's surmise is that the tree species Hopp found was first taken to coastal Virginia by early collectors where it eventually died out in an inhospitable coastal environment, but not before John Sands exported it to Long Island. The Long Island woodlots of shipmast locust, the botanists of the U.S. Department of Agriculture later concluded, must be clones from that single tree—the one brought thither by Sands—which accounted for the shipmast's inability to propagate from seed.

The tree that Hopp found was what the mountain people all along have called yellow locust, never knowing or caring whether it was found or lost, or named or unnamed, by the government experts and university professors who so casually relegated it to the status of variety. One wonders which is a variety of which. According to Orie Loucks, the yellow locust may well have preceded the black locust in the evolution of the species. He explains that during the Tertiary period, the tallest, strongest genotypes would tend to win out in the contest for survival. Only in later and climatologically gentler times could a weaker, smaller tree like the black locust evolve. An academic argument perhaps, but an interesting one from a political standpoint. "It's a people's tree," says John Flynn, "a great strong tree which like the people themselves has been misunderstood and ignored."

I asked Joe Aliff about it. "Oh, the yellow locust is dying too," he said. "It's going down fast, like the red oak." I asked about regeneration. "Not the yellow locust. Fact is, the only regeneration I've seen is in the papaw over to the other side of the hollow," he said.

After my visit with Joe Aliff and John Flynn, Orie Loucks and I discussed matters of tree death in a quiet corner of the lobby of a small hotel in Foggy Bottom. He said that recent mast studies (studies of the seed stock of the forest—acorns, hickory nuts, and the podded legumes of the locust) in woods similar to Joe Aliff's revealed that some species were experiencing a 50 to 80 percent reduction in mast. The statistic is fraught with meaning: no seed, no regeneration.

He comes to Washington, D.C., often, does Orie Loucks, for he is a leading acid-rain researcher, a major participant in as well as an outspoken critic of the National Acid Precipitation Assessment Program (which he fears is so politically tainted that its final assessment is "unlikely to be viewed as credible in the scientific community").

Like Joe Aliff, Loucks is bearded and quiet-spoken, and has an equally passionate commitment to "Lucy's woods," which Loucks, virtually alone among his scientific peers, believes should be studied assiduously. He himself has had the dream of studying it since his graduate school days in the mid-1950s, when he pored over Lucy Braun's book and toured the region.

Loucks accounts for the lack of scientific interest in the mixed mesophytic with the question, "How many people do you know who have a summer home in the Coal River Valley of West Virginia?" The point is that this place is unlike the Adirondacks, which have attracted the wealthy for over a century, or Vermont, where the rich and famous summer and then retire, or even the eastern slopes of the Appalachians, where Biltmore was built near Asheville, North Carolina, and where, farther north, the riding-to-hounds elite of Virginia chase after terrified foxes. Where the money and media are, says Loucks, is where the forest research gets done. Otherwise, the funding is harder to come by. And so Orie Loucks, unfunded and consequently without site-specific research findings to rely on, is puzzled about why the trees are dying in the mixed mesophytic. But he has some theories, the primary one being that the trees are dying from acid rain (originating mainly from coal-fired industrial plants of the Ohio Valley) and ozone (originating from high-compression engines, among other sources). And he is surprised by it.

"Until quite recently," said Loucks, "I was saying that there were no air-pollution effects on the north slopes of the mountains of this region or on the flats. I believed in the paradigm that the rich soils in these localities have tremendous stocks of calcium to buffer the acid, and the trees were therefore not going to be affected. But then I went to the Coal River Valley and found the forest was falling down all around me on the very same rich soils. It was very troubling." Loucks peered at me to see if I was with him so far.

"Anyway," he continued, "out of that experience I was sensitized to two processes that I was aware of, but that I hadn't really thought through. The first has to do with ozone. We were accepting the fact that an oxidant, such as ozone, was interacting with tree leaves and probably decreasing growth, but not necessarily having a profound effect on forests. But if you keep decreasing the total photosynthesis of a plant you will eventually produce major effects on the root system." Loucks said that foliage damage in Eastern deciduous forests on as many as twenty species had been well documented, with damage to another ten species likely but not yet validated experimentally. He had observed the same kind of damage in a wide range of species in the mixed mesophytic.

Loucks explained that the roots were where trees get the first "share" of energy-giving carbohydrates from the growing foliage, so that the tree can maintain its basic delivery system for water and nutrients. "But if you decrease the available carbohydrates by ten or fifteen or twenty percent, this translates into the decrease in roots of ten or fifteen or twenty percent. You've created a feedback."

Thus a kind of vicious cycle is developed. The roots are made smaller by the oxidant damage, leading to a decrease in nutrient and water uptake, which permits even greater impacts from ozone the next year on the weakened tree, until, finally, "the whole system accelerates to create a completely stressed tree."

Loucks drew a breath, still peering at me, wondering perhaps how good a student I might be. I realized that I was in the presence of a very gifted teacher, as well as scientist, but not one to mollycoddle the intellectually frail.

"The second effect," resumed Professor Loucks, "has to do with the enrichment of nitrogen. We're accustomed to adding nitrogen to corn, but corn happens to be a plant that will open its stomata and take up more carbon to create a balance. So the more nitrogen you give it, the more carbon it'll take up. But most species in the forest won't grow very much faster no matter what you give 'em. Now, our emissions [from factories and automobiles] have tripled the nitrogen that they get. And since they don't take up any more carbon, the whole system has an altered carbon-nitrogen ratio in the plant tissue. That means that all the secondary metabolytes, the materials that the plants produce to resist disease and insects, are altered. The Europeans have been working on this, and though they don't know the mechanism, they have identified the tolerances that trees have for nitrogen. Based on their calculations, our trees here in the Eastern United States are receiving about three times their tolerance for nitrogen. This does not mean three times the optimal level, but three times the *tolerance*."

Loucks went on to explain that the altered carbon-nitrogen ratio permits penetration of the tree by pathogens—the fungi that create the rot, which could not penetrate previously. Thus, due to the loss of roots from ozone and the penetration of pathogens as a result of the carbon-nitrogen imbalance induced by oxides of nitrogen, in the form of acid rain or other acid deposition from air pollution, the trees have been falling over or snapping off in the Coal River Valley, and elsewhere in the mixed mesophytic, at a rate that could in no way be considered natural.

Research is also needed, Loucks said, to determine the exact rates of death and decline on a species-by-species basis in various locales. The normal "background" mortality rate in the era before the long-range transport of air pollution (that is, before the 1950s) was between 0.5 percent and 0.7 percent per year, Loucks told me. Walking through such a forest, he said, you would see snags and down wood—"a few downed trees." One out of every 100 or 150 living trees, he said, no more than a half dozen or so on a given acre of thickly wooded forest land. The fallen trees would tend to accumulate, of course, each lasting two or three years, or perhaps ten, depending on the species and the degree of rot prior to falling, before disappearing into humus. But even accounting for that, the rate of death that I had seen on Joe Aliff's place was nothing like what Loucks was describing as pre-pollution normal. In fact, Loucks estimates that in the *least*-affected areas he has visited in the mixed mesophytic forest, the mortality rate is between 3 and 4 percent, between four and eight times higher than normal. "Anything over two to three percent death each year," said Loucks ominously, "is a disaster."

The effect of this level of mortality is that a forest, even if forever uncut, can never reach a natural state with trees of many species and many ages, including some forest giants with four-foot trunks that have been growing for two or three hundred years. Posterity is cheated of such woodlands, no matter how many are "preserved" by the Nature Conservancy in nature sanctuaries or by governments in local, state, and national parks. As Loucks wrote in a letter to a colleague, "Decadal mortality rates of 30 to 40 percent, which we have observed during the 1980s for dominant species at various study sites in Ohio and Indiana [similar to the mixed mesophytic], show clearly that old growth forests are inconceivable."

In effect, then, the forest is moribund, obsolete. So much for the treasure trove of broadleaved diversity.

There are, of course, some who choose to argue with the palpable evidence of tree death such as I witnessed (and Orie Loucks explained) in the woods behind Joe Aliff's place in Rock Creek Hollow. Indeed, for reasons that have seemed to me to be more political than ecological, an argument is still raging in the Coal River Valley, in West Virginia, and in corporate and government offices in New York and Washington, about just what *is* happening to the mixed mesophytic forest. It all started because a great reporter, my friend John Flynn, who was one of the earliest to break the acid-rain forest story in national media, came home again.

Flynn grew up in this country; he was born and spent his childhood right here in Rock Creek. After graduating from West Virginia University, he began newspapering, first as a sportswriter, then as a science writer. He held positions at several big-city newspapers, the last of which was at the *Detroit Free Press.* Then in 1985 he was eased out of his job by people who seemed to him to be more concerned about the state of the automobile industry than the health of trees and people. He is not the first environmental reporter I know to whom this sort of thing has happened. Mostly, they find a job at another paper. But by this time, John Flynn was in his fifties, and wondered if that wasn't the end of newspapering for him. His wild blond hair had turned white and hung to his shoulders. Too old to get another slot in such a young man's game. So, after a bit of indecision, he finally decided to quit full-time reporting and come back after a long absence to his beloved hollow, where he hoped to get over his bitterness. Only when he got there, he found the woods around his "homeplace" a victim of the very crisis he had been reporting since the early 1980s.

I spoke with Flynn at Sible's restaurant and rooming house in Naoma, just a bit down Route 3 from Rock Creek Hollow. "Right after I got back," he told me, "I was walking along the road at nine o'clock at night. It was warm and perfectly still. Then a tree fell, *bang!* Then one came right behind it. *Bang!* I jumped about five feet in the air when I heard this. I've seen fallen trees completely clothed—fully foliaged trees—lying on the forest floor, having fallen when there had been no wind, no rain. A basswood, a red oak. They just fell down."

It was then that he decided to write the story of "the falling forest," which appeared in the *Beckley Register-Herald* on Sunday, October 6, 1991. He called his friend Orie Loucks, who made several trips to the area, and interviewed other acid-rain scientists to make sure he was on solid ground. The resulting articles presented a well-reported and responsible account of what had been happening in the mixed mesophytic forest of the Coal River Valley. Copies were distributed far beyond West Virginia to scientists and officials concerned with the effect of air pollution on Eastern forests.

But it was not long before a backlash began. A month after Flynn's pieces were published, some West Virginia members of the Society of American Foresters (as they described themselves) organized by a public-relations executive of the Westvaco Corporation who was then chairman of the society's West Virginia chapter, telephoned William Byrd, editor of the *Register-Herald*, demanding equal time. What they had in mind was that the senior staff of the newspaper meet with them for a session that would deconstruct Flynn's analysis. Since the economics of a small-city newspaper are a bit different from those of a giant corporation like Westvaco, Byrd sent a young but experienced reporter, who in this account remains nameless at her insistence. "I don't ever want to go through that again," she told me.

As it turned out, when she arrived at the paneled conference room where the meeting was held, she was confronted with a roomful of hostile foresters armed with a slide show, written materials, and an orchestrated discussion that dissected Flynn's pieces for several hours and berated her paper for publishing them. "The dissenting foresters," she wrote in the November 3 *Register-Herald*, "were shocked by the suggestion that the Appalachian forest is in jeopardy, an idea they term as 'sensationalism.' On the contrary, the group maintains, the Mixed Mesophytic Forest referred to in the stories is in 'robust' health, and the state's forests are flourishing as never before." Curiously, in surveys of forest health, John Flynn later told me, the U.S. Forest Service does not count any fallen trees as dead—only "standing dead" are enumerated. This method would not merely understate the mortality in the mixed mesophytic, it would, given the nature of the symptoms—toppled trees and snap-offs—almost wholly conceal the true condition of the forest.

Despite the fact that, as editor Byrd put it, "she was manhandled by those guys," the reporter dutifully absorbed the blows and turned out a story representing the Westvaco viewpoint. The conferees (who included a representative of the U.S. Forest Service), she wrote, were annoyed that one of their number had not been interviewed for the stories, that their statistical analyses had not been included, and that the tree death report was local and did not discuss forest health or the lack of it elsewhere in the region. If there was any tree death (which they doubted), it had to do with something besides pollution—such as fires and gypsy moths. Anyway, they said, trees grow quickly and die out after a period of time. Inadvertently they made Orie Loucks's point for him—the period of time being fifty or seventy-five years signaling premature death rather than the three hundred years trees ought to live.

All of this was powerfully annoying to Loucks, Joe Aliff, and John Flynn, who were hoping that the government's response to Flynn's article would show at least some concern, if not constructive action. But the Forest Service did not break ranks with Westvaco. Indeed, its hostility was directed at me as well when I published a brief account of my visit to Aliff's place and my interview with Orie Loucks in *American Forests* magazine. For my trouble, a midlevel U.S. Forest Service official wrote several letters of complaint to the publishers of the magazine, the American Forestry Association, suggesting that writers like me ought not to be allowed. These were not letters to the editor for publication (one of those was sent, too, that was much less hysterical), but official Forest Service communications with copies to board members of the association. I quickly came to appreciate why the *Register-Herald* reporter wanted to lie low. Robert Bruck, the North Carolina State University scientist whom the Forest Service has tried (and failed) to make a pariah, says of incidents like these (and there are many): "The Forest Service is speaking through a bunch of leftovers from the Reagan and Bush administrations who participated in NAPAP and continue to push the old political line."

Writers on public issues have got to be thick-skinned, and I suppose I should have quickly forgotten the incident, but I was taken by surprise. What could possibly be wrong with proposing that research be considered, based on the concerns of a very senior forest ecologist in the person of Orie Loucks? Moreover, Loucks was not alone in his findings. I had dug up an earlier report (by the U.S. Forest Service, in fact) of substantially the same kind of tree death occurring in the Tennessee section of the mixed mesophytic. There, during an eight-year period in the late 1970s and early 1980s, large trees began dying in rapid succession. Eighteen percent of the red oak and white oak over seventeen inches DBH (diameter at breast height) had mysteriously died, and 26 percent of the hickory, a pattern reminiscent of what was happening on Joe Aliff's ridge. But not one of the West Virginia dissenters or their aides and allies had visited Aliff's place to see what Loucks might be talking about.

At length, a year later, Westvaco did organize a group to visit the property—"the Gang of Nine," Aliff called them—which included representatives of the Forest Service, the West Virginia Department of Agriculture, and some faculty members of West Virginia University's Department of Forestry. They produced a lengthy report making essentially the same points, but this time rather explicitly suggesting that if there was a problem, it had nothing to do with acid rain. It was the landowner's (Joe Aliff's) fault—for letting his cattle graze in the woods, for high-grading (cutting the biggest trees), for fire. The only problem was that the group, which spent all of three hours on the property, did not visit the areas visited by me or by Orie Loucks, where there had been no fire, little recent cutting, and no grazing. ("Maybe a lost cow or two," said Joe when I asked him about it.) In fact, Loucks had earlier told some of the members of the group to avoid the very area they visited, since the tree death there was untypical of the phenomenon he was concerned about.

When the government fails to meet the needs of the people, as it showed every indication of failing in the case of the tree death crisis in Lucy's woods, then the people must take matters into their own hands. This they appear to be doing, via the Appalachia Forest Action Project, a citizen-science effort meant to provide an independent, objective measurement of just what is going on in woodlots like Joe Aliff's in southern West Virginia, eastern Kentucky, and north-central Tennessee. The project is operating under the auspices of Trees for the Planet, a national group; Appalachia Science in the Public Interest; an interstate ecological task force organized by the Sierra Club; and the Lucy Braun Association for the Mixed Mesophytic Forest, a membership organization put together by John Flynn, Orie Loucks, and a number of other scientists, policy experts, and writers—including me.

The appeal of the notion of citizen science has been so great that even the Forest Service has had to pay attention. The local West Virginia office eventually offered to help train some of the volunteers, perhaps reflecting the reform efforts of the Clinton Administration's new chief forester, Jack Ward Thomas. One of his earliest acts after appointment (in December 1993) was to send a memo to all senior

Forest Service officials, with the instruction that the contents be conveyed to their subordinates. Six "messages" were promulgated by the new chief, the first three of which were: Obey the law; tell the truth; and implement ecosystem management. That these were necessary to articulate says more about what many environmentalists have maintained is a "rogue" agency than perhaps Dr. Thomas should have revealed. But one hopes that the messages will be taken to heart. Indeed, there was evidence of a new candor in a major 1993 report in which the Forest Service stated that, nationally, timber mortality had increased 24 percent on a volume basis between 1986 and 1991, "in all regions, on all ownerships, and for both hardwoods and softwoods." Hardwoods were especially affected, most particularly in the South, where the mortality increase was 37 percent.

After I had come down off the ridge overlooking Rock Creek on Joe Aliff's ORV, John Flynn, Joe Aliff, and I were standing around in Aliff's farmyard in Rock Creek Hollow, the ORV's engine making small tinkling noises as it cooled. I was still a bit choked up, noticeably so, over the amount of devastation I had seen up there. "Anybody Joe takes up to the ridge, or anyplace they want to go," said Flynn, "comes back convinced we have a serious problem here." I said I could believe it.

"You pick out the mountain," said Aliff. "I'll take you there, and you'll see. I don't need to say nothin'. You just need to look."

Aliff, known locally as a serious and accomplished naturalist, presented me with one of his natural history text books. He opened the book to the flyleaf, which he had been using as a kind of guest register for all the people he has carted up the mountain on the back of his four-wheeler, and I added my name and a comment.

We shook hands. Flynn and Aliff told me to come back, in that cordial Southern mountain way. But I said I didn't know how soon that might be. I told them that I couldn't remember when I had spent such a wrenching day just interviewing people. I was sick at heart.

Since then, John Flynn has written me many letters about his sad, beautiful mountains. Here is one of them, composed while he was staying at his Grandfather Rorrer's house that now belonged to his aunt. He was finishing a book about his works and days as an investigative science reporter, and writing articles about the mixed mesophytic forest while staying at Aunt Ressie's place. Flynn wrote:

> Dear Uptown Charles [his name for me, just as mine for him is Holler John], I hope this letter finds you feeling better. It's a cloudy rainy day here in the hollow; beautiful however, with the Sarvis bush and redbud blooming. I have spent considerable time in the mountains since I returned from newspapering. The wild flowers of these coves are gorgeous at this time of year; whole beds of them as if they had been cultivated. I sat high on the right-hand ridge at twilight yesterday, peering down at the home-place, which is greening up. I heard wild turkeys gobbling and saw white-tailed deer. As I mentioned to you before, it's beautiful here even in the various stages of death. I must re-emphasize to you that what is occurring here is profound. The more one looks, the more the deterioration of the system becomes apparent. Most startling is the rapidity of the poplar disease, the girding that progressively eats through the bark about a foot or two off the ground until the tree is dead. These people need the yellow poplar for saw-wood—but the girding's in all of them, to one degree or another. I have come to accept Joe Aliff's premise that not a single species is unaffected by the rot taking place. The whole forest, at least in Rock Creek hollow, is simply rotting on the stump and falling. This is a hard story to tell, especially in the establishment press, because the public perception is so far behind the reality. The sadness in Joe Aliff's eyes, and in Ernie Scarbro's and in Bobby Wills's, is related to the awareness of what is taking place. We're losing 100 million years of evolution in less than a hundred, Charles. This is a tragedy.

I am sorry that I never got a chance to meet Lucy Braun, that she died before I had learned anything about the mixed mesophytic forest, even the name of it. On the other hand, perhaps it's a mercy that she and Annette did not have to see what is happening here, that forever fixed in a gentler time is the image of the diminutive sisters, bumping along the dirt roads of the Appalachian hollows in their 1934 touring car, remarking to each other on what a splendid woods these are, and what a joy it is to study them.

9

PANDEMIC

Our inability to assign definite values to the causes of the disturbance of natural arrangements is not a reason for ignoring the existence of such causes in any general view of the relations between man and nature, and we are never justified in assuming a force to be insignificant because its measure is unknown.

—George Perkins Marsh,
Man and Nature *(1864)*

After I published the brief article on the death and decline in Lucy Braun's mixed mesophytic forest in *American Forests* magazine, the editors received the following letter from a private forestry consultant named E. Gerry Hawkes.

> Finally, an article which echoes my own observations, feelings, and frustrations on the forest health issue. For over twenty years I have watched the health of our forest worsen to the point where there is now widespread decline and rapidly increasing levels of mortality across a broad range of species on a wide variety of sites. Despite this graphic evidence, many foresters deny there is a serious problem, and not only refuse to sound the alarm, but also warn against listening to the so-called "alarmists." Count me as an "alarmist." We should have been alarmed years ago. . . .

Forest trees are beset with all kinds of creatures that do not wish them well. Historic evidence of tree mortality and forest declines shows that from time to time the bugs and fungi get the upper hand, especially in trees weakened by drought or bitter cold. A natural phenomenon. But in recent years, as forester Hawkes points out, an extraordinarily large number of species have been hit hard by dieback and decline, with levels of mortality never seen before. The causes of death are manifold, just as they are in humans. But in most cases (and certainly in the severe episodes), human actions are, to one degree or another, implicated—as I have described in previous chapters. But there is more tree death, and there are more causes of it, than a handful of chapters can contain. Let me therefore add a few significant details at this point concerning some effects and causes not yet covered.

To begin with, the sugar maple. A Vermonter, Mollie Beattie, sent me a clipping about this tree, a tree that most Americans think is indestructible. "Hard maple," it is called. "Rock maple." Beattie, now the director of the U.S. Fish and Wildlife Service in the Clinton administration, was, at the time the clipping arrived, between jobs, having been replaced as the commissioner of forests and parks in a change of governors in Vermont. It is always useful to get mail from people like Mollie Beattie—a face card in the officialdom of environment and natural resources of the kind that magically pops up in marvelous places at appropriate moments. The clipping she sent me came from *The New York Times.* The headline said, SUGAR MAPLES SICKEN UNDER ACID RAIN'S PALL. The dateline was from a town in Vermont. Beattie attached a little slip of yellow stickum paper to the clipping: "Check this out," it said.

I did, and as it happens, not only are the high-elevation red spruce in northern New England dying from acid rain (reduced to less than a quarter of their former numbers, as I reported in Chapter 2), but the beloved (and profitable) sugar maple (*Acer saccharum*) in the United States and adjacent Ontario and Quebec (Canada produces more than 70 percent of the world supply of maple syrup) is in its most severe decline in history.

The decline of the maple began in 1912, in Pennsylvania, and reached the far north in 1932. In recent years—since the mid-1970s—decline episodes have been increasing in frequency and severity. In Quebec's Appalachian mountain region, researchers found that the number of maple trees showing symptoms of decline had reached 91.3 percent in 1988—meaning that in effect the entire forest was affected, since maples constitute two-thirds or more of the trees in lower Quebec. The area of greatest damage was south of Quebec City, the land that lies between the Saint Lawrence and the borders of Vermont, New Hampshire, and Maine. This is the part of the province that receives the heaviest dose of air pollutants carried by the prevailing winds from the tall stacks of Midwestern industry, especially in the Ohio valley.

In Ontario and Quebec, and throughout New England, the rainfall, according to researchers, has been ten times as acidic as normal. Accordingly, in southern Quebec, the Canadians found that the soils in which the maples were growing had developed deficiencies in magnesium, potassium, and phosphorus—evidence that the pollution was probably contributing to the decline, since acid deposition will leach these nutrients from the soil as well as from leaf tissue. Moreover, excess nitrogen deposition from long-range transport of pollutants also, according to Canadian researchers, produces a nutrient imbalance in a maple forest. Though nitrogen is usually considered a nutrient in itself, an excess, as Orie Loucks explained to me in connection with the mixed mesophytic forest, can be toxic. According to a Canadian report, "Excess inorganic-N availability in soil could reduce fine root biomass and produce a loss of ectomycorrhizal symbionts thereby decreasing the uptake of water and P by the trees." The reference here is to the helpful, orange-colored, spongelike mycorrhizal fungi described in earlier chapters, which attach to the fine tree roots, helping them to take up nutrients such as phosphorus, as well as water. In any case, the result of this complex of actions and reactions set in motion by pollution deposition was a pattern of dead and dying maples whose topmost branches were devoid of leaves—crown dieback, this condition is called—accompanied by decreasing rates of growth.

What is more, the maple decline has ramified destructively throughout the maple-forest ecosystem. Canadian researchers have discovered that the defoliation of the crowns has decreased the abundance of birds that rely on the canopy for food and shelter. More pertinently to human concerns, lichens and some other sources of deer and moose food have been found to accumulate toxic metals from air pollution deposition on poorly buffered soils. These metals, cadmium especially, become concentrated in the organs of animals ingesting them. In some areas of Canada, the cadmium level has been so high that the government has declared that the livers and kidneys of moose and deer are unfit for human consumption.

In Vermont, where the sugar maple is every bit as symbolic as it is in Canada, sugar makers became seriously alarmed about the dieback and decline by the mid-1980s. Reported *The New York Times* in 1986, "Fears of a mass sugar maple extinction surfaced last month at an international maple syrup producers' conference in Rutland, Vermont. Botanists from Vermont and Canada presented environmental evidence to support their dire forecast and sugar makers confirmed their findings with reports of extensive deaths and serious production losses." Wilson Clark, a sugar maker from Wells, Vermont, and president of the Vermont Sugar Makers Association, told the *Times* that Vermont had been hit with a 36 percent drop in maple syrup production that year. (Today, the main product of the sugarbush is maple syrup. However, producers are nevertheless called sugar makers or sugarers, a holdover from the days when maple sugar was shipped in bulk from New England as a general sweetener—a commodity, not a luxury item. Maple was the only source of sugar during Colonial times, and remained competitive in price with cane until the latter part of the nineteenth century.)

Two years after the *Times* story, in the spring of 1988, the pear thrips invaded. The thrips (the word is from the Greek and has no singular form) are pests commonly associated with vegetables, tobacco, and fruit trees, not the hulking maples of the forest. And yet, adventitiously perhaps, given the weakened state of the declining sugarbush, the pear thrips virtually took over southern Vermont, ripping into some half a million acres of forest, after having infested Pennsylvania maples beginning in the late 1970s. The thrips are tiny winged creatures, scarcely one-twenty-fifth of an inch long, but enough of them can cause mortal damage to a drought- or pollution-weakened tree in a single season. The thrips larvae bore into the leaf buds in the early spring, causing the buds to produce small misshapen leaves that are puckered with white or yellow blotches and that wither and fall long before autumn.

Northern Vermont was spared the heavy infestations of thrips until the early 1990s, but the pollution damage to the sugar maples continued apace. In 1991, the last thrips-free year in the northern part of the state, Dr. Mel Tyree, head of the University of Vermont's Proctor Maple Research Center, told a *New York Times* reporter, "We think we are looking at the early stages of an epidemic problem," adding that the scientists at the Proctor Center projected a continuing regionwide decline for the next fifty or one hundred years. Tyree said that amending forest soils with applications of calcium, reducing logging, and using only ecologically safe pesticides might slow the decline a bit, but that "the ultimate solution is to reduce acid rain."

Shortly after the Proctor Center's research findings were announced, the U.S. Forest Service took the following contrary position:

> Decline of sugar maple in the northeast U.S. recently has been reported in various newspapers and magazines. [It was, in fact, also reported in a number of refereed scientific journals.] An evaluation of information from three independent [of each other—all were U.S. government sponsored] surveys, Forest Inventory and Analysis, the North American Sugar Maple Decline Project, and Forest Health Monitoring show that *this is not true* [emphasis added].

The Forest Service assured everyone that 90 percent of the sugar maples surveyed in these studies were healthy and that overall, the numbers and volume of sugar maple were increasing.

The key government study was the North American Sugar Maple Decline Project, an effort led by the U.S. Forest Service (which included Forestry Canada in a secondary role) that began in 1987 to evaluate the condition of sugar maples in unmanaged forested areas as well as commercial sugarbushes. The survey technique was an annual (1988, 1989, and 1990) visual assessment of crown condition in 171 plot "clusters" (five plots per cluster) scattered throughout seven northern states (Maine, Massachusetts, Michigan, New Hampshire, New York, Vermont, and Wisconsin) and four Canadian provinces (New Brunswick, Nova Scotia, Ontario, and Quebec). A U.S. Forest Service summary paper on the project asserted that "quality assurance," referring to the validity of the data, was a high priority.

The specific crown conditions measured by the survey were "dieback," wherein the top of the tree shows dead branches, and "transparency," wherein the amount of light that could be seen through the crown of the tree is suggestive of a tree in decline. The normal dieback is 5 percent, the normal transparency, 25 percent. If there is more than 15 percent dieback or more than 55 percent transparency, the tree can be considered to be in trouble.

According to this survey, not only were the maples not in trouble, their health was improving. Overall, the amount of dieback in 1988 was claimed to be only 9 percent in sugarbushes and 7 percent in unmanaged forest areas, well within the "normal" range. In 1989, dieback figures were 8 percent and 6 percent respectively, and in 1990, 7 percent and 6 percent. The transparency measures, also within the normal range, were similarly unremarkable. In 1988 transparency in the sugarbush was 18 percent, in unmanaged areas 16 percent. In 1990, the government researchers moved the transparency figures even lower—to 15 percent for the sugarbush and 14 percent for unmanaged areas. In the high production areas for sugaring—Vermont and Quebec—the crown dieback and transparency were said to be on a par with the study region as a whole. Moreover, the condition of the maple trees' crowns allegedly bore no statistical relationship to air-pollution patterns, as measured by "high versus light sulfate deposition loads" (as an indication of acid deposition) in the plot cluster areas.

"Sugar maple is doing well on a regional basis," reported the Forest Service. In fact, not only was it doing well, nothing out of the ordinary had *ever* been the matter with it, and especially not air pollution. While admitting that a few localized stands or individual trees might have problems, the government report concluded that these should be attributed to "insects, pathogens, mismanagement, weather conditions, and/or poor growing conditions for sugar maples"—not to acid rain.

The variance of the findings of the university scientists at the Proctor Center in Vermont, and of a significant number of official Canadian studies (even though Forestry Canada was involved in the USFS's crown-condition project), with the Forest Service's crown-condition assessment could not have been greater. The Canadian version of the United States' official ten-year acid-rain study (the National Acid Precipitation Assessment Program), called the Canadian Long-Range Transport of Air Pollutants and Acid Deposition Assessment, stated an entirely different view. In the Canadian LRTAP 1990 report on "terrestrial effects" is the following: "There is general agreement that the current episode of forest decline, particularly the sugar maple component, is both more severe and extensive now than has occurred in the past, and that exposure to atmospheric pollutants is a contributing factor."

It is perhaps possible for government bureaucrats simultaneously to agree with both statements—the Canadian one directly above, and the

U.S. findings quoted a few paragraphs back—but not for me. I needed to visit the trees myself.

The person to see (Mollie Beattie told me) was David Marvin, proprietor of one of the larger sugarbushes in Vermont, a top sugar maker, a trained forester, and an industry leader in national and international trade associations. His place of business was two flights up in a converted house along the main street of Johnson, Vermont, a small town about thirty miles south of the Quebec border.

I had scarcely taken my seat in Marvin's ample, sunny office when he said: "If you are here to find out if we are experiencing maple decline, the answer is yes. And we are also experiencing mortality, in some areas very rapid mortality. We've lost a lot of trees." Marvin, a soft-spoken, open-faced man in his forties, was sincerely worried. He was worried about the impacts of air-pollution deposition on the livelihood of sugar makers; he was worried about the dramatic shift, quite possibly a result of global warming, in the geography of sugaring, wherein syrup is now being made in northern Quebec, New Brunswick, and northern Maine, places where heretofore the winters proceeded directly into summer without pausing at the freeze-and-thaw early spring season needed for good sap production.

And he was worried, too, because the U.S. scientific establishment —those conducting government- and industry-funded research—has become so politicized that it seems no longer capable of candor. That pained him most of all, since he believes that what is happening might very well be remedied by proper public policy choices.

After a briefing in the office, Marvin invited me to pay a visit to his sugarbush, located out of town on a south-facing slope, the very best situation for maximizing the sap run. No one completely understands why a sugar maple can produce "sweetwater" season after season (from late winter to early spring, when the temperature alternates between nighttime dips into the twenty-degree range and near-balmy daytime temperatures) with no appreciable harm to the tree. Marvin said that he knew of a sugarbush with trees that had been fully tapped every year for 175 years with no reduction in quantity or quality of the syrup produced.

After we arrived at the Marvin homeplace—an attractive farmhouse with the sugarhouse and vats just across the narrow road—Marvin put the pickup into four-wheel drive and we lurched up a rutted track deep into the sugarbush. The trees were garlanded with green plastic tubing that stays in place year-round and delivers the sweetwater from the trees to the sugarhouse at sugaring time: eighty miles of tubing from twelve thousand taps producing twelve thousand gallons of sap from which three thousand gallons of maple syrup is made.

It was now late summer, and the leaves were already turning. "We've experienced a good production year," said Marvin, "but the signs of stress are very evident right now. The color changes come very early, the leaves fall early, and we've seen tremendous seed crops, which can be a warning of a quite severe forest decline." Marvin directed my attention to the tops of the trees, which were spikey with bare, leafless branches at the crown; some had large dead branches. A few trees had recently fallen.

As we walked among the maples, thickets of raspberry canes kept clutching at my trouser legs. "The raspberries are new," said Marvin. "We never used to have them here—they grow because there's more light now on the forest floor from the thinning crowns." He stomped down the canes in front of him. "I hate them," he said. "And the light. Because of the dieback, the summer woods now have a sickly lime-green color, not the healthy deep forest green the way it should be."

The practical problem, Marvin told me, was that he is no longer able to improve his maple tree stands. The idea in sugaring is to thin out the smaller and less productive trees in such a way that the remaining maples are properly spaced throughout the sugarbush. Maple trees are sensitive to sudden increases in sunlight, having grown up in the dimmed ambience of sheltering neighbor trees. The sudden growth spurt that comes with a flood of new light produces soft, unhardened wood that makes the tree vulnerable to winter-burn and depletes the sugar stored in the roots during the summer, which is needed for the tree to withstand the hard freezes of December, January, and February. Accordingly, it is a careful kind of arboriculture that sugarers must practice. And it is the labor of a lifetime, suitable only for people with a long view; it takes forty years before a seedling maple matures into a worthwhile, high-production member of a first-class sugarbush. "The trouble is not just that we lose trees," Marvin explained, "but that we lose the opportunity to improve our stands. Instead of us making the decisions about thinning, the decision is made for us—by air pollution and other stresses."

In fact, air-pollution deposition entrains quite a number of long-term difficulties for the fifteen thousand maple-sugar producers in North America (three thousand of them in Vermont) who rely on the sugarbush for their livelihood, or at least a substantial part of it. In Canadian studies of the impacts of air pollution on Ontario sugar maples, researchers found that even the sugar chemistry changes in the syrup in declining maples, with greater amounts of arabinose and galactose replacing the "true sugar"—sucrose—that characterizes normal maple sap. Further, the sap from such trees also contains aluminum, manganese, iron, sodium, and barium, while healthy elements such as calcium and potassium are absent. In general, Canadian researchers have found, pollution-impacted Ontario trees show a growth rate only two-thirds that of unpolluted trees, meaning that it might take sixty years rather than forty for maples to reach maturity for sugar makers like David Marvin.

If, as the U.S. Forest Service study asserts, the crown condition in sugar maples actually has improved between 1988 and 1990, this potentially good news may suggest that the reduction in sulfate in rainfall is having some benefit (despite the official view that air pollution is not involved in decline or mortality of sugar maples). The bad news is that, even if the crown conditions are somewhat less grim-looking than before, this does not by itself mean that long-term maple decline has been reversed. Although a reduction in acid content of the rain might lessen the potential for toxic aluminum to enter the trees' vascular system, the forest soils nevertheless remain lacking in essential nutrients, these having been leached away by many years of acid deposition. According to a 1992 paper, two Quebec scientists, R. Ouimet and J.-M. Fortin, in correlating nutrient loss with foliar loss, found that general decline over twenty-five million acres of forest in lower Quebec was continuing apace in terms of reduced radial growth of the maple trees during the same period when the U.S. government was suggesting that there was nothing to worry about. In fact, radial growth was slower in 1988 and 1989 than it was in the preceding four years, 1983 to 1987, a finding that contradicts the Forest Service's claims.

Orie Loucks, himself a Canadian scientist (though he now works in the United States), has studied the effects of air pollution on deciduous forests perhaps more than anyone else. In his exhaustive Ohio Corridor study for the U.S. National Acid Precipitation Assessment Program (NAPAP), Loucks found "that the pattern of change being observed in the sensitive soils and forest of the study area are consistent with hypotheses relating long-term acid deposition to these changes." In Loucks's view, the thinning crowns and dieback of deciduous trees such as the maple may come and go in pollution-afflicted forests in "pulses," as he calls them. This means that improving crown condition by itself may not be a meaningful measure of the long-term damage done to the forest ecosystem by years of acid deposition, excess nitrogen, and tropospheric ozone. Significantly, the U.S. Forest Service research on sugar maples, unlike that of Ouimet and Fortin (and unlike that of Loucks in the American Middle West), dealt only with a visual assessment of crown condition, not with measurements of growth rate. Based on this evidence, the Forest Service presents the sugar maple as being better off than ever before, with the only problem, presumably a minor one in their view, being that other studies have shown, as they put it, a "short period of poor growth in response to below-normal precipitation and insect defoliation."

David Marvin is appalled at such dissembling, and in general at the degree of resistance shown by U.S. government- and industry-supported scientists in terms of acknowledging the impact of acid rain on sugarbush maples. "There are a lot of people in the forestry community who pooh-pooh the idea of acid rain and air pollution," he said as we walked along his forest road. "There is good evidence that pollution has damaged the white pine and the high-elevation spruce, but there are those who say, 'You can't prove to me that there's a problem with maple.' Seems to me that the burden of proof ought to go the other way. The correlative evidence that there's a problem gets stronger every day.

"I have scientists come to my farm to look at my dying trees," Marvin continued, "and they say it's tent caterpillar that's killing them, or canker, or maple sap-streak. They can always find a disease organism somewhere as a way of dismissing the idea of air pollution. But the point is that these organisms don't work in a vacuum. Let me tell you, Charles, those people have tunnel vision; they can't seem to put the whole picture together. We need to look at root causes, not just symptoms, and at the whole forest ecosystem, not just one tree at a time."

We walked a bit further, in silence, with Marvin casting his eyes upward at the thinning crowns. "I don't want to condemn our forest scientists as a group," he said suddenly, "but I am very concerned that a great deal of forest research is funded by the federal government, by chemical companies, and forest industry companies—and it's very difficult for people who depend on that funding to stick their necks out or to help influence policy that might go counter to what the funders are interested in. Many scientists I talk to will not publicly say anything about the connection between air pollution and forest decline, but privately, to a person, they tell me, yes, we've got a problem."

Driving back down the forest road in the pickup, Marvin stopped momentarily at a clearing that provided us a panoramic view of Vermont's Green Mountains stretching southward to the horizon, interrupted only by small clusters of white houses and red barns here and there, and steeples. The dying light of afternoon was catching the first autumn splashes of maple color on the mountainsides opposite us—patches of yellow-gold merging into saffron, orange into coral, reds beyond reds: crimson, magenta, scarlet, vermilion, ruby—all of it set against the cobalt sky. "My Godfrey," said David Marvin softly, "that is so beautiful. What a shame it would be to lose it."

The plight of David Marvin's sugar maples is, however, only part of a rapidly escalating toll of death and decline of what most of us would consider to be "the great American trees."

Quite probably, the first casualty among native trees after the arrival of the Europeans on this continent was the lovely franklinia, discovered in Georgia by the botanist-explorer John Bartram in 1770. Bartram named the tree after his friend, scientific colleague, and fellow Quaker Benjamin Franklin.

Only thirty feet high, the franklinia grew in the shaded coves of the Southern woods. The outstanding feature of the species was its large and showy flowers, cups of pure white measuring three inches across, with golden stamens, and opening in succession over several weeks in the late summer. We know of this tree only because Bartram collected seeds, which he propagated in his botanical garden on the banks of the Schuylkill river near Philadelphia. Curiously, the franklinia simply disappeared from the wild—not a single naturally growing specimen has been found since 1790.

More than a century was to pass before the next mortal event would take place in the forests of North America. This was the chestnut blight, first identified on the grounds of the New York Zoological Gardens by a forester named Herman Merkel in 1904. Hybridizers anxious to increase the commercial value of the American chestnut (*Castanea dentata*) by combining the board feet of the big native trees with the larger nuts of its Asian cousins, had brought in chestnuts from China, and with them a deadly fungus, *Cryphonectria parasitica.* Despite heroic efforts to stem the march of the fungus, which choked the tree to death by cutting off the transport of water and nutrients, the disease moved quickly through the Eastern forests, northward and southward, its front traveling at the rate of fifty miles per year. By the 1930s, it was pretty much all over for *Castanea dentata.* The great spreading tree that had constituted between a quarter and a half of the canopy of the Eastern forest was gone—the only remnants the gray, leafless, barkless snags, and the treasured paneling and furniture that this most useful of all forest trees, whose trunks could reach eleven feet in diameter, had provided.

Next came a little bark beetle that would cause the death of another of America's most beloved trees, the American elm. The bug (*Scolytus multistratus*) was discovered in 1909, just five years after forester Merkel reported the dead chestnuts at the Bronx Zoo. By itself, the beetle, a European import, was harmless, and it remained harmless for two decades. Then scientists discovered that the tiny creature, scarcely bigger than a gnat, had become a vector for a deadly fungus called *Ceratocystis ulmi,* which the beetle carried on its body. It was this fungus, originating in Asia and reaching Europe in 1919, that produced Dutch elm disease, so named because during the 1920s it devastated the elms whose roots held the soil of the dikes of Holland in place. American arborists once again conducted heroic efforts, this time to keep the fungus away from our local beetles—both the exotic European elm bark beetle and the native elm bark beetle (*Hylurgopinus rufipes*), which could also serve as a vector—through rigorous quarantine of imported trees and shrubs. Nevertheless, the disease was discovered in Ohio in 1930. The experts converged on the outbreak, cutting and burning all infected, or possibly infected, trees, thus exterminating the beetle, and therefore presumably the fungus. Or so they thought. Three years later, nearly four thousand trees in New Jersey, as well as a score of trees in Connecticut, were found to be diseased. Not long after that it was acknowledged that the fungus could not be contained. Today, half or more of our American elms have been killed. Most of the survivors are ornamental trees; only a very few remain in natural forests.

As it turned out, the fungus had come into the country not through nursery stock, but embedded in English elm logs that American cabinet makers had imported for veneers. English elms contain lumpy growths—burls—which when sliced by veneer knives produce the fanciful swirling grain pattern that can be seen in some Victorian furniture and even modern pieces. The veneers are lovely, but the logs from which they were cut were swarming with fungus-infected European elm bark beetles. Now there is worse news, for a new strain of the fungus has appeared in recent years, possibly originating in the United States, that grows even more aggressively in the elm bark and therefore is able to infect more beetles, which in turn can reach remaining live trees more effectively. Yet another new form may have arisen in the Near East, writes Chris Bolgiano in *American Forests*, that may be moving this way. This one may actually be a new species of fungus, provisionally named *Ophiostoma novo-ulmi* sp. nov. by a British plant pathologist.

Looking at the history of tree death along a time line, one can see that—excepting the case of the franklinia, whose anomalous disappearance was doubtless a natural event of some sort, however mysterious—the dramatic incidents of widespread tree mortality among native species have occurred mainly in this century, in the industrial age, and have taken place in the *replacement* forests after the great national orgy of tree felling and land clearing between 1860 and 1890.

And now, as we have seen, the tempo of catastrophe has been increasing in the post–World War II era. The lovely flowering dogwood appears to be doomed in its native setting. High-elevation spruce and fir along the Appalachian ridge from Vermont to North Carolina have been reduced to a fraction of their original numbers. The great ponderosa pines are beset by ozone drifting to the mountains from polluted California valleys. Ruthless logging has changed the composition of the forests of the intermountain West, rendering them vulnerable to pests and death and, finally, mass fire. The gypsy moth has opportunistically followed the axe and plowshare southward and westward through weakened forests from its unfortunate Medford, Massachusetts, starting point. Residual tree death attends the scalping of the Cascades in Washington and Oregon, where ancient forests are sacrificed in the politics of jobs. In the mixed mesophytic forest, one of the two oldest temperate-zone forests on earth, ecologist Orie Loucks estimates that as many as eighty tree-size woody plant species, including the near-extinct red mulberry tree and local populations of chinquapin and butternut, are showing the effects of years of oxidant concentrations and acid deposition driven eastward by prevailing winds from the industrialized river valleys of the Midwest and the Southern border states. The impact, Loucks believes, may permanently reduce the biological diversity of this extraordinary ecosystem.

To this cheerless list, as I learned courtesy of Mollie Beattie and David Marvin, the sugar maple must be added, for it too is in danger—or at least thought to be by Canadian and independent U.S. scientists. Certainly Mollie Beattie thinks so, backing up David Marvin all the way.

After visiting Marvin, I arranged to interview ex–Forest Commissioner Beattie in the lounge of the Woodstock Inn. Amid the tinkling glasses of the tourists—early-arrival "leaf-peepers" come for the grand seasonal display—she spoke candidly and earnestly, as is her way. "If you ask me if there's a connection between pollution and the maple dieback," she began, "I would say yes. If you want proof, that's another matter. The problem is that neither science nor the funding sources for science are reacting at all to the way forests are changing. In the chronology of a forest, a decline taking twenty-five years is a sudden eruption, but human consciousness does not take it in that way. To us the change is so slow as to be unobservable. So we have people saying that the forest has always been like this. But the fact is, it's only been like this for their adult lifetime. Nobody knows what the natural level of mortality is. It's not that there's no science. It's that science is asking the wrong questions."

Beattie and I also discussed the fate of other forest trees in New England. How the beech had been dying at the rate of 10 percent a year over in the Adirondacks of New York State. (In fact, the largest U.S. fabricator of stairway parts—the Visador Corporation—now finds it can no longer count on beech wood for lumber, in view of its decline, and must substitute tulip poplar, a somewhat weaker hardwood.) How the white pine, a species sensitive to ozone in the same way as its Western cousins the ponderosas and the Jeffreys, seemed to be disappearing. And the butternut—which Beattie believes might actually become extinct. The severe white ash dieback, said Beattie, may be caused by a mycoplasma organism, a wall-less cell that causes an affliction called "ash yellows." What has energized the organism to become so widespread and virulent is a different question, and may relate to air-pollution effects weakening the white ash sufficiently to give this disease organism (and others) an opportunity not present before. And it goes on like that, through species after species. "About the only tree that isn't threatened up here," said Beattie, echoing the view of Joe Aliff in the mixed mesophytic forest, "is the red maple. Everything else is in trouble to one degree or another."

The hemlock was on Beattie's list, too, although it grows more spectacularly in the central Appalachians than in New England. One of the most striking trees in the Eastern forest, it is now in grave peril from an infestation of the hemlock woolly adelgid, which has been killing hemlocks from southern New England to southern Virginia. Both the Canadian (Eastern) and the smaller and less common Carolina hemlock (*Tsuga canadensis* and *Tsuga caroliniana*) are subject to adelgid assaults. Although most of the great old-tree Canadian hemlock groves were destroyed in the rapacious hunt for tannin in the nineteenth and early twentieth centuries, some sizable stands still remain and are worth searching out. Dim, silent, and cathedral-like, they are sylvan treasures unlike any other in the Eastern forest. Now, it would seem, what the tanners didn't get, the adelgid will.

The hemlock woolly adelgid (*Adelges tsugae*), a cousin of the balsam woolly adelgid discussed in Chapter 3, is thought to be an Asian import. It was first reported on the West Coast in the 1920s, and in the East —in Virginia—in the 1950s. Since then, the Eastern adelgid has spread slowly northward. In recent years, however, its rate of spread and its virulence have become particularly dramatic.

According to plant pathologists, the adelgids' egg sacs are attached thickly by the female to the underside of the hemlock's newly grown outer branches and needles, making them appear as if they had been sprayed with some sort of fuzzy white paint. The pest itself is a pinhead-size red-brown creature that can withstand freezing cold. During the winter, when the tree is most vulnerable, the adelgid sucks the hemlock's sap and simultaneously injects a toxic saliva. The result is quick discoloration and desiccation of the needles and their branches, followed by the death of the tree within one to four years. I can personally attest to the validity of these observations, as I had to clear-cut a grove of adelgid-killed *T. canadiensis* on my own property in Maryland. Although not exactly an extensive stand, these four trees were afflicted even more decisively than our dogwoods, which were also dying.

Mark S. McClure, of the Connecticut Agricultural Experiment Station, who has been studying the hemlock woolly adelgid for more than a decade, declares that the devastation now being caused by the pest can be compared only to that of the chestnut blight and the Dutch elm disease. McClure and others who have scoured Japan for natural predators have come across a mite that feeds on the insect's egg coating, thus disrupting reproduction. Experiments so far are "encouraging," although there is no guarantee that the introduced predator will survive in its new environment, or that the mite will not become a harmful pest itself. Gardeners can spray their trees with horticultural oil (at considerable expense), but this remedy is out of the question for forest trees.

A possible—if not likely—reason for the sudden increase of adelgid-caused mortality in forest stands of hemlock in recent years is that the insect seems to thrive on nitrogen. McClure conducted a test of this theory by fertilizing a group of adelgid-infested hemlocks with nitrogen and comparing the effects with another group of adelgid-infested trees not given nitrogen fertilizer. On the trees to which nitrogen had been added, the adelgid population densities were five times higher than on the other group. Moreover, hemlock growth was not enhanced at all by nitrogen, as might be expected. Instead, the *un*fertilized trees grew faster than the fertilized ones, and the foliage on the fertilized trees became discolored.

According to Edward Whereat, a forest ecologist at the University of Maryland, McClure's research suggests a connection between the excess nitrogen deposition caused by air pollution and the recent virulence of the adelgid. "There is good reason to assume that increased nitrogen deposition in forests could stimulate adelgid populations via increased soluble nitrogen in leaves," Whereat writes, although he is cautious about applying the nitrogen-deposition thesis at the "ecosystem level." A possible mechanism, according to Whereat, is that "when plants are subjected to stresses such as drought or air pollutants and growth decreases, there is often a rise in the soluble nitrogen in leaves," to which the adelgid is attracted. He goes on to explain that "even as the plants' need for nitrogen is falling, nitrogen availability [from deposition] is not changing," thus producing a surplus for the adelgid. "Some people theorize that in this way, abiotic [i.e., pollution] stress may predispose plants to insect attack." It is this kind of interaction, says Whereat, as well as the deposition of nitrogen itself, that contributes to the adelgid's success.

To put the matter in the most unvarnished terms, one could say we may well have turned a problem bug into an effective tree killer that becomes more and more deadly as it feeds on our pollution. And there seems to be no reprieve. Writes McClure, "No host resistance to this adelgid has been observed in either native hemlock species in the East."

There is a certain hemlock grove in the Toe River valley of the North Carolina Blue Ridge, a secret, uncut place known to my cousins and me, where huge trees grow. The trail into the grove we and others keep concealed at the juncture where it begins, off a fire road somewhere in the Pisgah National Forest. On a recent visit, I checked the undersides of the branches of five-hundred-year-old hemlock trees hanging across a creek. Creeks need hemlocks to keep them cool enough for trout. No adelgids yet. But I took some pictures anyway, just in case this dark and lovely spot, where the wind and rushing waters sound like organ music, will one day be no more.

Let us return to the American beech (*Fagus grandifolia*), for a triple tragedy is in the making here, as this tree is often found to be growing alongside the Canadian hemlock, with an understory of flowering dogwood. In healthy stands, the bright patches of light-colored beech contrast with the dark hemlock in groves that are intricately layered by the horizontal dogwood branches. The effect is of an ancient Japanese garden designed over the centuries by Zen Buddhist priests of exquisitely refined taste. All three trees which so agreeably grow together are afflicted—the hemlock with the adelgid, the dogwood with its unstoppable and deadly anthracnose fungus, and now the beech with a scale insect (*Cryptococcus fagi*) that severely stresses the tree, which allows a deadly fungus (*Nectria coccinea* var. *faginata*) to finish the job.

The beech scale, in heavy infestations, produces whitish patches on the trunk near the base of the tree, and sometimes on the lower sides of branches. In time (two to five years) the scale, a sucking insect, pits the thin bark of the beech, creating an "infection court," as Edward Ketchledge of the State University of New York at Syracuse described it to me during an interview at Saranac Lake—in the midst of beech-death country, the Adirondacks. The infection court, said Ketchledge, permits the fungus to enter the cambium layer and the sapwood through the aggregated wounds. The fruiting bodies of the fungus are red in color, showing up against the bluish bark of the beech and the whitish patches of scale: death in red, white, and blue. Large areas of bark die, and the fungal lesions coalesce at the base of the tree, choking off the uptake of water and nutrients. According to entomologist Whiteford Baker, "The fungus is entirely dependent on the scale for its incidence and spread." For the beech, which in eastern forests is already stressed by ozone and acid deposition, this is an unholy alliance if there ever was one.

The scale, a late-nineteenth-century European import, became especially virulent in the post–World War II era, moving rapidly throughout the beech tree's northern range—from Maine to Ohio and into southern West Virginia. Forest entomologists describe the movement of the scale in terms of three broad belts of affliction: the advancing front, the killing front, and the aftermath zone. One would hope that in the aftermath zone (an area that now includes most of upstate New York and New England), the beech might somehow regenerate healthy, resistant trees. Such is not to be, however, for when the beech regenerates after a scale infection it does so not by saplings grown from the large number of seeds that might come from a nearly healthy beech's spiny pods, but almost entirely by sprouts of trees that are dead save for their roots. The sprouts then grow into thickets of small, weak trees—thickets so dense that they crowd out all other species. Moreover, since most of the thicket trees are genetically identical to the killed tree from which they sprouted, they are themselves vulnerable to a return of the disease. In such a case, great swaths of regrown forest can be revisited by the beech bark scale, which in a pure-beech thicket will leave nothing behind except phalanxes of small, dead snags.

In an old country church somewhere in the Southern mountains, or in the Northeast or the Middle West for that matter, if the altar is carved of a lustrous and satiny wood, a light brown with bands of paler sapwood, it might well be made of butternut. The nut itself is sweet-tasting, but encased in an oblong, heavy shell whose covering is made up of sticky, rusty hairs, almost impossible to remove from hands or clothing. During the Civil War, some Confederate soldiers colored their uniforms with a yellowish-orange permanent dye drawn from the shells and from the inner bark of the tree. So common was the practice that these soldiers were, in fact, called "Butternuts."

Unlike hemlocks or sugar maples, the butternut—or white walnut, as it is sometimes called (*Juglans cineria*)—doesn't grow in stands but is distributed thinly throughout its range, which is most of the Eastern deciduous forest region, save that of the deep South. Moreover, it is not a particularly prepossessing tree, unlike the black walnut for which it might be mistaken, for although its frondlike pinnately compound leaves are quite similar to those of the black walnut, at one hundred feet the black walnut is twice as tall as the butternut.

Despite its size, this is a "grand old American tree," as Donald Culross Peattie described it in 1950. He did not know that it may very well become extinct.

The proximate cause of butternut mortality is a canker, first identified in 1967 on the East Coast, but not much recognized for another twenty years as the serious problem it was to become. The butternut canker is now found throughout the tree's range—as far west as Minnesota, which has banned cutting the tree on state-owned lands since so few remain. The canker—a "sore" caused by the fungus—begins as a tiny spore entering the tree through an injury to a limb, twig, or trunk. Then the lens-shaped cankers, necrotic lesions of the bark and cambium layer, spread throughout the tree, even to the nut husks, eventually girdling the main limbs and trunk and causing the tree to die. The death is slow, taking several years, but certain. According to Mike Ostry, a plant pathologist in the U.S. Forest Service's Saint Paul, Minnesota, labs, there is no certainty whether the canker is a recent import or an old disease that has mutated into its present deadly form. One mystery concerns how the fungus has been able to move from butternut to butternut, since these trees are so widespread. In any case, in an article by naturalist-writer Rich Patterson appearing in *American Forests*, Ostry revealed that he is no optimist about the fate of the tree. The butternut, he told Patterson, "is more threatened than even the American chestnut." For that reason, the butternut is the first tree to be added by the Fish and Wildlife Service to the list of candidates for protection under the Endangered Species Act. The U.S. Forest Service, not usually in the ecological vanguard, has ruled that no butternuts may be cut in national forests.

At the Great Smoky Mountains National Park, National Park Service scientists have been working with canker-afflicted butternuts since 1987, having identified some seventy trees that they keep track of. Many have since died, but even among those still living, the rate of reproduction of the butternut has fallen to near zero. The Park Service is now collecting "scions"—detached shoots—from the trees that are left, in a near-hopeless effort to find a canker-resistant genotype.

The experimental work on butternut mortality in the park is part of a concerted effort by park scientists to deal with a quite widespread pattern of tree death and decline in the Southern mountains stemming from air pollution. Park personnel have identified some ninety different tree and native plant species that have manifested "ozone-like foliar damage." Forty-six of these species have been subjected to controlled ambient ozone conditions in fumigation chambers. Of these, nearly two-thirds were affected, showing that tropospheric ozone, produced by emissions from Tennessee Valley industry and from automobiles, was indeed damaging trees and other plants in the park. According to the National Park Service, "Almost 100 percent of the black cherry and sassafras trees in the highest elevation sites exhibit ozone symptoms with up to 75 percent of the leaf area injured."

In the Shenandoah National Park in the Virginia Blue Ridge, which is subject to similar air-pollution effects, Superintendent Bill Wade likens (as have others) the impacts of acid deposition on the park's trees to those of AIDS on human beings. A *Washington Post* account reported that the park's trees have been so severely weakened by air pollution deposition that "the park's defenses are down, and the symptoms are getting harder to ignore. Acid rain—from power plants and factories as far away as Illinois—is slowly killing the streams and vegetation. Ozone and other pollutants are assaulting the trees, increasing their vulnerability to disease and insects. The park's panoramic views are often obscured by a blanket of haze. The air gets so bad on some summer days, that health advisories are posted at park entrances."

The connections between air pollution, in the form of ozone and acid deposition, and the mortality of the butternut (among other trees) are not always clear, but National Park Service officials say that despite the elevation and remoteness of the Appalachian parks, they are nevertheless among the most polluted in the country. As a result, the Park Service is seeking "the strictest possible regulations" on factory and automobile emissions.

Such regulations may someday come to pass, but perhaps not soon enough for the butternut. And thus the provenance of the place names will be forgotten—like David Marvin's Butternut Farm, and my own Butternut Road, where I once lived in veterans' housing while attending college, and all the hollows and hamlets from Vermont to Tennessee to Iowa named for the tree as a way of giving due homage to it. The little tree will be a mystery to the generation now being born, grandchildren who will never again find the sticky husks on a woodland path, never again crack them open with a stone to get at the sweet center. The "grand old American tree" will be no more.

There are still more examples of the mounting toll—and in surprising places and for what may be quite surprising reasons. One of these is the giant saguaro cactus (*Cereus giganteus*) of the Sonoran Desert of Arizona and the adjoining state of Sonora in Mexico. Yes, this cactus is actually a tree according to the standard definition: a woody plant that is fifteen feet or more at maturity, with a trunk at least several inches in diameter (must be a single stem, not a clump), and a distinct crown with upright branches. Donald Culross Peattie, in his *A Natural History of Western Trees*, says the saguaro looks to him like a tree "designed by someone who had never seen a tree." He further describes it as having a "goblin" look, an Easterner's view to be sure. For to me the saguaro is somewhat reminiscent of Saint Francis with his arms upraised as if in praise or benediction of what is surely the most beautiful and garden-like desert on earth.

For reasons that are not fully understood, the saguaros are dying out—and not just from delinquents taking potshots at them from motorcycles, or from midnight cactus rustlers illegally uprooting specimens for the gardens of wealthy Arizonans. According to Kate Kajtha, a biologist at Boston University, the 63,000-acre Saguaro National Monument near Tucson has lost more than 50 percent of its giant cactuses in the last fifty years to a mysterious affliction that turns the cactus brown prematurely and causes the trunk and branches to lose their spines. "They're dying," Dr. Kajtha told a reporter. "Their arms are falling off. They're keeling over."

Some scientists suspect that air pollution from local mining smelters may be involved, but the affliction is not confined to the Tucson area; it can be found even in remote parts of the Sonoran Desert in northern Mexico. This has led researchers to consider the possibility that the currently rapid spread of the disease may be linked to increased ultraviolet (UV-B) rays leaking through the thinning stratospheric ozone shield, the result of the destruction of the O_3 molecule by chlorofluorocarbons released from air conditioners, refrigerators, and aerosol cans. Cactus disease symptoms appear on the south side of the plant, the side getting the most sun and therefore the most UV-B rays. Tellingly, in shaded saguaros, the disease is not found at all.

The ultraviolet connection is not as farfetched as some might think. The discovery of an ozone "hole" over Antarctica led to an international protocol in 1989 to replace the chlorofluorocarbons (CFCs)—widely used since the 1950s—with less ozone-damaging variations. As was outlined in an earlier chapter, CFCs are suspected of being responsible for upwards of three-quarters of the depletion of the stratospheric ozone layer by "consuming" the O_3 molecule. And because the chlorine that does the consuming is not broken down in this process, a single chlorine atom, according to the Air and Waste Management Association, can destroy as many as ten thousand ozone molecules before it finally descends from the stratosphere to the troposphere. Thus, for every 1 percent of ozone-shield depletion, there is a 2-percent increase in the ultraviolet rays striking the earth. In temperate zones of the world, such as in North America, the rate of depletion has been 3 to 4 percent, with brief surges to 10 or 15 percent in the early 1990s that may have been affected by the volcanic eruption of Mount Pinatubo in the Philippines.

Until recently, however, scientists have not been able to show that a significant increase in ultraviolet rays was actually obtaining at ground level in temperate zones due to shielding by clouds and, perversely, air pollution. In a study released in 1993, Canadian scientists J. B. Kerr and C. T. McElroy showed that, over five summers and four winters, from 1989 to 1993, ultraviolet radiation did, in fact, increase as the ozone shield decreased. The research, conducted in Toronto, revealed that harmful UV-B rays (with wavelengths between 290 and 325 nanometers) had increased by 6.7 percent a year in summer and by 35 percent during the winter.

In 1994, after unusually high levels of UV-B radiation reached as far south as the Ohio Valley the summer before, Orie Loucks, who had noted what he thought was radiation damage on the leaves of deciduous tulip poplar trees, developed a way to determine such damage over time—by examining the needles of coniferous trees, whose leaves are not dropped annually like the tulip tree's. New needle clusters are put out each year, with each year's growth separated from the last, thus permitting the comparison of possible damage from one year to the next. Loucks found that one conifer, the white pine, "showed evidence that a portion of the population has suffered damage to the foliage in 1993, but not in 1992, and on the south, but not on the north (shaded) side of open grown trees in 1993." Loucks went on to describe the damage symptoms, which include "a sharp bend or deflection in the normal linear development of the needles," together with "necrotic lesions typical of sun scald." On severely affected branches, the needle loss exceeded 50 percent in the high–UV-B year of 1993, Loucks found, versus "virtually 0" in the low–UV-B year of 1992. Over all, 13 percent of the white pines he examined were severely affected by the 1993 UV-B bombardment, which, Loucks points out, is "nearly three times the proportion of this species that is severely affected (the sensitive, so-called 'chlorotic dwarf') by ambient rural ozone levels in the north-eastern U.S."—ozone being, heretofore, the most toxic of all pollutants on the white pine.

Further evidence of UV-B damage has been demonstrated by laboratory tests. UV-B exposures of loblolly pine, which like the cactus and Orie Loucks's white pine is a non-leaf-shedding evergreen plant and therefore subject to UV-B damage year round, have shown that the growth rate of such plants can be affected not only by a high-level bombardment of rays during a bad year, but on a cumulative basis at lower levels of UV-B exposure. During the first year or two, in an experiment conducted at the University of Maryland, the pines showed little growth reduction, but after five years, the equivalent of a simulated 16-to-20-percent ozone depletion produced a growth reduction of 12 to 20 percent. The effect of extended ultraviolet radiation is interference with photosynthesis, which produces discoloration and the death of the surface cells of trees and plants.

Thus do the causes—direct or indirect—proliferate, a growing list of human actions that so modify the natural environment that tree death and forest decline eventuate: too much ground-level ozone and not enough stratospheric ozone; acidified soils over vast forest regions; a pattern of nutrient loss and an excess of other nutrients, such as nitrogen, that prove toxic; the deposition of heavy metals—cadmium, lead, copper, zinc, mercury—and the mobility of poisonous aluminum normally locked in the soil; the loss of beneficial mycorrhizal fungus; the destructive edge effects from clear-cutting, and the modification of forest composition from a century of overcutting; the genetic weakness of replacement trees in impacted ecosystems; a host of plagues and diseases anxious to take advantage of the debilitated trees and forests; the unwonted effects of too-rapid climate change. And this by no means exhausts the list of possible, and perhaps probable, anthropogenic impacts on trees and forests.

One of the impacts not often dealt with in the standard scientific literature of tree death and forest decline is the "Petkau effect." Abram Petkau, a Canadian physician and biophysicist, discovered that low doses of nuclear radiation, not just high ones, could have a perversely devastating effect on living cells. According to Ernest Sternglass, M.D., of the University of Pittsburgh School of Medicine, Petkau showed how "cell membranes which could *withstand* radiation doses as large as tens of *thousands of rads* when exposed to a short burst of X-rays without breaking, *ruptured at less than one rad* when subjected to low intensity, protracted radiation such as that produced by radioactive chemicals [emphasis added]." Significantly, the Petkau effect's cell damage derives mainly from artificially created radioactivity rather than from natural background radiation. Thus, the implications for trees and humans living downwind of a nuclear power plant, a storage or waste facility, a uranium mine, or an A-bomb testing range might well be significant.

Certainly author-engineer Ralph Graub, a Swiss who has devoted many years to investigating the effects of atomic energy, thinks so. In his book *The Petkau Effect*, he cites research on tree damage near nuclear power plants in Germany and France "that could not be explained by other pollutants." Moreover, European research has shown that "the toxicity of SO_2 becomes much more acute in the presence of radioactivity. It may be increased dramatically when the radioactivity acts together with aerosols and fog, or with rainfall."

Yet other potential tree killers not often taken up in the U.S. scientific literature are the chemical compounds used for dry cleaning, degreasing, and as components of some popular herbicides. These are the halocarbons, which can accelerate the effects of UV-B radiation, and, in the case of TCA (trichloroacetic acid), a herbicide, damage trees directly. TCA has been found in the needles of firs at high elevations, in remote areas where no other pollutants have been recorded. In fact, a study by the U.S. Geological Survey found traces in twenty-three states of agricultural herbicides which had entered soils and waters through rainfall.

These artificial agents—from atom bombs to TCA to plain old acid rain—created by and for an industrialized America, combine with the already plentiful natural causes of tree death and forest decline. And beyond the scores of dying trees already mentioned in this chapter and the ones preceding it, there are scores more from every point of the compass right here in North America, never mind the tropics, Europe, or Asia. In the rain forests of the Alaskan panhandle and British Columbia, there's the Alaska cedar, a tree so valuable for export that a single bole can sell for thousands of dollars. And many have been sold, along with many another species in the rampant clear-cutting of the Tongass National Forest and its Canadian counterpart. But the cedar is dying for other reasons, and at an increasing rate since the mysterious die-off was first reported over a hundred years ago. Researchers do not now believe that the dying of the cedars is caused by a biotic agent. Quite possibly human-induced climate change has contributed to the problem. According to forest pathologists P. E. Hennon, E. M. Hansen, and C. G. Shaw III, a warming trend has been taking place in Alaska during most of this century which coincides with the decline of the Alaska cedar as well as an increase in atmospheric CO_2. This warming trend may lead to the death of the trees from frozen roots, since they are no longer adequately protected by snow during winter. The researchers found that in high elevations the tree is well protected by the annual snowpack, and remains perfectly healthy; but at or near sea level, accumulating protective snows have all but disappeared in recent years due to the warming trend.

At the opposite corner of the United States, there is a similar mystery—the Sabal palms (*Sabal texana*) are dying. Francis E. Putz, a botanist with the University of Florida, has found that the Sabal palms—medium-tall (to fifty feet) cousins of the palmetto—were dying along a two-hundred-mile stretch of Gulf Coast shoreline in Florida. The palm loses its fronds and the top of the tree finally snaps off, leaving the trunk looking like some sort of tropical telephone pole. E. L. Barnard, a Florida forest pathologist, tested the stricken trees for palm weevils, bud rot, fungus diseases, and lethal yellowing, which had afflicted coconut palms in south Florida at one point, although the Sabal was thought to be immune. As in the case of the Alaska cedar, a biotic agent did not seem to be involved. Therefore, it might be environmental. Since Sabal palms were *not* dying on sites at some elevation above sea level, the scientists' best guess is that the steady rise of the sea, permitting toxic levels of salt water to bathe the palm's roots, is the culprit. As Francis Putz told a *New York Times* reporter, "Areas that today support salt marsh vegetation were forested in the 1940s. Twenty million years ago Florida was a series of islands. Maybe it is going to be that again." If the global warming scenario suggested by the National Academy of Sciences is correct, sea levels may rise as much as two feet by the end of the twenty-first century, which would take care of not only the palms but most of the land mass of the state of Florida. As the National Academy puts it, "No credible claim can be made that any of these events is imminent, but none of them are precluded."

The compass is boxed. From the cedars of Alaska to the palms of Florida, from the maples of Canada and New England to the saguaro cactus of Sonora. The incidents of death and decline are increasing at an increasing rate. Science vainly struggles to keep up, offering hypotheses implicating all manner of causes and suggesting all manner of effects.

To be sure, there are some who may argue that the ramifying progression of tree death and forest decline in this century, and especially since World War II, is either coincidence or simply a matter of selective reporting. Everything is all right. Not to worry. It's just a natural ebb and flow of nature. But that is not what I have heard from the scores of scientific scholars I have interviewed, or the mountain of papers I have studied. They say something else. E. Gerry Hawkes had it right: "Count me an 'alarmist.' " It seems to me that what he and Mollie Beattie and David Marvin and Mel Tyree and a dozen Canadian scientists and Orie Loucks and Mark McClure and Mike Ostry and Kate Kajtha and all the others whom I personally visited or whose papers have been quoted in this and in preceding chapters—what these distinguished people are describing is, when aggregated, a pandemic.

Which means an epidemic that is everywhere.

10

The Treesavers

Nature is a temple where living pillars
Sometimes emit confused words.
—*Baudelaire,*
The Flowers of Evil

A few years ago, I was driving with my son, Charles, up Oregon's I-5 from Eugene, where he operates his flower farm (both cuts and drieds, as they say in the trade), to Portland, where I needed to get on an airplane. Suddenly, a logging truck pulled onto the interstate ahead of us, a bright red diesel it was, blatting through the morning-misty flats of the Willamette Valley. A huge Doug-fir log had been mounted on its semitrailer, a trophy brought down from the mountains, one of many that was now headed toward a wharf where it would then be loaded on a freighter bound for Japan.

"My God," I said, "look at the size of that tree!" And as we sped by, both of us silent, my son watched it diminish in the rearview mirror as I peered out the back until at last the tree was gone from sight—but not yet gone from the hidden creases of our minds.

The awe was genuine, the reference to deity not merely a casual blasphemy, for a god had lived in that tree—a forest god feared and revered from the very beginning of our time on the planet, when proto-humans first left the forest, stood upright, and with an opposed thumb, a hungry belly, and year-round estrus came to dominate the world. Our sense that forests are sacred survives, as these lines from the anonymous English poem "Castle Howard" (ca. 1773) suggest:

Here the smooth Beach and rev'rend Oak entwine
And form a Temple for the Pow'rs Divine:
So Ages past from ancient Bards we've heard,
When Men the Deity in Groves rever'd.
A Tow'ring Wood superior in its Kind,
Was to the worship of the Gods assign'd.

According to the great Scottish anthropologist Sir James Frazer, among the Druidic Celts the "old word for sanctuary [in its primary definition as a place of worship] seems to be identical in origin and meaning with the Latin *nemus,* a grove or woodland glade." The sacred grove is our sanctuary, our temple.

And yet, contrarily, we fear and distrust the forest, for we are a savanna species, having arisen in the Great Rift Valley of East Africa millions of years ago, when the distant forest was the home of creatures wishing to do us harm.

These days, members of our species, representing these atavistic inclinations in varying degrees—reverence or fear and loathing—have taken to arguing with one another about whether we should cut certain trees, in Amazonia or Oregonia, or leave them uncut (the argument was settled for that one Douglas fir, of course) so that ecosystems can remain in balance for the sake of posterity. We also argue whether or not trees are being killed by acid rain and other industrial emissions, including the emissions of my son's elderly van, an O_3 producer if there ever was one. Charles is concerned about pollution and the felling of the Brazilian forest, but he remains a bit ambivalent about cutting some (though not all) the remaining Oregon old-growth Doug firs, being in sympathy—a kind of man-of-the-soil solidarity—with the woods workers who would be displaced by a decision that the big trees could no longer be taken off public land or even private land. In the Northwest, says Charles, people believe that the spotted owl—the proximate agent of the federal government's plan to reduce logging in old-growth forest areas—is a kind of curse, like Coleridge's albatross. That said, our witnessing of a four-hundred-year-old tree carried like a corpse along the highway troubles him, too.

It is not altogether idle to speculate about what seems to be driving the private ambivalence and the public controversy. Between my son and me, it produces a mild argument for a minute, then agreement.

But for others it has brought murder and hatred. In Brazil, the most famous case is that of Chico Mendes, a rubber-tapper and conservationist who was murdered at the behest of ranchers. But we need not rely on exotic jungles for examples of the foul deeds of retaliation against those who insist on conservation. In New Mexico, Leroy Jackson, a militant Navajo who worked tirelessly to save a sacred forest of ponderosas high in the Chuska Mountains, was found dead under suspicious circumstances in his pickup near Chama. State police suggest that it may have been an overdose of methadone—a drug used to help addicts kick a heroin habit; but absolutely no one in a position to know anything about Jackson believes this for a minute. It was murder. In California, Judi Bari, who wanted to save the coast redwoods, was permanently crippled by a pipe bomb placed in her car. There, the authorities, offering no evidence whatsoever and no credible motive, said that the bomb was of her own manufacture.

In the eastern United States, the incidents are possibly less bloody, though I myself was once delicately admonished by a friendly Mafia emissary to lay off a case of road builders illegally mining gravel from a New York State trout stream. More often than threats or acts of physical violence, careers are jeopardized or destroyed. Those scientists who have warned of extensive damage to our forests by air pollution have often been treated like pariahs by government officials and even their own academic colleagues. Grants can be withheld from those whose findings prove what others who set policy do not want to hear. Journalists, and I can name some of the first rank, are pressured to resign for writing too accurately about the impacts of pollution on forests and other resources. Meanwhile, in the lumber-town barrooms of the Pacific Northwest, more violence is promised if the old growth cannot be cut.

There are many who wish simply to avoid the argument—indeed, to obviate it if they can. Sometimes the avoidance arises from timidity, but often it derives from a genuinely positive attitude about environmental issues, reflecting an American trait that de Tocqueville admired—when something needs to be done, we form a citizen committee and get to work. In this instance, such citizen organizers may be called the "treesavers," those who instead of being fractious about tree death and forest decline want to replant the fallen forests, to modify forest ecosystems—cut and uncut—so that trees can regenerate and grow, to change the genetic makeup of trees so that they can resist the stresses of the modern-day industrial environment.

I will tell you this right up front: I am conflicted about the treesavers. On the one hand, what they do, and the energy and goodwill they bring to it, are admirable. Who could fault a person who wishes to plant trees or to help them grow or to find new techniques to bring sick or cut-over forests back to health? On the other hand, I fear that many of the treesavers miss the message of the dying forests, which to me is that the basic argument cannot be obviated but must be joined, for there is no technical way, however benign, to get around the implications for our society and the ecosphere in which we live of widespread and disturbingly synchronous mortality of scores of tree species in the forests of North America, Europe, and Siberia, as well as in the tropics of Africa, Southeast Asia, and South America.

Let me examine, then, what some of the treesavers are doing with an appropriately generous spirit, albeit one that does not cloak objective analysis. I'll begin with the effort to protect the vanishing oak lands in the state where I grew up, California.

If there is such a thing as a normative (if not ideal) human landscape, by which I mean the most appropriate place for human beings to live, the savanna, such as those where the California oaks grow, is it. A savanna—wild grasses and scattered trees (without an intermediate understory of vines and shrubs)—is the originating landscape of our species. If all species have a habitat to which they are innately suited, the savanna is ours, despite our recent capacity for adapting artificially (via clothing, shelter, and the use of complex organizations and tools for food-getting, i.e., making a living) to a wide range of relatively hostile regions of the globe. Our adaptability has placed us nearly everywhere—in deserts, arctic tundra, dark jungles, steppes, mountain passes, boreal forests, and humid lowland swamps. For purposes of human self-validation, many of us come to regard the new (non-savanna) habitat in which we happen to reside as exemplary simply because we understand it and are inured to its disadvantages. Social-science research has confirmed this. One well-known preference study has shown that children, selecting among pictures of various kinds of landscapes, tend to pick their own place out as "the best."

But, remarkably, a savanna-picture is almost always selected as *second* best. This happens because for *Homo sapiens,* at some level below the conscious mind (as may be most clearly revealed by children who lack an overlay of encrusted cultural values), the savanna bespeaks easily available food, effective personal safety, and a benign climate. It is home. The openness of the landscape permits us to spot game and permits us as well to spot competing predators that might do us harm, including predators of our own species. The place looks like a park, mainly because the normative landscape of the savanna is, and has ever been, the model for the designers of public landscapes.

And so, any little kid (such as I) from the small cismontane valleys attending the chain of port cities—San Diego, LA, San Francisco—or from the interior foothills of the Sierra and the Coast Range between Tehachapi Pass and Shasta Lake, in an oval belt of oaks and grassland more than a thousand miles in length circumscribing the agriculturally industrialized Central Valley, knows instinctively that the best place to be in all the world is perched on a stout cantilevered branch of a California oak. With the dappled shade from above concealing your presence, you look out across the distances of a tranquil world of golden grass and deep green trees—the oaks dotted singly on the hillsides or huddled into groves along the swales. For me and the generations of other children born to this landscape—from a time long before Sutter's Mill or even the chronicles of Father Junípero Serra—the oak tree has ever been what California is all about.

Indeed, so abundant, so unexceptional, were these trees—one-fifth the land area of the state is "oak land"—that without anyone really noticing until quite recently, large areas of the quintessential California oak landscape have become in peril of simply disappearing. The causes are manifold and have been in progress since the beginnings of European settlement. When Father Junípero and his Franciscans set up their missions in Alta California in the 1700s, often located in the midst of oak woodlands, the establishment of the Mexican ranchos was not far behind. The ranchos were large feudal settlements, often using the Native American population as slave labor (though Serra, the "Apostle of California," abhorred the practice) in an economy based entirely on animal husbandry and agriculture. And this economy persists to a substantial degree, courtesy of both the climate and exploitable migrant and illegal-alien labor.

Inevitably, the boundaries of the ranchos later became the boundaries of modern towns and cities that bear their names, such as La Cañada, where I grew up—originally Rancho de la Cañada, a *cañada* denoting a ravine or, more generously, a narrow valley.

In my narrow valley, the original economy was based on grapes and oranges. (It is now merely real estate.) In other places in southern and central California, the rancheros appropriated vast acreages for cattle, which, in less than a century, quickly consumed the nutritious bunchgrasses that grew beneath the oaks. The native perennial grasses were well adapted to the feeding habits of local herds of indigenous deer and elk, but not to the heavy-footed *ganados* of the *ranchos grandes* that not only tore the tender grasses up by the roots but severely compacted the soil so that only weeds could grow. By the 1860s, more than three million head of cattle and one million sheep grazed the oak savannas of the interior foothills and adjacent pasturelands of California's great Central Valley—twice the livestock pressure that obtains today. In short order, the rancheros had replaced virtually all the native bunchgrasses with the tough, invasive Mediterranean annual grasses brought to California from Spain as a substitute. Before the Franciscans arrived, 33 percent of the land area of the state of California was covered with bunchgrass. Now the figure is 1 percent. Many botanists believe that the European annual grasses are so pervasive, ineradicable, and well adapted that they have become, in effect, the "new natives."

New natives or not, the oaks among which these Mediterranean grasses now grow have been unable to adapt to *them.*

The main problem derives from the difference between the root structures of the bunchgrasses and those of the annual grasses, the effect of this difference on acorn germination, and the ability (called "recruitment") of oak seedlings to survive beyond a season or two. Whereas the perennial bunchgrass roots descend downward deeply into the soil directly beneath the tufts and hummocks of the individual plants, the annual grasses' roots spread laterally throughout the upper layers of soil. The effects of this pattern on germination and recruitment have been twofold. First, the imported grasses have created an almost impenetrable, seamless turf, with few interstices wherein the acorn can be cradled and shaded so that its first rootlet can reach the soil. Second, the roots of annual grasses, growing outward instead of downward, greedily deplete the moisture uniformly from the upper layers of the soil, so that none is available for an oak seedling. Unhappily, the new oak seedlings need moisture at the very time—early spring—when the grasses are greening up and in the process hogging all the soil moisture. The overall effect, in botanical terms, has been to change the ground-level ecosystem from mesic (meaning middling moist) to xeric (meaning dry). Most ecologists now believe that, because of grazing, not only have the exotic grasses and herbs brought from Europe become permanent residents, but even the complex soil ecosystems of the oak savannas have been permanently altered.

Of the eighteen species of oak in California (there are several hundred worldwide), only nine are tree-size. Three of these species are severely affected by regeneration problems: the deciduous valley oak, which once dominated the valley bottoms of the Central Valley; the blue oak, denizen of the foothills, also deciduous; and the partly evergreen Engelmann or mesa oak, which grows only in a small, rapidly developing area north of San Diego. Studies have shown that in the areas where these particular trees grow, very few individuals are younger than seventy-five years old. According to one ecologist, K. J. Rice, who has closely studied the blue oak, "substantial recruitment has not occurred for up to 200 years." By contrast, the oaks of my southern California childhood, the coast live oaks and interior live oaks, both evergreen, are tolerant of xeric conditions and therefore less subject to regeneration problems—albeit more subject to extirpation by the developer's bulldozers.

Other oaks include Oregon white oak, the black oak, the canyon oak, and the island oak, which is found only on Santa Catalina and the Channel Islands. In addition, there are eleven named and ten unnamed hybrid species. As a result, identification becomes a chancy thing even for the experts. But they are all fine trees, every one, and worth saving. In fact, the botanic name for oak, *quercus,* is a combination of two Celtic words, *quer,* meaning tree, and *cuez,* meaning fine. All of them moderately long-lived—usually two hundred to three hundred years, though some live to six hundred—the oaks will grow to a weight of several tons. Characteristically, even when oaks grow in clusters, only rarely do the limbs overlap or even touch one another, which is what makes the grass-and-trees oak savanna landscape seem so parklike. When the English explorer George Vancouver happened on the oak groves of the Santa Clara Valley (now Silicon Valley), he commented that the place "could only be compared to a park which had originally been closely planted with true old English oak."

The tree that recalled the benign landscapes of rural England to Vancouver's mind was the valley oak, the species that has suffered by far the most grievous assaults since European settlement. The valley oak is the loftiest of all, though as a group the California oaks tend to be wider than they are tall. The current "champion" valley oak, located near Covelo, California, is 163 feet tall with a trunk over 9 feet in diameter. As the species found growing along riversides and on flat land, the valley oak has proved to be the most vulnerable of all the oaks to the incursions of industrial agriculture—an economic activity in which California has no serious competition—and urban sprawl (ditto). Douglas McCreary, a University of California Agricultural Extension Service expert on oaks, told me that the accounts written by early settlers described "fantastic" riparian forests of these great oaks—the forests that grew along rivers and streams. "There were once nearly a million acres of valley oak riparian habitat," McCreary said, "but only twelve thousand acres of it today." The rivers throughout the great Central Valley, as well as in the smaller patches of farmland, have been ditched, dammed, and diverted for agricultural and urban water use to near-extinction during the last century or so. And the riversides have long since been plowed out so that every available acre can be planted to profitable crops, of which the valley oak was not one. By the beginning of the twentieth century, 90 percent of California's valley oaks had been destroyed. In more recent times, the valley oak—all oak trees for that matter—have been displaced by residential and commercial development.

But now, at last, Californians have begun to realize they are about to lose their landscape heritage. The California oaks are so insignificant economically—good only for firewood (but very, very good for that, giving a hot, long-lasting blue flame)—that only recently have scientists been able to secure serious funding from the federal government in order to study the species. To the contrary, between 1945 and 1965, Doug McCreary told me, the government was in the business of funding programs to clear rangelands of oaks to benefit the cattle industry. Now the greatest loss of trees is to development (which is also government-subsidized, by highways, low-cost mortgages, and other inducements). "We're losing eighty to ninety thousand acres a year,"

McCreary said. A significant datum in this regard is that some 80 percent of oak savannas and woodlands are privately owned and thus unable to withstand development pressures, unlike, say, the famed California redwoods, which grow on public lands.

It is this impact—the loss of trees to development—that has energized the treesavers in California, as opposed to the more subtle effects of the loss of native bunchgrasses and continuing grazing pressures. Since the cooperation of landowners is needed for any oak regeneration project, treesavers tend to downplay the effects of unrestricted grazing, for much of the natural oak savanna and woodlands is owned by large cattle ranchers. Nevertheless, grazing greatly exacerbates the water-loss impact of annual grasses on oak recruitment by further reducing soil moisture through compaction. One study comparing a grazed blue oak savanna with an adjoining area that had been ungrazed since 1972 revealed that in the ungrazed area green leaf tissue in seedlings was between 23 and 46 percent greater than in the grazed area; this suggests significantly higher rates of recruitment.

As local citizen treesavers busily plant trees and fight off developers, ecologists are studying more primary matters—the dynamics of recruitment. According to ecologist Bruce M. Pavlik and colleagues, authors of *Oaks of California*, a splendid book published by the California Oak Foundation, "the efforts of the scientific community have largely focussed on the issue of oak regeneration."

Nevertheless, the strategy as enunciated by the California Oak Foundation, which provides information services to local groups and leads the fray on a statewide basis, includes both citizen action and ecosystem research. The foundation encourages the planting of acorns or seedlings in areas where regeneration is poor or nonexistent, or where trees had previously been removed; the preservation of tracts of oak savanna and woodland; and field trials to determine how oak woodland and savanna habitats might be restored to something approximating their original ecological function.

When I visited with Douglas McCreary, the oak expert at a University of California field station located in the midst of an oak savanna near the aptly named Grass Valley, I learned how compelling the idea of oak restoration is to the tree lovers of the state. As we were walking through the parking lot on our way to an experimental plot, McCreary, who is a board member of the Oak Foundation, motioned to his car, a sedan decidedly drooping in the rear. "When the word got out we were doing replanting studies here," he told me, "people from all over the state sent me acorns. I've got five hundred pounds of 'em in the trunk of that car."

In this regard, McCreary had become a human analogue to the acorn woodpecker, whose life's work it is to drill perfect, to-the-millimeter, acorn-size holes in dead or dying trees (or in telephone poles) in order to create cooperative acorn granaries for a family group. An industrious woodpecker can drill five thousand holes a season. Trees with as many as fifty thousand acorn holes have been recorded, McCreary told me.

Doug McCreary's acorns (carefully selected from local trees, not from the trunk of his car) are planted in test plots at his field station to determine how citizen groups and governments can successfully replicate an oak savanna or woodland, if they have time, manpower, and energy. As it turns out, it's not a simple process for human beings to "recruit" a young oak tree.

As a general rule, McCreary advises, it is better to plant an acorn than transplant a seedling grown in a pot. The way to proceed is to find a nearby oak situated in roughly the same environment as the area selected for planting. The acorns should be picked from trees, not the ground. Then, the caps should be removed and the acorns rinsed in lukewarm water with a bit of bleach. After this cleansing, they should be dried, placed in small Zip-loc bags, and refrigerated for one month to improve the chances of germination. It is important to use *small* bags, since a large number of acorns together will generate heat.

The best of all planting times is November. The acorns should be placed only one inch deep in the soil (as if cradled between tussocks of the bunch grass of yore), located in a sunny spot. McCreary suggests that the hole be dug deeper and refilled to loosen the soil. Some experts recommend that three acorns be planted together in the hole and later thinned.

There is more. The growing area should be fenced to keep livestock or large wildlife away. And to guard against bugs, birds, and smaller animals making short work of the germinating acorn, the general practice is to make a collar for it, fashioned from a plastic cottage cheese carton with the bottom cut out. Around that a small wire cage should be made of window screen for the first year or so, gathered at the top, and then replaced with a hardware-cloth cage after the seedling (if it appears) grows a bit. Further, it is essential that all the existing grasses and weeds in the planting area be completely removed to a diameter of three feet. If you do not wish to keep weeding around the planted acorns, then black plastic "mulching" sheets can be used, fastened to the ground with six-inch wire staples.

During hot weather the oak-grower should water two or three times a week—though not too much. McCreary advises that the seedlings that appear should be carefully tended until they get about four or five feet tall, when they might be judged to have been "recruited," which is to say when they are about that many years old. A 50-percent success rate would be wonderful.

Given the difficulties that California treesavers confront when standing in for the now-bygone bunchgrass ecosystem, most oak tree planting is on a garden or yard basis, or to produce street trees. According to Amy Larson, executive director of the California Oak Foundation, CalTrans, the California state highway agency, promised to plant one million oaks along state highways in 1994. As for the replanting of those millions of acres of lost valley, blue, and Engelmann oak savannas and woodlands, McCreary thinks that in general, the requirements for site preparation, maintenance, and protection are too elaborate and difficult for more than a limited number of committed volunteers to meet, and too expensive for governments to undertake.

This may be one of the reasons why the Oak Foundation and other groups emphasize the preservation of existing trees as the first line of defense. Oak tree protection has a long and honorable history in California, dating to the early 1920s in Visalia, a small Sierra foothill town that was once named Oak Grove City. Alarmed by the loss of valley oaks to agriculture and city expansion, a local nursery gave away five seedlings to any resident willing to plant them. Since then the population has grown too much for such largesse, but the local government still plants two hundred oaks a year, year in and year out. Moreover, Tulare County, of which Visalia is the county seat, levies a five-hundred-dollar fine for illegally cutting an oak. In fact, more than one hundred cities and counties in California now have regulations protecting native oaks, and the California Oak Foundation is undertaking to persuade all local governments to add oak protection language to their planning and zoning ordinances.

The most limited effort made by the oak-savers of California relates to the only solution that might actually have a chance of working—to restore the bunchgrass habitat and to protect what existing habitat remains where the oaks thrived prior to the arrival of the Spaniards. In the Bald Hills of Redwood National Park, for example, where Oregon oaks grow, researchers have removed cattle from the savannas and reintroduced fire (which encourages perennial grasses and kills off much of the annual grasses and weeds) to sustain the relict bunchgrass prairies and woodlands. In Yosemite, park scientists not only have replanted black oaks, but also have extirpated exotic plants, replacing them with native understory species, and have begun systematic controlled burning to mimic the fire ecology of a natural bunchgrass ecosystem. According to Bruce Pavlik, writing in *California Oaks*, these and other experiments are tantalizing in terms of their future possibilities, but at the same time any large-scale implementation of habitat restoration "may prove too costly and labor-intensive for application."

Still, according to the California Native Plant Society, such restoration is the only true remedy for the disappearing oaks of California. With regard to the seriously threatened Engelmann oak in San Diego County, merely saving large trees is not enough. Writes Thomas A. Scott in the society's bulletin, *Fremontia*, "Educational efforts need to emphasize the maintenance of the entire Engelmann oak ecosystem in order to promote sustainable woodlands."

This is, in fact, a heartbreaking prescription, for Pavlik and McCreary are surely right about costs and complications. To restore the pre-Columbian perennial grass ecosystem on millions of acres of grazing land from which cattle would have to be largely excluded (though herds can be shifted from one grazing area to another to replicate the original levels of feeding by ungulates such as deer and elk), and to treat such restored prairies with prescribed-burn groundfires (even though 50 percent of existing grazing land is within five miles of urban development) in order to grow oak trees the natural way, seems, for all practical purposes, impossible.

Thus, even though optimism and a California can-do spirit pervade much of the activist oak-saving literature, in many citizens there remains, underneath, a sense of permanent loss. Writing in the Oak Foundation's newsletter, Kenneth Lamb, a Livermore, California, surveyor (Livermore being a smallish community about fifteen miles west of Oakland), tells how during his researches some years ago in old survey records, he unearthed an 1851 account of a mighty valley oak that had, apparently, stood not many miles from his home. The description told of a tree with a five-foot trunk that had been blazed as a "witness tree" in a survey of metes and bounds. The spread of the tree was even more remarkable—"3.18 chains," the early surveyor had written. Since a chain is 66 feet, this meant the tree had a limb-spread of about 210 feet, an area of roughly three-quarters of an acre. Given the oaks' typical root-spread of 100 feet beyond dripline, this one, single tree dominated an area of no less than three acres—a patch of land that to my suburban way of thinking is simply enormous.

Lamb says that he first looked for the tree in 1969, and found it. Although it was much reduced by age, he was sure of the identification, since the characteristic witness-tree blaze mark was clearly visible. By careful examination, Lamb estimated the age of the tree at five hundred years. Having made the find and recorded that spot, he did not revisit the tree for nearly fifteen years. Then, in 1983, he returned. Sadly, only a ragged stump remained. It was such a personal loss to him that he was moved to write a verse about the venerable old grandfather tree that somehow stood for all the great trees now dying in California. The verse begins:

Long-scourged by wind and rain and staring sun,
This sentry at the New World's birth and rise
Is fallen now. His passing mourned by none,
His gnarled limbs no longer span the skies.

As the California oak experts like Doug McCreary have learned, the instinct to plant trees is a powerful one in the hearts of American civic activists, as it is in perhaps a majority of us, especially now that the carelessness of past (and present) generations is becoming so manifestly plain. It was this insight that led Neil Sampson, a friend and colleague of twenty years, to invent a program called Global ReLeaf. The idea is to recruit volunteers to plant trees—millions of them. A hundred million, in fact.

Sampson, who may well be Washington's most imaginative policy expert in the natural resources field, is the chief executive of the American Forestry Association (now American Forests, in a recent name-change), the oldest (since 1875) citizen conservation organization in the United States, founded to champion the cause of "forest reserves" (later the national forests). Once the reserves had been established (1897), the association encouraged the reforestation of the ravaged woodlands of the East and Middle West. In recent years, Sampson has reinvigorated that early tradition with a thoroughly modern program that seeks not only to grow more trees for forestry, but to reduce global warming.

Neil Sampson, like many others in Washington, was stunned by the testimony of NASA scientist James E. Hansen, before the Senate Committee on Energy and Natural Resources in June 1988, that global temperatures during the previous two decades had been the highest recorded since mankind had been keeping records, and that the rate of global warming, due to CO_2 and other greenhouse gases, was increasing much more quickly than climatologists had earlier predicted. During the searingly hot drought summer of 1988, Hansen's data became front-page news, as the corn and beans withered on the baked cropland of the Middle West and mass fires blackened half the acreage of Yellowstone National Park. Meanwhile, the felling and burning of the Amazonian rain forest had also become a major story.

For Neil Sampson this seemed like an opportune moment to ask large corporations, government agencies, and civic organizations to work with American Forests in mounting a major citizen-action tree-planting effort. There was a good story to tell. For example, growing trees can absorb forty-eight pounds of CO_2 a year—ten tons an acre; what is more, growing trees that also provide shade to buildings and streets can multiply this CO_2 absorption by fifteen times. Thus, three trees shading a house can cut air conditioning needs by up to 50 percent. Planting one hundred million trees could save American consumers four billion dollars a year on their energy bills alone and drastically cut global-warming CO_2 emissions into the bargain.

As far as Sampson was concerned, the global-warming crisis was real and tree planting was a way that ordinary people could help deal with it. As he later told me, "With 5.6 billion people on earth we have neither the space nor the time to use major sections of the planet as an ecological observation laboratory for the next one hundred years. We now face the problem of finding a way to live on earth. We simply have to be aggressively restorative and aggressively managerial about our trees and forests. Global ReLeaf won't fix everything, but it's a start."

It is something of an understatement to say that the corporations, civic groups, and government agencies took his message to heart. Four months after Hansen's grim testimony on Capitol Hill, Sampson and his colleagues had developed a Global ReLeaf plan, officially launched by Senator Timothy Wirth of Colorado, by the head of the Forest Service, and by other dignitaries. The theme, "Plant a Tree, Cool the Globe," was so utterly apt after the hot summer just concluding that the event was picked up by the news media and given national exposure. Articles appeared in major magazines and metropolitan dailies. COOL THE GREENHOUSE, PLANT 100 MILLION TREES, read the headline of a piece bylined by Sampson in the *Los Angeles Times.* "We'll enter the 21st Century with millions of trees," he wrote. "Millions of people who recognized a threat took action." In 1989, public-service ads appeared in thirty-nine national magazines with a readership of twenty-nine million. One hundred and fifty communities and schools signed on with Global ReLeaf as tree planters. Amway, the door-to-door retailing giant, became a corporate sponsor, as did the E. & J. Gallo Winery, which put up the money for tree-planting projects in ten cities and donated Global ReLeaf in-store displays, coupons, and advertising to get the message across. By the end of the year, fifty-two business and corporate sponsors had joined the campaign, and fourteen state legislatures inaugurated official Global ReLeaf programs for their states. Los Angeles announced it would plant five million trees, and 113 other cities followed suit with their own ReLeaf programs.

In the following years, the pace hardly slackened. Texaco donated one million dollars, and put their staff members to work on tree planting as well. "I saw four hundred Texaco people in mud up to their knees," Sampson said, "wrestling trees that weigh four hundred pounds apiece. Thirty-five-foot trees. They converted the entrance of the Houston Medical Center into a tree-lined boulevard. And in New York, we've got Bronx kids reclaiming their neighborhood through tree planting." Local programs were started as well in Denver, New Orleans, and Houston. McDonald's agreed to produce educational posters and give tree seedlings to children in nine cities. Later that year, Global ReLeaf International was launched in Canada, Costa Rica, and Hungary. Sampson, who is a mud-on-the-shoes kind of conservationist, traveled to Budapest, where, with Arpad Gontz, president of Hungary, he planted a row of trees along the Danube. By the end of 1991, ten nations had joined the program. McDonald's expanded their program that year and gave away nine million seedlings nationwide. In Aspen, Colorado, a two-day jazz festival donated its proceeds to Global ReLeaf. Sampson and his staff received a presidential citation that year, together with an Award of Excellence from the Natural Resources Defense Council.

Several offshoot programs were established along the way: Heritage Forests, an effort to replicate original woodlands in areas where they had long since been converted to cropland or urban development; the Famous and Historic Tree Program, which provided seeds and cuttings from trees with historic associations, such as George Washington's oaks at Mount Vernon; the New Communities program to work with developers not only to save trees, but to plant them, too; and a ReLeaf program with farms and ranches that harks back to the Dust Bowl days, when the Roosevelt administration urged farmers to plant shelterbelts to break the prairie winds. Many did, and then cut them down in the 1970s when large tractors demanded long runs without turns. Now Sampson and company are reviving the shelterbelt tradition. A ReLeaf-inspired Cool Communities program, mounted in concert with the U.S. Environmental Protection Agency and the Department of Energy, is designed to save energy and reduce heat in inner-city areas.

Indeed, in the field of "urban forestry," American Forests has made particularly impressive strides, providing organizational structure and professionalism to an enterprise that can make cities more attractive, decrease air pollution, increase property values, and reduce energy requirements dramatically. According to Gary Moll, American Forests' urban forestry director, the cost of planting a city tree will be earned back in energy savings alone. That cities cut tree programs first rather than last in this era of tight budgets, he says, is a false economy that defies logic.

Moll told me that the average life of a downtown street tree is seven years, mainly because we do not provide them a proper place to grow—not enough space, not enough soil, not enough water, not enough light, too many utility wires, too much pollution, too much salt spread during winter, too much vandalism, too much hot air ejected onto the street from too many air conditioners, too many dogs peeing on the trunks. "Trees will last only thirty-two years in the city as a whole," he said, "and only seven years in downtown locations. Not only that, four trees are dying for every one planted in cities." He said that in the old days, the street trees were elm, maple, and ash. The first, a victim of blight, has virtually disappeared from city streets; the other two can't manage the modern environmental assaults.

These days, trees are engineered to work in an urban environment —the ubiquitous Bradford pear, a special cultivar of the Comice pear, being the best example. Tidily pyramidal in shape, the smallish Bradford pear looks artificial, and doesn't work so well either in terms of providing shade. Despite the difficulties with pears and other street-tree species now favored, urbanites as well as suburbanites are planting as many as they can, anyway. The trouble with uncoordinated volunteer city-tree planting, according to Gary Moll, is that little is being done to correct the underlying problems that will cause the planted trees to die in seven years, or maybe thirty-two years out in the suburbs.

Urban complications aside, by the end of 1993, the Global ReLeaf program had collected millions of dollars in corporate and individual donations and spawned substantial new state and federal tree-planting programs as well. Corporate sponsors number in the hundreds. The annual rate of tree planting in projects directly managed by American Forests has increased by fifty times since the first full year of the program, including some in cities. But the overall program has become so various and self-starting that Sampson has no idea how many millions of trees can be said to have been planted under the aegis of Global ReLeaf. Something in the tens of millions might not be far off the mark. The one hundred million trees that Neil Sampson thought might be simply a good round number in 1988 now seems to be very much a possibility, if not within this decade then shortly after.

All of the foregoing is so decent and positive that only a curmudgeon would fault it. "What good does it do," I asked Sampson anyway, "to plant trees only to have them afflicted by acid rain or depleted soils, or some other assault from our industrial society, or simply chopped down? Wouldn't it be a better use of your time and money and everyone else's time and money to try to change air-pollution policy and stop clear-cutting?" After due reflection, Sampson answered the questions in turn: "A lot," he said, and then, "No."

Sampson's view is that people can work backward from a "partial" solution such as tree planting to an understanding of the whole problem. To engage large numbers of citizens (as well as corporations and government agencies) in the process of planting trees is to recruit them into coming to grips with the crises of global warming, planetary pollution, and the wreckage we have made of natural forest ecosystems. "Everyone who plants a tree for the environment's sake has a stake not only in the tree but in the environment," he told me, emphatically.

The formulation is reasonable but still gets an argument from some environmentalists. In *Audubon* magazine, for example, nature writer Ted Williams severely took the Global ReLeaf program to task in 1991, describing it as a wrongheaded exercise conducted by environmental dilletantes: "Only God can make a tree, but any environmental illiterate can plant it in the wrong place. All of a sudden Americans are rushing around the country like Johnny Appleseed on applejack. We need to slow down and think about what we're at before we do more harm than good." Indeed, Auduboners are so troubled about planting the wrong trees in the wrong places, says Williams, that a regional vice president of the society "politely declined when Global ReLeaf offered her chapters ten thousand Afghan pines to hand out at the malls. 'They're garbage trees as far as wildlife goes,' she told me." Moreover, he makes the telling point that "a more effective means of greenhouse postponement than planting trees is not cutting them—at least when they are very old. The ancient forests of the Pacific Northwest are the most efficient carbon sinks on Earth."

What also distresses Williams is that too often the enterprise has been a corporate PR smokescreen without any real commitment to environmental quality. On the sponsorship of Global ReLeaf by the Geo Division of General Motors, Williams pointed out that there was something fishy about a "bloated U.S. automaker that led the successful fight to sabotage fuel-efficiency legislation . . . to turn over a new leaf and find beneath it magic seeds from three trees that may or may not belong in your area."

Of course, Sampson knows a great deal about which trees belong where, and does not need instruction in such matters from *Audubon* magazine. The very nature of the ReLeaf program is to let it ramify at will—and it often goes off into odd directions unbeknownst to American Forests. What is more, Sampson believes, and I would agree, that it is just a little bit precious to claim that a serious error is being perpetrated by the good-hearted tree planters inspirited by Global ReLeaf. One doubts that any great ecosystem will crash from an ill-advised project here and there. In addition, Sampson would argue, and has done so, there is nothing in Global ReLeaf that works against reform in air-pollution policy or in keeping the Doug firs standing in the ancient forests of Washington and Oregon.

The either-or argument is of course as unfair as it is fallacious. As for the sequestering of carbon, a tree planter can rightly claim that bringing new trees into the world causes more carbon to be sequestered, not less. And especially if wood or wood chips from those trees are used for fuel. This is the proposition Sampson advanced in an intriguing 1992 analysis meant to justify massive tree planting at an even greater scale than the one hundred million trees he had earlier proposed. Sampson suggests that if we were to use for energy wood derived from fast-growing trees planted specifically for this purpose on marginal cropland, instead of using fossil fuel, we would replace a "non-recycling carbon source" with a recycling carbon source. The unused coal, oil, and natural gas, by remaining safely sequestered in the earth, would not add to the CO_2 burden, whereas the growing of fuel trees would absorb more CO_2 than they would produce in the process of being consumed as fuel, thus reducing net CO_2 emissions over time—and maybe taking some pressure off forests that should be managed as ecosystems rather than exploited as a resource into the bargain.

However appealing this notion, it does seem to me a bit too blue-sky to do us much good in the polluted here and now, where the trees are dying faster than even a whole population of tree planters can keep up with. As for Ted Williams's complaint, what concerns me most about what he likens to a bunch of Johnny Appleseeds high on apple-jack is not that they are planting the wrong trees in the wrong places, but that in the process, some of them might come to believe they have absolved themselves of the sacred duty of every citizen in these environmentally parlous times to come to grips with the mounting evidence that our poor beat-up planet will not tolerate any more environmental burdens heaped upon it by a heavy-handed industrial civilization. That is the hard message of the dying trees, simple and direct, and nothing should get in the way of our hearing it.

The treesavers, of course, have many other strategies besides tree planting. One of them is to modify or restore to health the natural ecosystems in which trees grow. In California, as I described earlier, experimental projects have been mounted to reintroduce the native bunchgrasses. But there is an even more elementary approach than this, dealing not just with what grows next to the soil in a forest ecosystem but with the soil itself. This is the cause of the *remineralizers,* who approach their efforts with evangelical, if not apocalyptic, zeal.

The remineralization movement—which has New Age adherents around the world, and some scientific support (rather more in Europe than in the United States)—derives from the theory, propounded by John Hamaker, an American soils scientist, that the increases in CO_2 from industrial and automotive emissions and the deforestation and burning of tropical forests will bring on a new ice age, not because the globe will become cooler, but because it is becoming warmer.

The generally accepted view is that ice ages—eight of them have occurred in the past million years—are caused by long-term cyclic changes in the earth's orbit around the sun and in the tilt of the earth on its axis that obtain periodically, every 23,000, 41,000, and 100,000 years. Recently, some scientists have proposed that these astrological effects may be modified by shifts in ocean currents which can precipitate an ice age. Others suggest that the buildup of mountains by tectonic movement may also serve as a trigger, by altering air currents. Hamaker argues that because we are at the end of an interglacial cycle, the dire effect of global warming will be to trigger the onset of a new ice age. This would obtain because the warming would be just enough to increase snowfall in northern hemisphere polar regions but not enough to melt existing glaciers in the arctic or subarctic areas such as Greenland and Alaska. Thus the ice sheet would expand. Once triggered, the glacier would move southward ineluctably, based on the principal of self-potentiation. There is, actually, some precedent for this prediction. Just before the last ice age began, according to Gifford Miller of the University of Colorado, "temperatures got a little warmer, just as they are getting a little warmer today."

Hamaker and his followers believe that the mineral nutrients created when rocks are pulverized under the incredible weight of an advancing ice sheet are now depleted, having been leached away for thousands of years. At a discussion of Hamaker's work, Joanna Campe, a movement leader and editor of the periodical *Remineralize the Earth*, told me that "forest death typically happens at the end of an interglacial period. And we are speeding it along." Evidence suggests, she has written, that "as forests begin to die off worldwide, giving off carbon dioxide, the climate of the Earth is altered, triggering the transition from the warm interglacial period to an Ice Age. We are hastening this process with the burning of fossil fuels. Undertaking the task of remineralization is urgent to restore our agricultural soils and to save the dying forests of the temperate latitudes and stabilize our climate." Hamaker's own description of the crisis is apocalyptic: "Within a few decades the growing season may have decreased so much that millions of people will starve, in the richer nations as well as the poorer."

The way out of the crisis is not only to reduce greenhouse gases but to "re-create Eden" and postpone a new ice age at the same time. This could be done, Hamaker and his followers insist, by a massive application of manmade rock dust, replicating the effect of glaciation, in agricultural and forested areas of the northern hemisphere. The result would be to stabilize CO_2 and reduce the climate change extremes—drought, storms, bitter cold, and scorching heat—that affect the growth of trees and plants. The remineralizers point out that the best rock dust is glacial gravel, which would replicate minerals that would be subject to glacial pulverization. Apparently, simply adding lime to depleted forest soils does not work well, since the lime kills off needed soil organisms, whereas rock dust does not.

The literature is vague on the mechanisms by which plants take up and utilize rock dust (some adherents think that such dust contains healthful living microbes, and dose themselves directly with it as a medicine), but those who have measured the results of application claim some astonishing statistics. The *Remineralize the Earth* newsletter reports that in Germany a 1986 study "showed four times the timber volume in a forest where pine seedlings were planted versus the controls. One application of basalt rock dust lasts 60 years." In 1991, the EarthDance Institute of Asheville, N.C., together with graduate students from North Carolina State University, planted thousands of Fraser fir and red spruce seedlings and applied eight tons of rock dust on test sites. Twelve weeks later, the rock-dust treated red spruce had grown 27 percent higher than those on non-treated sites, and Fraser fir 19 percent higher. Robert Bruck, the North Carolina State plant pathologist, is monitoring the results on the off chance that the remineralizers may be on to something. Other tests have shown that rock dust can help restore mycorrhizal fungus, the helpful symbiont that increases the ability of tree feeder roots to take up nutrients and water.

Acceptance of Hamaker's theory that a new ice age is imminent is not necessary for a sober analysis of the efficacy of rock dust used to improve the soils of forests like those atop Mount Mitchell, whose nutrients have been leached away by decades of acid precipitation. Therefore, the salient question for the treesaver is whether or not grinding gravel to dust and distributing it in the beset forests of the northern hemisphere is at all practical. On the most elementary basis, would the energy required to distribute rock dust produce more CO_2 than would be absorbed by the possible new growth that the applications would produce? A partial answer may be found in the introduction in 1991 of a relatively low-cost and fuel-efficient pulverizer, the invention of Richard Ewing, an American engineer, and Geurt Kreutzelman, a Dutch engineer living in Eugene, Oregon. With only two moving parts, the Ewing-Kreutzelman "Cyclone pulverizer" (as manufactured by Buker Enterprises of Springfield, Oregon) can process three tons of gravel an hour powered by a small 20-horsepower gasoline engine or electric motor. The advertised price is $16,765.45. Some remineralizers envision a kind of global civic movement in which every locality buys a pulverizer, stokes it with rocks and gravel, and distributes the dust in nearby forests and on cropland, perhaps by helicopter. Others believe that large military transport planes should be used to distribute the dust, pouring it out of cargo doors onto the forestlands below. In either case, the prospects of making much of a dent on the vast stretches of boreal and temperate-zone forests of the northern hemisphere, from Scandinavia across the taiga of Siberia, to the coniferous forests of Alaska, the Pacific Northwest, and Canada, from the Laurentians down to the southernmost Appalachians, seems a daunting task indeed. *Newsweek*'s Gregg Easterbrook, a skeptic about many environmental issues, writes, "Hamaker believes that finely ground rock dust, such as that deposited by retreating glaciers, should be dropped on the forests of the world.

This would activate the tree-growth spurts that accompanied the end of the last ice age, returning the carbon balance to a benign level." The whole business, Easterbrook writes, is "loony," and out of the "scientific mainstream." Quixotic, to be sure, but maybe *loony* is too facile, given the state of northern hemisphere forests today.

Aside from the acorn planters and soil amenders, there are those who wish to save the trees by trying not to destroy the forest ecosystems that give them nurture. To this end, Jerry Franklin, the University of Washington professor introduced in Chapter 7, has created a new approach to logging called New Forestry. Beginning in the 1980s, Franklin and his colleagues at the Andrews Ecosystem Research group, a Forest Service–university consortium located in Blue River, Oregon, sought to develop a "kinder and gentler" forestry that better accommodates ecological values while allowing for the extraction of commodities.

After a multitude of studies to determine (as well as any human can) the primary elements that differentiate a working ecosystem from a working tree farm, Franklin and the Andrews group, with a special assist from the volcanic eruption of Mount Saint Helens, developed the concept of "biological legacies." Such legacies, they theorized, are the means by which a ravaged ecosystem can regenerate. They noticed that after the fires set off by the Mount Saint Helens eruption and the deposition of a killing blanket of volcanic ash, the landscape was not as sterile as it appeared. Underneath the devastation, says Franklin, "We found incredible legacies of living organisms and dead organic matter." In studies of the aftermaths of other natural catastrophes, such as wildfire, tree-flattening windstorms, and floods, the researchers identified much the same kind of biological legacies as at Mount Saint Helens. Such disturbances "often leave green trees and do not consume much of the wood, which remains behind in the form of snags and downed logs," Franklin observes.

Franklin says that traditional cutting, including the so-called "shelterwood" and "selective cutting" previously thought to be kinder and gentler, focuses on the regeneration of trees and destroys essential ecosystem linkages in the process. In contrast, the natural forests that reappear after catastrophic events such as windstorms or wildfires—or even a volcanic eruption—are "complex and rich in structures and organisms." To mimic this complexity within the context of commercial logging, Franklin and the Andrews group have recommended that each area selected for harvesting identify "leave trees"—large trees that would remain standing through the next rotation of eighty years or so. Moreover, snags and downed logs should be left on the site, along with slash, and cut-over patches should not connect in order that the microclimates in the uncut areas are not so drastically affected by a tree-destroying "edge effect."

To show how New Forestry might operate in the future, Franklin cites the prospect of the endangered spotted owl. "On the Olympic peninsula," he writes, "the owls are known to use multi-aged stands that were created by windstorm and wildfire some 70 to 90 years ago. By adopting New Forestry practices, we may recreate spotted owl habitat in a matter of 90 years, rather than having to wait 200 to 250 years as with current practices."

While New Forestry is still in an experimental stage and has not yet been adopted by the forest products industry and their associates in the U.S. Forest Service, Franklin and the Andrews group have probably had a significant effect on the thinking of commercial and public forest managers, and will continue to do so. At the very least (and I hope this does not sound too cynical), the precepts of New Forestry can provide public-relations "cover" for the industrial forestry establishment, now beset with such severe criticism from the environmental community that "old" forestry may be at least partially legislated out of existence.

But the environmentalists are not too happy about New Forestry, either; they dub it nothing more than a "sloppy clear-cut." Wildlife ecologist Chris Maser (also introduced in Chapter 7), an early collaborator in Franklin's work, has more recently tried to distance himself from New Forestry, claiming (accurately, I believe) that it is more commodity-oriented than ecology-oriented. He describes it simply as "a new look at old forestry." In defense of his environmental correctness, however, Franklin can point to Professor Bill Atkinson of Oregon State University, who in disparaging the work of the Andrews group fears that if its precepts ever become required practice, it will be the ruination of the forest products industry as well as the U.S. Forest Service.

A much more radical prescription for forest management has been offered by the adherents of "ecoforestry." The approach here, philosophically, is to upend Franklin's New Forestry. Whereas Franklin proposes a way to harvest trees and still maintain a part of the biological legacy, the ecoforesters propose a way to maintain natural forest ecosystems and still have the option of cutting some trees. The process, as practiced for example by Merve Wilkinson, a British Columbia forest owner, is to do selective cutting in an ecologically sensitive way. "What you need," he told a *Seattle Post-Intelligencer* reporter, "is multiple ages, multiple heights, and multiple species."

To accomplish this, Wilkinson's selective cutting method leaves the biggest and oldest trees, choosing instead trees that might be shading out an area where seedlings have sprung up. The trees cut are widely separated, and skidded out of the forest one at a time. Wilkinson claims that his production is only a bit below that of more commercially oriented tree farms, and that the total amount of wood on his property is roughly the same as what it was when he started managing it more than half a century ago.

Tree farmers like Wilkinson, along with forest ecologists and environmentalists, have been brought together by the newly organized Ecoforestry Institute, which hopes to set up "natural selection ecoforestry" demonstrations throughout the Pacific Northwest in both Canada and the United States, as well as in other areas of North America. The outfit has a definite New Age flavor. States the current board president in an institute publication, "The Ecoforestry Institute is dedicated to Holistic Natural Selection Ecoforestry, which is the result of applying the platform principles of the Deep Ecology Movement to the use of forest and the practice of forestry. . . . Ecoforestry is perennial forest use based on respect for the wisdom of the forest. Ecoforestry assumes that nature knows best how to grow and maintain forests; human activities in relation to forests must respect and learn from this wisdom."

The experiments, whether by Franklin or the Ecoforestry Institute, are all to the good, of course. But meanwhile, the Clinton administration produced a compromise decision—the Option 9 plan—regarding the spotted owl controversy, that will start the chainsaws rattling again in the ancient forests of Oregon and Washington. Option 9, supposedly protecting a large part of the old growth, has loopholes, as Alexander Cockburn writes, "through which 500,000 logging trucks could happily drive each year for ten years, the duration of the plan." As finally modified, the plan calls for opening 4 million acres for regular logging, 7.5

million acres for thinning and salvage logging, and 1.5 million acres for "experimental" logging techniques (i.e., New Forestry). "It still leaves one-third of the ancient forest open to logging," said Brock Evans of the National Audubon Society. "It's still not a legal plan." According to James Monteith of Save the West, Inc., which is bringing suit against the Option 9 plan (although it was supported by most of the major environmental organizations), "The President's Forest Plan will not accomplish crucial biological objectives or even meet the standards required by law."

While the remineralizers and the ecoforesters, among others, seek to improve the biology of forests to make them more hospitable to trees, there are others who wish to change the trees themselves, to make them less susceptible to natural and unnatural forest stresses.

The best-known experiments in tree-saving bioengineering are those taking place with the American chestnut and the American (white) elm, two beloved species either gone (the chestnut) or nearly gone (the elm), as I recounted in the previous chapter. In both cases, the hunt for ways to save (in the case of elms) or reestablish (in the case of chestnuts) these forest trees has consumed many millions of dollars over the last half century. Regarding the elm, a search has been on for decades—at the University of Wisconsin and at experimental plots throughout the Midwest and East—to find a Dutch elm disease–resistant cultivar. The general approach has been to raise seedling elms, inject them with the disease spore repeatedly, and see what survives. From this laborious process, Wisconsin researchers generated the American Liberty elm. As naturalist George Laycock writes in *Audubon* magazine, the tree was selected from the "parent plants of the survivors of more than 60,000 inoculated seedlings." The Liberty elm has been available since 1983 from the Elm Research Institute, which holds a plant patent on the tree and distributes seedlings at low cost to individuals as well as cities and towns. The trees are all clones from a single genotype. Among the thousands distributed, only one has succumbed to disease.

In Kensington, Maryland, a registered historic district where I lived for many years, the town forester planted a Liberty elm in front of my house, in between some large maples whose days are numbered. It looks like a regular elm, does this clone, and I am assured that it will eventually become the beautiful, vase-shaped, old-timey Victorian tree that once grew here. Its progeny, however, will probably not be resistant to the Dutch elm disease fungus, which means that while we may have elms along our streets again, we shall not soon find them in our forests, if ever.

As for the chestnut, geneticists have been trying to develop crosses with the smaller Chinese chestnut, which is resistant to the American chestnut's fungal blight, in hopes of creating a fungus-resistant hybrid that would still grow wide and spreading and tall, with a plethora of tasty nuts—mast for a wide variety of wildlife now much diminished since the loss of the tree in Eastern forests.

Chestnut tree savers have also been searching for an unblighted specimen surviving somewhere—an "Eve tree" that might provide in its fruit a new beginning for the species. In fact one such, the "Ross" tree, almost, but not quite, fills the bill. This specimen, located in rural Virginia, is more than sixty years old, is forty-five feet tall (less than half the height of a large mature tree in pre-blight days), with a trunk diameter of about a foot (would be four feet at maturity). Why it has survived, no one knows. How much longer it will survive is also a question. It is resistant, but still affected by the fungus—*Endothia parasitica.* Accordingly, the experiments in "back-crossing" with hybrid American-Chinese trees continue apace as still the best hope. Eventually, proponents believe, continuous back-crossing will eliminate every characteristic of the Chinese chestnut save one—resistance to the blight.

Another approach to chestnut-saving involves the development of a hypovirulent strain of *Endothia* to produce a benign "infection" in the chestnut that will "wall off" the fungal disease that is killing the tree. Researchers at Michigan State University discovered that within a small stand of barely surviving chestnuts located in Michigan, some of the lesions caused by *Endothia* were healing and the trees were more or less holding their own. The Michigan researchers found that the *Endothia* infecting the trees was itself infected by a virus, creating a "hypovirulent" version of the fungus—meaning that the fungus could be transmuted to a less deadly form. The only trouble with infecting seedlings or shoots with the hypovirulent fungus (thus, in turn, infecting the lethal form present) was, the Michigan scientists found, that strains of the fungus elsewhere were resistant to the virus in the imported hypovirulent strain. Stalemate.

One way around this dilemma was to engineer a strain of hypovirulent *Endothia* that would more efficiently infect a wide range of fungal strains. At the Roche Institute of Molecular Biology in Nutley, New Jersey, Donald Nuss, in the course of a long-term basic research effort to understand how a virus could affect the virulence of a fungus, came across a means to create a hypovirulent fungal strain that would, unlike the Michigan strain found in nature, be much more efficient in infecting *Endothia* in a wide variety of circumstances. After examining the fungus at the molecular level and cloning a hypovirulent strain through recombinant DNA techniques, Nuss found that his laboratory-produced viruses were transmitted to the fungus through mating, which resulted in the creation of "hypovirulent offspring." As Nuss wrote in the newsletter of the American Chestnut Foundation, "This new mode of transmission, not available to natural hypovirulent strains, is likely to circumvent one of the major barriers to the spread of hypovirulence in North America." Two problems, potentially big ones: First, because Nuss's hypovirulent strain of *Endothia* was created by recombinant DNA techniques—which means it is "unnatural" and potentially dangerous—its release is strictly regulated, and in fact may not be permitted. Moreover, though his invention works in the lab, there is no evidence that it will work in a natural forest.

Meanwhile, over at the College of Environmental Science and Forestry at Syracuse, New York, another genetic engineering project is taking place. Here, molecular biologists have isolated a protein substance in a fungus-eating snail (the escargot snail, in fact) that is resistant to *Endothia,* and possibly to other fungi that affect forest trees. Now they need to find the gene in the snail, clone it, and then figure out a way to transfer the fungus-resistant genes into the living tissue of a tree. "The first step," forest geneticist Charles A. Maynard told the *Syracuse Herald American,* "is to get the gene into a plant cell. Then you have to grow that into a full tree. It's easier said than done." Nevertheless, according to Maynard, gene transfers have been successful in a hundred different plant species.

The American Chestnut Foundation, which collects and disseminates the findings of the many researchers working on the revivification of the beloved *Castanea dentata*—or something closely approximating it—believes that a viable cultivar can be developed before the end of the century. And in general, those who are conducting the various research projects are optimistic, even though few of them will give themselves a deadline. Indeed, some believe that the chestnut can once again become a dominant tree in the natural forests of the East and Midwest. Such is the optimism of the new science of gene-splicing and tree engineering.

But those who see the reinstatement of old *Castanea* as the king of the broadleaf forest will be in a race with other cloners and splicers, one group of which would like an oriental exotic, the Royal paulownia (*Paulownia tomentosa*), to become a commercial hardwood that can replace native oaks and other trees now beset with plagues and diseases. The paulownia is an ornamental that has escaped and taken up residence in Southeastern woodlands. It resembles a catalpa tree and produces sprays of deep purple flowers before the leaves appear, so that seen from a distance in the spring it looks very much like a dead tree which has been done in by a vigorous wisteria vine in full florescence. The paulownia is, in fact, both sturdy and fast-growing, with a light yet surprisingly strong wood, a quality greatly sought by those who wish for a fast-growing hardwood to match the fast-growing softwoods in the tree plantations of the South. In fact, the geneticists have found that they can actually improve on the paulownia's growth rate. One experimental model has been shown to mature in seven years.

All of the wonderful citizen energy, and the foundation grants, and the scientific breakthroughs to save the trees should, perhaps, bring us a sense of hope. And we are 100 percent on the side of hope. Hope is good. Hope is American. Are the blue oaks failing to regenerate in the California foothills? No problem, we'll just regenerate them ourselves with plastic collars and window-screen tents. Is our planet warming from CO_2? Relax, we'll plant a hundred million trees, or maybe even a billion and a half, and change over from fossil fuels to woodchip energy. Troubled by the leaching of nutrients from forest soils by acid rain? Don't be; just spread some rock dust around. Worried about losing the ecosystem functions of the Ancient Forest? Calm down, your friendly neighborhood tree feller can leave a mess behind after a clear-cut, downed logs and such, which makes it more like a natural catastrophe than a manmade one. Beloved forest trees going extinct on you, old man? Be cool, call a geneticist.

I do not wish to be cynical about the good-hearted people who are trying to save the trees. But I do worry about the decoupling—about not understanding that the system is sick and that while we can rush in with palliatives and first aid here and there, we cannot cure the underlying illness by this means. It surely is the human industrial society that has brought this tree sickness on. But I do not think we can automatically assume that the same genius at organization and technological innovation that produces automobiles with climate control and DNA cow-injections to increase milk production and the Mario Brothers on Nintendo machines to create what advertisers call a better life—that the same genius can use the same tools and techniques and capabilities that have been destroying the planet to make it well.

I love those who plant trees, despite the odds, and those who labor long in field tests and laboratories to develop a way around arboreal mortality. But the facts must be faced, and argued about, and then dealt with frontally, not eluded or suppressed or painted over by breathless good-news press-release optimism. "You are looking into fog," writes Wittgenstein in a self-chiding aphorism that we might well apply to ourselves, "and for that reason persuade yourself that the goal is already close. But the fog disperses and the goal is not yet in sight." We have a problem on this planet that we had better see clearly and not shrink from. Too many trees are dying.

11

On Crossing the Threshold

One planet, one experiment.
—*E. O. Wilson,*
The Diversity of Life

In his famous essay, "The Land Ethic," which is the culmination of *A Sand County Almanac,* published in 1949, Aldo Leopold declared that "no important change of ethics was ever accomplished without an internal change in our intellectual emphasis, affections, and convictions." It was once Leopold's hope, as expressed in an earlier version of this essay, written in the 1930s, that new understandings of ecology and the management of natural resources—in a way that we would now call "sustainable"—might be the "embryo" of a new consciousness that would produce a functioning land ethic. Trained as a forester, Leopold nevertheless looked upon the land with an inclusive view, as a natural ecosystem consisting of soils, waters, plants, animals, and their interactions. Of our treatment of the land ecosystem, he wrote: "We are remodeling the Alhambra with a steamshovel, and we are proud of our yardage."

In the final version of the essay, Leopold stated that the "proof" that the land ethic had not taken hold was that philosophy and religion had not yet heard of it. Implicit in this view, at least as I understand it, is that once those who guide us in our ethical perceptions *do* come to understand the dynamics of ecosystems and the fragility of the planet, why *then* the land ethic can emerge. Actually, it was scarcely twenty years after the publication of *A Sand County Almanac* (and Leopold's death the year before the book came out) before every teacher and preacher in the land with hair longer than the bristles of a toothbrush was proclaiming far and wide about our ethical responsibilities to nature. Should Leopold not have been pleased? The 1960s teach-ins on ecology, and the later outpouring of civic concern about the environment entrained by Earth Day in 1970, seemed so decisively to modify the perceptions of a whole generation that a Yale professor, Charles A. Reich, was constrained to pronounce, in his hopefully titled best-selling book, that we were witnessing nothing less than "the greening of America."

Alas, the facts of the case are now plain. Aldo Leopold, to whom every self-respecting environmentalist repairs when in need of understanding or a good quote, was wrong, as was Charles A. Reich in *The Greening of America.* Despite the blandishments of ethicists, the environmental consequences of corporation-induced "needs," from high-compression engines to cheap paper, have now brought us up to and beyond the point of crisis, with global impacts that would make the muttonchops of George Perkins Marsh—the nineteenth-century "father" of resource conservation—burst into flame. Every minute an acre of rain forest is destroyed. Every twenty minutes a species—a whole species!—is extinguished for eternity on this planet. I can introduce you to scientists who believe that the entire Eastern hardwood forest is dead ecologically, that it can never mend itself aright because of leached-out nutrients from acid deposition and the resultant ecosystem changes. The entire West is a torch waiting to be lit, transferring gigatons of carbon from trees to the atmosphere, changing the albedo—the electromagnetic reflectivity of the earth's surface—so drastically that worldwide weather patterns can be permanently altered. And perhaps already have been altered. There are Forest Service people in Idaho who say that the great American desert may soon curve up north of the Snake River and move well into Canada. Ecologists propose that the sugar maple will soon no longer grow within the borders of the United States. Global warming, at 3°C (5.4°F), will cause in one hundred years a change in climate that in the history of the planet has never taken less than ten thousand years.

One recent summer day, before my wife, Ila, and I moved to New Mexico, I was sitting out on our suburban Maryland front porch in the nice little Victorian village where we lived, talking about this sort of thing with my young cousin Jane, who had brought her new husband to meet us. She turned and looked at me hard. "We worry about all that, you know. The environment. We wonder if we should have children." It occurred to me then, more forcefully than ever before, that, put in these intimate terms, posterity is not some sort of abstract notion any longer, trotted out by environmentalists as it was in Leopold's day. Posterity was staring me in the face right there on the front porch.

What is worse is that I had not told her all of it—not even half of it. And yet I do not suppose for one instant that the information I have collected and presented in this book about the dying of the trees will signify in any important way, any more than the pronunciamentos of thousands of philosophers and theologians signified during the hopeful "greening" days a quarter century ago.

Here is the problem. We read of tree death in Europe and in the tropics, and I am telling you it is happening here in North America. Yet we look out the office window, and what do we see? Trees. In the Northeast, we live in neighborhoods so abundant with trees that fall leaf disposal is a major municipal solid waste problem, now that leaves can no longer be burned at curbside. Even in the arid West there are trees in abundance. The property we recently bought in the high desert of northern New Mexico is covered with piñon pine and juniper, small but healthy and seemingly durable. There are people who drive through West Virginia who are struck by the verdancy of the forest, the preeminence of the trees. Many will tell you that the return of trees after the loggers devastated the upper Middle West is one of the great achievements of American forestry. And in the Pacific Northwest, the "beauty strips" can still work their magic, making a drive through the Cascades an experience of arboreal splendor.

I remember what Joe Aliff told me when we were tramping through the "falling forest" in the Appalachian hollows. To see what is happening, he said, "All you got to do is look." By that he meant something more than having one's eyelids in the open position. He meant *look*. And when you *look*, then you see that the trees are dying. Some years ago, at the onset of middle age, I bought a quiet-running motorcycle called a Kawasaki 400 that seemed then to be of such exotic provenance that I might be the only one in Washington riding such a machine. And yet just a few weeks later, I noted that I was not alone in a throng of thrumming Harleys and snarling Suzukis. In fact, Kawasakis were everywhere as I rode to work at the Library of Congress. I had learned how to *see* them.

The Kawasaki effect now has me in its grip regarding trees. I see a world of dying trees: dying because the trunks have been bored into and the leaves have been stripped by adventitious pests; dying because fungi are girdling their bases and branches and turning their leaves to black corpses; dying because their shrunken roots can no longer absorb enough nutrients and water to keep them alive; dying from the direct effects of too much ozone in the troposphere and not enough in the stratosphere; dying because neighbor trees have been clear-cut, allowing unwonted cold and heat and drying winds into their precincts; dying because of being bathed too often in the sour gases of industry; dying because the weather patterns have changed and they cannot adapt quickly enough to them; dying, in fact, because they are dying.

The more trees die, the more trees will die, in the forlorn formulation of the famed ecologist George Woodwell. Woodwell's point is that climate warming from an increasing greenhouse effect can, in temperate forests especially, speed up the respiration rate of trees to the degree that it will surpass the rate of photosynthesis, so that the tree is no longer a net producer of oxygen, but a net producer of carbon dioxide. "The amount of carbon dioxide that could be injected into the atmosphere," wrote Woodwell and longtime associate Richard Houghton in *Scientific American*, "would depend heavily on the rate of climatic change in the forested zones of the middle and high latitudes. Although it is impossible to make any accurate calculation, an upper limit is given by the amount of carbon in these forested latitudes: approximately 750 billion metric tons, or about the same amount of carbon as there is in the atmosphere currently." Implied by analyses of this sort is, for the vast northern hemisphere forests, a devastating feedback loop in which forest trees, instead of mitigating CO_2 buildup, add to it, in a nightmarish cycle, similar to one suggested in an earlier chapter, whose finale could be a worldwide policy decision to cut down trees in order to protect oxygen supply.

The image is fanciful, of course, but not without a basis in fact. Recent research has demonstrated that forests are more effective in absorbing CO_2 and concomitantly producing oxygen for the benefit of planetary ecosystems (and replenishing the ozone shield) than was earlier thought. According to Jeff Amthour, a colleague of Woodwell's at the Woods Hole Research Center, early estimates on how much CO_2 can be taken up by a typical northern hemisphere woodland have understated the amount significantly; this suggests that these forests have a major role in maintaining the planetary carbon balance. Studies in the Harvard Forest in Massachusetts by chemist Steven C. Wofsy have shown that the carbon absorbed in this forest—with trees between fifty and seventy years old—was one-third greater than the early models of global carbon exchange would have predicted.

As for oxygen itself, a toxic gas, it has been an article of faith (and science) that the oxygen content of the global atmosphere is and ever has been, in modern geological times, a steady 21 percent. Should oxygen content rise above 25 percent in an orgy of photosynthesis, one single lightning strike would consume all the plant life on earth in a nearly instant conflagration. Should it sink below 15 percent, no fire could be started. Study after study has shown that the 21 percent, which is roughly the mean between 15 and 25, holds constant.

Except for a recent study by Ralph F. Keeling and Stephen R. Shertz of the National Center for Atmospheric Research in Boulder, Colorado.

Keeling and Shertz found that not only did the oxygen content change seasonally on an annual basis, which was expected, but that it was changing *interannually,* which was not expected. According to the NCAR scientists, the decrease in oxygen content "is consistent with the global rate of O_2 consumption from the burning of fossil fuels." The changes are quite small, to be sure, and not now serious in view of the abundance of oxygen in the atmosphere; but the data are discomfiting nevertheless.

What does this have to do with trees? The answer is, it has everything to do with trees. As one analyst puts it, "If the NCAR findings are correct, it would mean that the Earth's plants [including, if not especially, trees]—which transform carbon dioxide into oxygen—may be losing their capability to recycle the atmosphere's increasing loads of CO_2."

I did not tell my cousin Jane about the oxygen. She will have to read it here. She will also read here about another nightmare feedback loop. It has to do with what happens on the *other side* of the ozone shield. As we know, chlorofluorocarbons and other chlorine compounds have created a hole in the stratospheric ozone layer over the southern hemisphere, and have dangerously thinned it in the northern hemisphere, leading to the speculation that we are already seeing damage to trees, especially coniferous trees whose leaves (needles) are exposed year-round to destructive ultraviolet rays (UV-B). Since the signing in 1987 by the major industrialized nations of the Montreal Protocol to ban the use of CFCs for air conditioners and aerosol propellants, the general consensus has been that, while the earth will go through a period of higher-than-healthy UV-B bombardment, all will be well eventually. Indeed, Rumen Bojlov of the International Ozone Commission told members of the American Association for the Advancement of Science at their 1994 meeting in San Francisco, "When we reduce chlorine compounds in the next century, the destruction will become less and less—in that way the recovery will proceed. . . . We will have a few more percentage points addition to this destruction, after which it will go down." Such pronouncements have led to a relatively relaxed attitude on the part of U.S. policymakers, as compared to the urgency felt in the 1980s when the Environmental Protection Agency led the charge internationally, and the DuPont corporation set a policy to cease CFC production here before 1995, a year before the protocol's deadline. In 1994, however, the EPA, at the behest of Congressman John D. Dingell, representing the needs of U.S. automakers, asked DuPont *not* to end production, but please keep it going through 1995, since it would cost the auto industry money when, according to the EPA, given the relatively small effect on the ozone layer of just one more year, "it just didn't pay to phase out CFCs."

It is unlikely, but possible, that a continued nonphaseout could eventually send the integrity of the ozone shield past the tipping point in terms of self-repair. The fact of the matter is that the generation of chlorine compounds is only the starting point in the erosion of the ozone shield. In our solipsistic view of the greenhouse effect—wherein greenhouse gases such as carbon dioxide, methane, and, yes, CFCs trap heat in the earth's atmosphere, not allowing it to dissipate in space—we have been concerned about what it's like *inside* the greenhouse. But there is also an effect *outside* of the greenhouse, which is that, as the troposphere down here gets hotter and hotter, the stratosphere up there gets colder and colder.

The appalling datum relating to this condition is that the colder it gets, the easier it is to break down the O_3 molecule. And the more these molecules break down, the more UV-Bs will be delivered to the earth's surface. And the more UV-Bs are delivered to the earth's surface, the more trees will be killed or stunted, and the less photosynthesis will take place, which in turn takes up less of the CO_2 generated by burning fossil fuels, which in turn increases the greenhouse effect, which then makes it colder in the stratosphere, potentiating the further breakdown of the ozone layer. The great fear is that at some point the destruction of O_3 molecules will become automatic, will take place regardless of any change in the rate of chlorine compounds rising from Detroit's air conditioners, among other sources. At some point the cold is cold enough to maintain the destructive feedback loop on its own.

The more trees die, the more trees will die. Could, perhaps, the whole of the global ecosystem go spinning out of control?

The death of forest-associated correlative species strongly suggests extreme ecosystem imbalance. UV-B harms not only trees; now researchers at Oregon State University have found that the frogs living in the forest pools and streamsides of the Cascade Mountains are failing to regenerate. The increased UV-Bs have scrambled the cells of frog roe, which are laid in uncovered shallow water. Indeed, the decline of amphibians of all types has been noted since the 1970s. *Bufo boreas,* the common Western toad, is now absent in over 80 percent of its original range. The toad is the victim of a malfunctioning immune system. In a 1989 international conference on herpetology, researchers when they compared notes discovered that the loss of amphibians was worldwide. *Bufo periglenes,* the golden toad of Costa Rica, which would emerge by the thousands during breeding season, has not been seen since 1988. In Australia, the so-called gastric-brooding frog disappeared in 1980 and is presumed extinct. Another Australian species has also vanished. In Canada, the population of the northern leopard frog, *Rana pipiens,* has crashed, as have the Yosemite toad and the red-legged frog in California. In all, according to Emily Yoffe, writing in *The New York Times Magazine,* of North America's eighty-six species of frogs and toads, nearly a third are in trouble. On a worldwide basis, she writes, "Researchers estimate that one-quarter to one-half of the earth's species could be extinct in the next 30 years. Cut down a forest, drain a wetland, build a shopping center, and the local frog species die. No one puzzles as to why Southern California is virtually barren of most of its native frogs." Perhaps readers will recall University of Colorado biologist Jeffrey Minton's comment to me (Chapter 5) about the amphibian decline in Colorado: "Very clearly, here is a support group for the tree. . . . Did anybody notice that twenty and thirty years before the forests got hit, the frogs and toads disappeared?"

The causes of such declines and extinctions are, as in most ecological tragedies of this sort, hard to identify exactly. But acid rain and global warming are implicated, as well as massive changes in natural forest habitat. And now UV-B is suspected, too, since many of the species in trouble live at high altitudes.

In another example, the migrating woodland songbirds are seen less and less each year, the victims of diminished winter range in the forests of the tropics and of fragmented woodlands in North America. Some twenty-one species are thought to be severely affected in the eastern United States, with overall annual declines ranging from 1 percent for the oven bird to 11.6 percent for the Tennessee warbler. In specific locations the population differences can be dramatic. In one research area near Shelbyville, Illinois, between 1985 and 1989 seven out of thirteen species that had migrated from the tropics had declined by more than 50 percent.

Meanwhile, in European forests (and to a lesser degree in the United States) a mass extinction of mushrooms may be taking place. In research conducted in Holland, Eef Arnolds has found that in test plots the number of viable mushroom species declined from thirty-seven to twelve over a twenty-year period. In England, mycologists report that twenty species are in decline. In general, European researchers believe that the mushroom decline is bound up with the decline of forests from acid rain, excess nitrogen, ozone, and related causes. And on the forest floor in the Middle West, and presumably elsewhere, the earthworms are dying. According to ecologist Orie Loucks, studies of soil invertebrates in parts of Ohio and Indiana subject to air pollution deposition "show a 50 percent decline in the density of invertebrates and a 97 percent decline in the density of earthworms." These data are extraordinary, and have led Loucks (and now many others) to describe the mixed mesophytic as a forest with AIDS—a metaphor that concerns not only trees but all the myriad species that make up a forest ecosystem and keep it operating and functioning in terms of oxygen production and the sequestering of carbon.

In the tropics, the undisturbed forests have also sequestered many less attractive organisms, including the virus that produces AIDS, giving Loucks's metaphor a grisly twist of its own. In one of the finest pieces of science journalism I have ever read, Richard Preston writes (in *The New Yorker*) how nearly the eastern United States missed a viral plague that would have made AIDS seem like a case of the blahs. The agent of destruction was a filovirus, which like the AIDS virus originated in an African rain forest, in this case along the Ebola River in northern Zaire. It was suspected that this virus was accidentally imported, in monkeys, to a biological laboratory near Washington, D.C. In the event, there was a great panic that few knew about, and that ended well—although the outcome might have been altogether different. Unlike AIDS, which is quite difficult to catch, the Ebola virus can be transmitted through the air, so that it could be contracted on a bus or subway, in school, at work, just by being coughed on by a passing stranger. The virus takes two weeks (instead of eight years, as in the case of AIDS) to incubate, at which time a headache, the first symptom, begins. During the next week, the Ebola victim's blood clots, but at the same time there is profuse bleeding from orifices and tears in the skin, which becomes pulpy and insubstantial. The skin, as Preston vividly describes, "becomes speckled with purple hemorrhages called petechiae, and erupts in a maculopapular rash that has been likened to tapioca pudding. Your intestines may fill up completely with blood. Your eyelids bleed. You vomit a black fluid. You may suffer a hemispherical stroke, which paralyzes one whole side of the body and is invariably fatal in a case of Ebola. In the pre-agonal stage of the disease (the endgame), the patient leaks blood containing huge quantities of virus from rips in the skin. In the agonal stage, death comes from hemorrhage and shock."

It takes a week, and you are dead. The virus is 90-percent effective, Preston says. "A human slate wiper." In Zaire, villages wiped out by Ebola are burned, from a distance, with flame-throwers.

How is it that substances so deadly as the Ebola virus—and it is one of many, perhaps hundreds—can move into the human population? Preston: "When an ecosystem suffers degradation, many species die out and a few survivor-species have population explosions. Viruses in a damaged ecosystem come under extreme selective pressure. Viruses are adaptable: they react to change and can mutate fast, and they can jump among species of hosts. As people enter the forest and clear it, viruses come out, carried on their survivor-hosts—rodents, insects, soft ticks—and the viruses meet *homo sapiens*."

In the course of history, at least a third (though the figure is more often put at one-half) of the planet's forests have been destroyed. Today the destruction continues apace, from cutting, from pollution, from ultraviolet rays, from adventitious pests and diseases. What is to become of us now? Have we not crossed the threshold? Are we not dealing with nature in another zone? The endgame?

E. O. Wilson, the famed Harvard entomologist, asks, in the headline of a 1993 article in *The New York Times Magazine*, IS HUMANITY SUICIDAL? Suicide is, according to Wittgenstein, whom I have quoted earlier, "the elementary sin," arrived at by this logic: "If suicide is allowed, then everything is allowed." The global population, now 5.6 billion, is expected to double within the next fifty years, and at that level can, without stretching the point, be described as suicidal. As physicist James Lovelock has written, "If there were only 500 million people on Earth, almost nothing that we are now doing to the environment would disturb Gaia." But there is no chance of this, is there? Unless, of course, Ebola or some other virus wipes the slate clean, or nearly so. Wilson says, "The human species is, in a word, an environmental abnormality. It is possible that intelligence in the wrong kind of species was foreordained to be a fatal combination for the biosphere. Perhaps a law of evolution is that intelligence usually extinguishes itself." Lovelock says, "The maladies of Gaia do not last long in terms of her life span. Anything that makes the world uncomfortable to live in tends to induce the evolution of those species that can achieve a new and more comfortable environment. It follows that, if the world is made unfit by what we do, there is the probability of a change in regime to one that will be better for life but not necessarily better for us."

At ten a.m., Wednesday, November 18, 1992, the Union of Concerned Scientists, an international body of renowned academicians and heads of scientific agencies of governments, issued a statement entitled

"The World Scientists' Warning to Humanity." The statement noted that the signers of this declaration included 99 out of 196 living Nobelists. Wrote Henry Kendall, chairman of the Union of Concerned Scientists and himself a Nobel laureate, "This kind of consensus is truly unprecedented. There is an exceptional degree of agreement within the international scientific community that natural systems can no longer absorb the burden of current human practices. The depth and breadth of authoritative support for the Warning should give great pause to those who question the validity of threats to our environment."

The essence of the warning is this: "No more than one or a few decades remain before the chance to avert the threats we now confront will be lost and the prospects for humanity immeasurably diminished." And at the end of the statement they echo Aldo Leopold:

> A new ethic is required—a new attitude toward discharging our responsibility for caring for ourselves and for the earth. We must recognize the earth's limited capacity to provide for us. We must recognize its fragility. We must no longer allow it to be ravaged. This ethic must motivate a great movement, convincing reluctant leaders and reluctant governments and reluctant peoples themselves to effect the needed changes.

The silence after the issuance of this plea was profound. We have, you understand, remodeled the Alhambra with our steamshovels; and we are proud of our yardage.

A hand will be raised at the back of the room. "But what can we *do*?" the petitioner will ask. Do? What can we do? What a question that is when we scarcely understand what we have already done!

Plant trees? Yes, of course, plant billions, as Neil Sampson has instructed. But can we reforest the earth in such a way that it will stay reforested?

Reduce the pollution caused by gluttonous fossil-fuel energy use? Yes, of course. But not to the level of 1990, as the policymakers suggest and have legislated. Trees were dying long before that. Wouldn't the mid-fifties be closer to the mark, when the X-disease was discovered in

California pines and when the heavy metals entered the tissue of Vermont maples?

Stop the cutting of forests? Yes, of course. Zero cut on our national forests is a tiny beginning. Stopping the pillage of the rain forest is a given. But have too many atoms of carbon and too many species of virus already been unsequestered?

End the release of CFCs? Without question. But have the chlorine atoms that have already risen to the stratosphere entrained an unstoppable feedback reaction that will cause an increasing ultraviolet bombardment of trees and forests and frogs and us no matter what we do?

Control population? Absolutely. "New studies suggest," reports *The New York Times*, "that a country like Bangladesh can cut its birth rate significantly if it aggressively promotes the adoption of contraceptive methods." But would it not take a great deal more than this to return to James Lovelock's threshold five hundred million in world population? Or even ten times that many?

Environmentalism practices the language of crisis: to insist that something be done before it is too late. Even the Union of Concerned Scientists spoke to us in this way. But what we need now is a language, and the intellectual constructs that go with it, to deal with a *post*crisis environmental condition. And our response to the dying of the trees is central to this enterprise.

What my cousin Jane expressed to me on the front porch in Maryland was what I have come to call "environmental despair." I have heard it in different ways from many of her generation. When I was discussing environmental despair with my younger daughter, Katharine, a geologist who works to clean up the ghastly radioactive mess of a former bomb factory in Ohio, she acknowledged its presence, saying: "Well, no one really expects the human race to last forever, do they?" The wisdom of the young existentialist, too world-weary for her years. And my granddaughter, Julia, her mother (Dorothy, my older daughter) tells me, worries constantly about the environment; sometimes is sick with worry. She is twelve.

I have seen despair in the faces of scientists, too. I hope he will forgive me for this, but I have witnessed the energy drain out of Orie Loucks's eyes sometimes when he tells me what is happening to the Eastern forest. And I am least of all immune, having suffered an unwonted string of illnesses during the writing of this book that are so atypical that I must ascribe them, at least in part, to psychological causes. Despair.

I have learned things I wish I had not learned.

I have learned that the trees are dying. And that the more trees die, the more will die.

I have learned that we have crossed the threshold. And I simply do not know how we can get back safely to the other side.

William Wordsworth wrote, in *Tintern Abbey:*

> *. . . this prayer I make,*
> *Knowing that Nature never did betray*
> *The heart that loved her; 'tis her privilege,*
> *Through all the years of this our life, to lead*
> *From joy to joy: for she can so inform*
> *The mind that is within us, so impress*
> *With quietness and beauty, and so feed*
> *With lofty thought, that neither evil tongues,*
> *Rash judgments, nor the sneers of selfish men,*
> *Nor greetings where no kindness is, nor all*
> *The dreary intercourse of daily life,*
> *Shall e'er prevail against us, or disturb*
> *Our chearful faith that all which we behold*
> *Is full of blessings.*

That, I think, is the only antidote to despair: to stay firm in the belief that nature never did betray the heart that loved her.

And now we must love her as we have never been asked to love before. That is the crux of the matter: The trees could save us, if we would save the trees, for they *are* the threshold.

So might we *begin* a process—requiring at least a century, though likely more—of environmental repair, of letting nature heal herself. But I must tell you, Cousin Jane, it's going to be a bumpy ride.

NOTES

CHAPTER 1: IN THIS SIGN

page 2, "Stepping delicately": Donald Culross Peattie, *A Natural History of Trees of Eastern and Central North America* (Boston: Houghton Mifflin, 1950; Riverside ed., 1991), pp. 503–504. For tree lore as well as scientific data, I have leaned heavily on this wonderful book, in this chapter and others, and on its companion volume, *A Natural History of Western Trees.* The Peattie books, now in paperback, should be owned by anyone with even a passing interest in North American trees and forests.

page 3, 79 percent dead: Manfred Mielke and Keith Langdon, "Dogwood Anthracnose Fungus Threatens Catoctin Mt. Park," *Park Science* 6, no. 2 (winter 1986): 6–8; also an unpublished paper presumably written by Mielke and Langdon, and provided to me by James L. Sherald of the National Park Service, which updates this article to 1988.

page 6, first published account: Ralph S. Byther and Roy H. Davidson, "Dogwood Anthracnose," *Ornamentals Northwest Newsletter,* March–April 1979, pp. 20–21. These investigators subsequently published two-page updates in July 1979, October 1981, June 1984, and October 1986 (Pullman, Washington: Extension Bulletin 0972, Washington State University, Cooperative Extension Service).

page 7, "The dogwood trees are in trouble": P. P. Pirone, "Parasitic Fungus Affects Region's Dogwoods," *New York Times*, 24 February 1980, section 2, pp. 34, 37.

page 7, *Discula* identified as cause of anthracnose: C. R. Hibben and M. L. Daughtrey, "Dogwood Anthracnose in the United States," *Plant Diseases* 72 (1988): 199–203; M. L. Daughtrey, C. R. Hibben, and G. W. Hudler, "Cause and Control of Dogwood Anthracnose in Northeastern United States," *Journal of Arboriculture* 14 (1988): 159–164; D. S. Salogga and J. F. Ammirati, "*Discula* Species Associated with Anthracnose of Dogwood in the Pacific Northwest," *Plant Diseases* 67 (1983): 1290.

pages 7–8, signs and symptoms of dogwood anthracnose: Anne Bird Sindermann, Robert Rabaglia, and Ethel Dutky, *Discula Anthracnose of Flowering Dogwood*, a brochure (Maryland Dept. of Agriculture and University of Maryland, 1990); Manfred E. Mielke and Margery L. Daughtrey, "How to Identify and Control Dogwood Anthracnose," U.S. Forest Service (NA-GR-18), 1989.

page 9, land of optimists: for example, "Don't Give Up on Dogwoods," *Southern Living*, April 1991, pp. 76–77; Wallace Kaufman, "New Light on Dogwood Blight," *American Forests*, November–December, 1989, pp. 47–49, 76; Elwood E. Fisher, "Distressed Dogwoods—Doomed to Die?" *Harrisonburg* (Va.) *Daily News Record*, 3 September 1991, p. 12.

page 10, "probably little hope": F. S. Santamour, Jr., A. J. McArdle, and P. V. Strider, "Susceptibility of Flowering Dogwood of Various Provenances to Dogwood Anthracnose," *Plant Diseases* 73 (1989): 590–591.

page 10, "no reliable antidote": Charles Fenyvesi, "Go for the Gold—or Red," *Washington Post, Home* magazine, 25 October 1990, p. 23.

page 11, *Discula destructiva* Redlin: Scott C. Redlin, "*Discula Destructiva Sp. Nov.*, Cause of Dogwood Anthracnose," *Mycologia* 83, no. 5 (1991): 633–642.

page 13, rate of infection increased by acid rain: Robert L. Anderson, Paul C. Berrang, and John L. Knighton, "Correlation Between Simulated Acid Rain and Dogwood Anthracnose in the Greenhouse" (paper for meeting of the Dogwood Anthracnose Work Group, Athens, Ga., January 1991).

page 14, forest reduced to rubble: National Park Service, *Catoctin Mountains*, brochure, n.d.

page 14, "I can lime it": Arthur A. Schlesinger, Jr., *The Coming of the New Deal* (Boston: Houghton Mifflin, 1959), pp. 335–336.

page 16, Appalachian folk legend: My source is a funeral home booklet (Kirksey Funeral Home, Morganton, N.C.) that is devoid of any indication of the origin of this folk tale.

CHAPTER 2: VIGIL AT CAMEL'S HUMP

page 18, Vermont history: Charles T. Morrissey, *Vermont: A History* (New York: W. W. Norton; Nashville: Association for State and Local History, 1981), pp. 36–100, passim.

pages 20–21, tree death data: Hubert W. Vogelmann et al., "A 21-Year Record of Forest Decline on Camel's Hump, Vermont, USA," *European Journal of Forest Pathology* 18 (1988): 24–29.

page 21, "gray skeletons of trees": H. W. Vogelmann, "Catastrophe on Camel's Hump," *Natural History* 91 (1982): 8–14.

page 22, "The common excuse": H. W. Vogelmann, "Should We Wait for Proof to Know When It's Raining?" *Journal of Forestry* 80 (August 1982): 8.

page 22, "overmaturity": Robert A. Mello, *Last Stand of the Red Spruce* (Washington, D.C.: Natural Resources Defense Council/Island Press, 1987), p. 27.

page 23, 1950 shift in rainfall acidity: Mello, p. 29.

page 24, "They didn't believe me": from personal notes taken by John Flynn of the *Detroit Free Press* in an interview while Dr. Ulrich was lecturing in Canada. Quotation courtesy of Mr. Flynn.

page 24, "With the discovery of *Waldsterben*": F. H. Bormann and G. E. Likens, "Changing Perspectives on Air Pollution Stress," *Bioscience* 37 (1987): 370.

page 25, "Tree ring analyses": Richard M. Klein and Timothy D. Perkins, "Long-Term Fates of Declining Forests," in Dunnette and O'Brien, eds., *The Science of Global Change: Impact of Human Activities on the Environment* (Washington, D.C.: American Chemical Society, 1992), p. 361. This is as good a brief article on the mechanisms of pollution deposition on high-elevation coniferous forests as I have come across. Offprints may be available from the Forest Decline Program, Botany Dept., University of Vermont, Burlington, VT 05405.

page 26, results of aluminum absorption: drawn from a discussion with Edward Whereat, Botany Dept., University of Maryland.

page 26, no mycorrhizal fungi: Mello, pp. 77–78.

page 27, "complex cascade of causes": Klein and Perkins, p. 369.

page 27, "In the past five years": John D. Aber et al., "Nitrogen Saturation in Northern Forest Ecosystems," *Bioscience* 39 (1989): 378–386.

page 28, "Nitrogen-saturated forests": Aber, p. 385.

page 29, "operational flexibility": Editors of *Buzzworm* magazine, *1992 Earth Journal: Environmental Almanac and Resource Directory* (Boulder, Colo.: Buzzworm Books, 1991), p. 56.

page 30, roundup paper of nonpollution causes of tree death: Arthur H. Johnson and Thomas G. Siccama, "Decline of the Red Spruce in the High Elevation Forests of the Northeastern United States," in James J. MacKenzie and Mohamed T. El-Ashry, eds., *Air Pollution's Toll on Forests and Crops* (New Haven: Yale University Press, 1989), pp. 154–159.

page 31, Ninety-three percent healthy: Robert T. Brooks et al., *Summary Report: Forest Health Monitoring: New England* (U.S. Forest Service, 1991), p. 9.

page 31, "The best of science": Edward O. Wilson, *The Diversity of Life* (Cambridge, Mass.: Harvard University Press, 1992), p. 5.

page 32, latest findings from Camel's Hump: Klein and Perkins, pp. 361–364.

page 35, a sadness pervading Vermont: Morrisey, p. 24.

CHAPTER 3: ON TOP OF MOUNT MITCHELL

page 39, "At the three intensive sites": U.S. Forest Service, *Spruce-Fir Research Cooperative: Research Highlights* (Radnor, Pa.: U.S. Forest Service Northeastern Forest Experiment Station, 1989), n.p.

page 39, "Along ridges": R. I. Bruck and W. P. Robarge, "Change in Forest Structure in the Boreal Montane Ecosystem of Mount Mitchell, North Carolina," *European Journal of Forest Pathology* 18 (1988): 357.

page 40, "the high rate of red spruce mortality": Joseph E. Barnard et al., *NAPAP Report 16: Changes in Forest Health and Productivity in the United States and Canada, Acid Deposition: State of Science and Technology* (Washington, D.C.: U.S. Govt. Printing Office, 1990), p. 126.

page 41, "The data does not support": Philip Shabecoff, "Acid Rain Report Unleashes a Torrent of Criticism," *New York Times*, 20 March 1990, p. C4.

page 44, Karl Popper discussion: From Bernhard Ulrich, the dean of German acid-rain scientists, in "An Ecosystem-Oriented Hypothesis on the Effect of Air Pollution on Forest Ecosystems," in National Swedish Environmental Protection Board, *Ecological Effects of Acid Deposition* (Stockholm: 1984), pp. 221–222.

page 45, "Beyond all reasonable doubt": D. A. Godbold and A. Hütterman, "The Uptake and Toxicity of Mercury and Lead to Spruce (*Picea Abies* Karst.) Seedlings," *Water, Air, and Soil Pollution* 31 (1986): 509.

page 45, "new types of forest damage": Otto Kandler, "Epidemiological Evaluation of the Development of Waldsterben in Germany," *Plant Diseases* 74 (1990): 4.

page 46, "scientifically unprecedented changes": Ellis B. Cowling, "What's Happening to Germany's Forests?" *Environmental Forum*, May 1884, pp. 7–9.

page 46, another survey: Janet Raloff, "Where Acids Reign: Do Dying Stands of Bavarian Timber Portend the Future of Polluted U.S. Forests?" *Science News*, 22 July 1989, p. 56.

page 48, acid fog on Mount Mitchell for up to seventy days a year: David Shriner et al., *NAPAP Report 18: Response of Vegetation to Atmospheric Deposition and Air Pollution* (Washington, D.C.: U.S. Govt. Printing Office, 1990), p. 38.

page 48, Ducktown, Tenn.: Wilton Barnhardt, "The Death of Ducktown," *Discover*, October 1987, pp. 36–37.

page 49, "Ninety-percent certain": Philip Shabecoff, "Deadly Combination Felling Trees in the East," *New York Times*, 24 July 1988, p. 1.

page 52, "Because of the current political environment": Arthur H. Johnson and Thomas G. Siccama, "Decline of Red Spruce in the High-Elevation Forests of the Northeastern United States," in James J. MacKenzie and Mohamed T. El-Ashry, eds., *Air Pollution's Toll on Forests and Crops* (New Haven: Yale University Press, 1989), pp. 193–194.

page 53, "Available data show": G. D. Hertel et al., "The Effects of Acidic Deposition and Ozone on Forest Tree Species in the Eastern United States:

Results from the Forest Response Program" (conference paper, June 1991), p. 16. Manuscript supplied to the author by Dr. Hertel.

CHAPTER 4: THE CALIFORNIA X-DISEASE

page 58, "The foliage deterioration": James E. Asher, "Observation and Theory on 'X' Disease or Needle Dieback" (photocopied paper, Arrowhead Ranger District, San Bernardino National Forest, 1956), p. 1.

page 60, Paul Miller's earliest studies of ozone damage: Fields W. Cobb, Jr., and R. W. Stark, "Decline and Mortality of Smog-Injured Ponderosa Pine," *Journal of Forestry*, March 1970, pp. 147–149.

page 60, Miller's definitive study, 1973–1978: Paul R. Miller, "Concept of Forest Decline in Relation to Western U.S. Forests," in James J. MacKenzie and Mohamed T. El-Ashry, eds., *Air Pollution's Toll on Forests and Crops* (New Haven: Yale University Press, 1989), pp. 86–87ff.

page 62, regeneration of stratospheric ozone: Sagar V. Krupa and William J. Manning, "Atmospheric Ozone: Formation and Effects on Vegetation," *Environmental Pollution* 50 (1988): 114.

page 63, trees as polluters: Sam Atwood, "Trees Climb List of Southern California's Air Polluters," *Burlington Free Press*, 25 July 1991; photocopy.

page 63, Atlanta trees: "Leaves of Gas," *Discover*, February 1989, p. 20.

page 65, "The Tehachapie Mountains": Thomas A. Pittenger, *On the Air! Sequoia and Kings Canyon National Parks* (brochure, National Park Service and California Air Resources Board), n.d., n.p.

page 65, pollution at high altitude: data from Dan Duriscoe, personal communication to the author, 7 November 1992.

page 67, hourly ozone concentrations: Steve Nash and Mike Spear, "Ghost Forest," *National Parks*, March–April 1991, p. 20.

page 68, "cruise survey": Daniel M. Duriscoe and Kenneth W. Stolte, "Photochemical Oxidant Injury to Ponderosa Pine (*Pinus ponderosa* Laws.) and Jeffrey Pine (*Pinus jeffreyi* Grev. and Balf.) in the National Parks of the Sierra Nevada of California," in R. K. Olson and A. Lefohn, eds., *Effects of Air Pollution on Western Forests* (Pittsburgh: Air and Waste Management Association, 1989), pp. 261–267.

page 68, growth reductions in ponderosa pines: David L. Peterson et al., "Regional Growth Changes in Ozone-Stressed Ponderosa Pine (*Pinus ponderosa*) in the Sierra Nevada, California, USA," *The Holocene* 1 (1991): 58.

page 69, growth reductions in Jeffrey pine: David L. Peterson, et al., "Evidence of Growth Reduction in Ozone Injured Jeffrey Pine (*Pinus jeffreyi* Grev. and Balf.) in Sequoia and Kings Canyon National Parks," *Journal of the American Pollution Control Association* 37 (1987): 910–911.

page 71, "As a result of other states": Matthew L. Wald, "California's Pied Piper of Clean Air," *New York Times*, 13 September 1992, section 3, pp. 1, 6.

page 72, big three automakers: Oscar Sims, "Big Three Discuss a Joint Crusade Against California's Electric-Car Rule," *The Wall Street Journal*, 25 October 1993, p. A4.

page 74, "bioindicator": Krupa and Manning, pp. 114, 119–120.

page 74, "Earth's Largest Living Things": National Park Service, *Sequoia and Kings Canyon Official Map and Guide*, n.d., n.p.

page 74, coast redwood as tallest tree: Donald Culross Peattie, *A Natural History of Western Trees* (Boston: Houghton Mifflin, 1950; Riverside ed., 1991), p. 15.

page 74, "every second look at the crowns": Peter Schütt and Ulla Lang, "The 'Waldsterben' Reaches the New World," unpublished paper trans. by André Blum, Student der Forstwissenschaft, Albert-Ludwigs Universität, Freiburg, West Germany, n.d., pp. 1, 7.

page 76, ozone effects on redwood seedling tissue: Lance S. Evans and Michael R. Leonard, "Histological Determination of Ozone Injury Symptoms of Primary Needles of Giant Sequoia (*Sequoiadendron giganticum* Bucch.)," *New Phytologist* 117 (1991): 557–564.

CHAPTER 5: THE FIRE NEXT TIME

page 80, Forest Service literature referred to by Averill: R. L. Furniss and V. M. Carolin, *Western Forest Insects* (Washington, D.C.: U.S. Govt. Printing Office, 1977), pp. 357–359.

page 82, comparison of photographs: Thomas T. Veblen and Diane C. Lorenz, *The Colorado Front Range: A Century of Ecological Change* (Salt Lake City: University of Utah Press, 1991), pp. 29–32.

page 83, synchronicity in beetle outbreaks: Thomas W. Swetnam and Ann M. Lynch, "A Tree-Ring Reconstruction of Western Budworm History in the Southern Rocky Mountains," *Forest Science* 35 (December 1989): 977.

page 84, "A vicious, self-perpetuating cycle": Timothy Ingalsbee, "Learning to Burn: The New Fire Agenda," *Inner Voice* (Association of Forest Service Employees for Environmental Ethics), March–April 1992, p. 6.

page 84, change in Oregon forests: Johnstone Quinan and Dave Cook, "The Drastic Decline of a Forest Ecosystem," *American Forests*, September–October 1992, p. 35.

page 84, 53 percent of trees dead: U.S. Forest Service, *Blue Mountains Forest Health Report* (U.S. Forest Service Pacific Northwest Region, 1991), p. II–3.

page 84, "There is a growing concern": *Blue Mountains Forest Health Report*, p. i.

page 85, "There is relatively little ponderosa": Quinan and Cook, p. 35.

page 85, forest fires north of the Snake River of Idaho: U.S. Forest Service, "Boise National Forest: Forest Health Indicators," chart (n.d.) supplied by R. Neil Sampson of American Forests.

page 86, "in areas where the ground": R. Neil Sampson, "On the Fireline," *Resource Hotline* (an American Forests newsletter), 3 August 1994, p. 4.

page 86, "Everything about the fires": Stephen J. Pyne, "The Summer We Let Wild Fire Loose," *Natural History* 88 (August 1989): 45.

page 87, wartime fire history: Thomas Cox et al., *This Well-Wooded Land* (Lincoln: University of Nebraska Press, 1985), p. 239.

page 87, comparison of wildfire statistics: U.S. Forest Service, *1984–1990 Wildfire Statistics* (Washington, D.C.: 1992), n.p., 1988 table 1A.

page 88, "Careless Matches Aid the Axis": Ellen Earnhardt Morrison, *Guardian of the Forest: A History of the Smokey Bear Program* (Alexandria, Va.: Morielle Press, 1989), p. 7.

page 88, "Only You Can Prevent Forest Fires": Morrison, p. 10.

page 88, citizen organizations using bear image: Information and documentation supplied by Father Albert Fritsch, director of Appalachia Science in the

Public Interest, which in 1992 sought to persuade the U.S. Forest Service to halt clear-cutting in Daniel Boone National Forest (Kentucky). ASPI distributed a photocopied flyer with a figure of Smokey holding a sign reading, "Only *You* Can Stop the Forest Service." A Forest Service lawyer wrote the group a warning letter implying (though not directly threatening) dire consequences for this act.

page 90, Overriding concern with "mass fire": Stephen J. Pyne, "Fire Policy and Fire Research in the U.S. Forest Service," *Journal of Forest History* 25 (April 1981): 67–73.

page 90, number of fires cut in half: Cox, p. 239.

page 90, ten-year period: Pyne, "Fire Policy and Fire Research," p. 76.

page 91, "When the forty-niners": Eldon G. Bowman, "Has Smokey Bear Outlived His Usefulness?" *American Forests*, November 1968, p. 56.

page 91, "public opinion and expectations": Bowman, p. 13.

page 91, "To a bear who has been a hero": Morrison, p. 118.

page 92, "Wildland fire is not a precision instrument": Pyne, "The Summer We Let Wild Fire Loose," p. 46.

page 93, "It is well known": Stephen H. Schneider, *Global Warming* (New York: Vintage Books, 1990), p. 304.

page 93, consensus on global warming: Schneider, p. 13.

page 93, rate of increase: Robert C. Musselman and Douglas G. Fox, "A Review of the Role of Temperate Forests in the Global CO_2 Balance," *Journal of the Air and Waste Management Association* 41 (June 1991): 798.

page 94, "OMB marked up": David Goeller, *Environmental Action*, November–December, 1989, pp. 24–25.

page 95, "a misleading debate": Schneider, pp. 286–296.

page 96, 43 percent annual increase in carbon dioxide: Richard Hill, "Global Warming Could Destroy Forests," *Portland Oregonian*, 17 February 1992, p. 66.

page 97, "Each 1°C warming": Musselman and Fox, p. 801.

page 98, "During the transition": Schneider, p. 181.

page 100, "callous as an undertaker": Aldo Leopold, *A Sand County Almanac* (New York: Oxford University Press, 1949; paperback ed., 1968), p. 174.

CHAPTER 6: PATH OF THE GYPSY ROVER

page 101, historical context: drawn from Charles E. Little, *Cyclopaedia of Classified Dates* (New York: Funk & Wagnalls, 1900), pp. 266–269. (The compiler is the author's great-grandfather.)

page 102, misplaced gypsy-moth eggs: Thomas R. Dunlap, "The Gypsy Moth: A Study in Science and Public Policy," *Journal of Forest History* 24 (July 1980): 116.

pages 102–3, biology of the gypsy moth: drawn from Whiteford L. Baker, *Eastern Forest Insects* (Washington, D.C.: U.S. Govt. Printing Office, 1972), pp. 320–324; Cooperative Extension Service and Dept. of Entomology, Michigan State University, and Michigan Dept. of Agriculture, *Gypsy Moth in Michigan: Homeowner's Guide* (Lansing, Mich., 1991), pp. 1, 3; and Paula Ford, "At War with the Gypsy Moth," *Country Journal*, May–June 1990, pp. 46–47.

page 103, homeowners' reports: "A Plague of Pests: Lessons from the Gypsy Moth War," *Environmental Action*, November–December 1989, p. 27.

page 103, "There was not a place": Donald Dale Jackson, "Gypsy Invaders Seize New Ground in the War Against Our Trees," *Smithsonian*, May 1989, p. 50.

page 104, ever-widening circles: Jackson, p. 52.

page 104, early history of the spread of the gypsy moth: drawn from Dunlap, pp. 118–124.

page 106, DDT: Rachel Carson, *Silent Spring* (Boston: Houghton Mifflin, 1962), pp. 20–23.

page 107, "The gypsy moth programs": Carson, pp. 160–161.

page 110, rate-of-spread predictive model: Andrew Leibold et al., "Landscape Ecology of Gypsy Moth in the Northeastern United States," in Kurt W. Gottschalk et al., eds., *Proceedings U.S. Department of Agriculture Interagency Gypsy Moth Research Review 1990* (Radnor, Pa.: U.S. Forest Service Northeastern Forest Experiment Station, 1991), p. 113.

page 110, height and weight of Paul Bunyan: James Stevens, in Harold W. Felton, ed., *The Legends of Paul Bunyan* (New York: Alfred A. Knopf, 1955), p. 34; and the thirty-one trees: James Cloyd Bowman, in Felton, pp. 36–38.

page 110, "The unsigned tale": Mary Jane Hennigar, ed., "The First Paul Bunyan Story in Print," *Journal of Forest History* 30 (October 1986): 175–181. The story itself was ferreted out by Daniel Hoffman, author of *Paul Bunyan, Last of the Frontier Demigods* (Lincoln: University of Nebraska Press, 1983 [1952]).

page 111, "We'd placed our camp": James MacGillivray, in Felton, p. 335.

page 111, "It was Round River": Hennigar, p. 179.

page 111, "When the timber crew descended": John Eastman, "The Ghost Forest," *Natural History*, January 1986, p. 13.

page 111, "The white and red pine": Eastman, p. 12.

page 112, "No living person": Eastman, pp. 10–12.

page 114, description of insecticides: "A Plague of Pests: Lessons from the Gypsy Moth War," pp. 29–30.

page 115, cause of gypsy-moth "wilt": Robert Emmett Ginna, Jr., "Waging War on the Tree-Eaters," *Yankee*, May 1990, p. 60.

page 116, "Good news": Joan Lee Faust, "Around the Garden," *New York Times*, 4 August 1989, p. D-3.

page 117, examination of new fungus: Faust, p. D-3.

page 117, "Caterpillars from all over": Ann E. Hajek, "Enter the Fungal Factor," *Natural History*, June 1991, p. 42.

page 117, The kill was 85 percent: "Killer Japanese Fungus Curbs Big Appetite of Leaf-Eating Bugs," *Research and Development*, November 1990, p. 154.

page 118, "In a dry year": "Fungus Routs Gypsy Moth Outbreak," *Science News*, 4 August 1990, p. 77.

page 119, "The Asian female": Ann Gibbons, "Asian Gypsy Moth Jumps Ship to the United States": *Science*, 31 January 1992, p. 526.

page 120, plant species preferred by AGM: Gibbons, p. 526.

page 120, "The Asian gypsy moth": "Northwest Girds for Gypsy Moth Battle," *Harrisonburg Daily News-Record*, 25 November 1991; photocopy.

page 120, localities where AGM introduced: California Forest Pest Council, *Forest Pest Conditions in California—1991*, draft report prepared for U.S. Forest Service, 20 November 1991, p. 11.

page 120, "The U.S. Department of Agriculture": Don Richardson, "$15.2 Million to Come from USDA for Asian Moth War," Salem, Oregon, *Capital Press*, 20 March 1992, pp. 1–2.

page 121, "entomologists fear": Gibbons, p. 526.

CHAPTER 7: A HISTORY ONLY OF DEPARTED THINGS

page 125, "oak openings": George Perkins Marsh, *Man and Nature, Or Physical Geography as Modified by Human Action* (1864; Cambridge, Mass.: Harvard University Press, 1965), p. 120.

page 125, a form of redemption: Michael Williams, *Americans and Their Forests: A Historical Geography* (Cambridge: Cambridge University Press, 1989), p. 12.

page 126, "What could they see": Alfred Kazin, *A Writer's America* (New York: Knopf, 1988), p. 19.

page 126, "Proceeding on our return": Kazin, p. 23.

page 127, Romantic poets: Kazin, p. 23.

page 127, "Paradise, and groves": William Wordsworth, from Prologue to *The Excursion* (1815 ed.).

page 127, "The European community": T. H. Watkins, "The Travels of Turner," introduction to Frederick Turner, *Beyond Geography: The Western Spirit Against the Wilderness* (New Brunswick, N.J.: Rutgers University Press, 1992), p. xxiii.

page 128, "The amount of forests lost": John Perlin, *A Forest Journey* (New York: Norton, 1989), p. 256.

page 129, disquieting research: David Cameron Duffy and Albert J. Meier, "Do Appalachian Herbaceous Understories Ever Recover From Clearcutting?" *Conservation Biology*, June 1992, pp. 196–201.

page 131, After the eastern forests had been leveled: Thomas R. Cox et al., *This Well-Wooded Land* (Lincoln: University of Nebraska Press, 1985), pp. 51–73, passim.

page 132, definition of "old growth": Elliott A. Norse, *Ancient Forests of the Northwest* (Washington, D.C.: The Wilderness Society and Island Press, 1990), p. 7.

page 132, "the classic coniferous forest": Norse, p. 18.

page 133, felling of coastal and riverine forests: David Kelly, *Secrets of the Old Growth Forest* (Salt Lake City: Gibbs Smith, 1988), p. 9ff.

page 133, two-thirds of the forest still unlogged: H. Michael Anderson and Jeffrey T. Olson, *Federal Forests and the Economic Base of the Pacific Northwest* (Washington, D.C.: The Wilderness Society, 1991), pp. 14–15.

page 133, clear-cuts close together: Ted Williams, "Big Timber, the U.S. Forest Service and the Rape of the Northwest," *Forest Voice*, March 1990, p. 7.

page 134, a strange, fortuitous climate: Norse, p. 19.

page 134, "A nearly ideal coincidence": Norse, p. 19.

page 134, plantation trees only a tenth as valuable: Kelly, p. 15.

page 135, "add a foot of girth": Norse, p. 31.

page 135, 1,500 invertebrate species: Kelly, p. 10.

page 135, needles "comb" the heavy fogs: Jerry Franklin, "Toward a New Forestry," *American Forests*, November–December 1989, p. 40.

page 135, highest level of terrestrial biodiversity: Anderson and Olson, p. 13.

page 135, "nurse logs": Norse, p. 51.

page 136, "If my granddaddy": Brenda Peterson, "Killing Our Elders," in Peter Sauer, ed., *Finding Home* (Boston: Beacon Press, 1992), p. 59.

page 136, snags can remain standing: Norse, p. 48.

page 137, most nurturing effect: Des Kennedy, referring to comments by ecologists Jerry Franklin and Miles Hemstrom, in "Death of a Giant," *Nature Canada*, Spring 1991, p. 20.

page 137, "By treating 500- to 1,000-year-old trees": Norse, p. xx.

page 138, "a fecal pellet": Chris Maser, *The Redesigned Forest* (San Pedro, Calif.: R. and E. Miles, 1988), p. 36.

page 138, mycorrhizal fungi: Chris Maser, *Forest Primeval: The Natural History of an Ancient Forest* (San Francisco: Sierra Club Books, 1989), p. 18. Also Kelly, pp. 31–32.

page 139, "once the host species": Franklin, p. 41.

page 139, "It is these fungi": Kelly, p. 32.

page 140, 48 percent . . . 81 percent: Norse, p. 169.

page 140, "The climate in a clearcut": Norse, p. 239.

pages 140–41, "since temperature, humidity, and wind": Franklin, p. 42.

page 141, "Because of edge effects": Norse, p. 249.

page 141, "young growth" forest: Maser, *The Redesigned Forest*, p. 19.

page 141, 350 metric tons: Kelly, p. 63.

page 141, fallen logs 265 tons per acre: Chris Maser and James M. Trappe, quoted by Kelly, p. 44.

page 142, "If climatic change": Norse, p. 143.

page 143: "confusing landscape": Jeffrey St. Clair, "Any Way You Cut It," *Wild Forest Review*, March 1994, p. 12. This modest journal, edited by St. Clair, has consistently provided the most thoughtful analysis of the old-growth issue.

CHAPTER 8: LUCY'S WOODS

page 146, corporate ownership of West Virginia: David Liden, quoted in "Poverty and the Wealth of the Land," *American Land Forum*, Spring 1985, p. 19.

page 147, "Many of the trees": John Flynn, "Mixed Mesophytic: World's Best," *Beckley Register-Herald*, 6 October 1991. Reprinted in John Flynn, ed., *The Falling Forest* (Oxford, Ohio: Lucy Braun Association, 1992), p. 13.

page 150, "moonshine manners": "The Sisters Braun: Uncommon Dedication," *CMNH Quarterly*, spring 1988, p. 11.

page 151, "all of the Cumberland Mountains": E. Lucy Braun, *Deciduous Forests of Eastern North America* (Philadelphia: Blakiston, 1950), p. 39.

page 151, "luxuriant tropical selva": Braun, p. 42.

page 151, canopy trees: Braun, pp. 40–41.

page 152, coverage of American chestnut: Braun, p. 77.

page 154, shipmast locust variety: Oran Raber, *Shipmast Locust, A Valuable Undescribed Variety of Robinia Pseudoacacia*, Circular 379 (Washington, D.C.: U.S. Dept. of Agriculture, 1936), pp. 1–8.

page 154, would not propagate from seeds: Charles F. Swingle, "Experiments in Propagating Shipmast Locust," *Journal of Forestry* 35 (1937): 713ff.

page 154, yellow locust brought to Long Island: S. B. Detwiler, "The History of Shipmast Locust," *Journal of Forestry* 35 (1937): 710.

page 154, discovery of ancestral form: Donald Culross Peattie, *A Natural History of Trees of Eastern and Central North America* (Boston: Houghton Mifflin, 1950; Riverside ed., 1991), pp. 420–421.

page 154, shipmast clones from single tree: Henry Hopp, *Methods of Distinguishing Between the Shipmast and Common Forms of Black Locust on Long Island, N.Y.*, Technical Bulletin 742 (Washington, D.C.: U.S. Dept. of Agriculture, 1941), p. 20.

page 158, "decadal mortality rates": Orie L. Loucks, personal correspondence to James Runkle of Wright State University, 1 December 1992; supplied to the author by Dr. Loucks.

page 161, "The Forest Service is speaking through": John Flynn, "The Falling Forest," *Amicus Journal*, Winter 1994, p. 36.

page 161, an earlier report: Charles E. McGee, *Heavy Mortality and Succession in a Virgin Mixed Mesophytic Forest* (New Orleans, La.: U.S. Forest Service Southern Forest Experiment Station, 1984), p. 1ff.

page 162, reform efforts by Jack Ward Thomas: Al Kamen, "Code of the Forest (Service)," *Washington Post*, 22 December 1993, p. A19.

page 163, a major 1993 report: Douglas Powell et al., *Forest Resources of the United States 1992* (Fort Collins, Colo.: U.S. Forest Service Rocky Mountain Forest and Range Experiment Station, 1993), p. 2.

CHAPTER 9: PANDEMIC

page 165, "Finally": In "Forest Forum," *American Forests*, July–August 1992, p. 2.

page 166, maple decline in Ontario and Quebec: R. G. Pearson and K. E. Percy, eds., *The 1990 Canadian Long-Range Transport of Air Pollutants and Acid Deposition Assessment Report*, part 5: *Terrestrial Effects* (Ottawa: Federal/Provincial Research and Monitoring Coordinating Committee, 1990), pp. 5–39.

page 166, most severe decline in history: S. L. Walker, et al., *History of Crown Dieback and Deterioration Symptoms of Hardwoods in Eastern Canada*, part 1 (Downsville, Ont.: Environmental Integration Services Branch, Atmospheric Environment Service, 1990), pp. 14–15.

page 166, early history of maple decline: Walker, pp. 5–40.

page 167, rainfall ten times as acidic as normal: Peter V. Fossel, "The Sugar Maples Are Dying," *Country Living*, September 1987, p. 34. The figure is corroborated by Dr. Robert I. Bruck of North Carolina State University.

page 167, Canadian soil deficiencies: Pearson and Percy, p. 42.

page 167, "Excess inorganic-N": Pearson and Percy, p. 37.

page 167, wildlife impacts of acid rain in Canada: S. Milburn, et al., *The 1990 Canadian Long-Range Transport of Air Pollutants and Acid Deposition Assessment Report: Executive Summary* (Ottawa: Federal/Provincial Research and Monitoring Coordinating Committee, 1990), p. 25.

page 168, "Fears of . . . sugar maple extinction": "Sugar Maple Faces Extinction Threat," *New York Times*, 7 December 1986, p. 69.

page 168, pear thrips in southern Vermont: David R. Houston et al, *Sugarbush Management: A Guide to Maintaining Tree Health* (Radnor, Pa.: U.S. Forest Service Northeastern Forest Experiment Station), p. 24.

page 168, description of thrips: Allan R. Gold, "Forests of Vermont Severely Damaged by Flea-Size Insect," *New York Times*, 23 June 1988, p. A16.

page 168, damage by thrips larvae: Houston, pp. 24–25.

page 168, "early stages of an epidemic": "Sugar Maples Sicken Under Acid Rain's Pall," *New York Times*, 15 May 1991, p. A18.

page 169, "Decline of sugar maple": from one-page photocopy of U.S. Forest Service statement supplied to the author by Gerard D. Hertel, Assistant Director of Forest Health Protection, U.S. Forest Service.

page 169, findings of American Sugar Maple Decline Project: Imants Millers et al., "Sugar Maple Crown Conditions Improve Between 1988 and 1990" (Radnor, Pa.: U.S. Forest Service, Northeastern Area State and Private Forestry Division, 1992), n.p.

page 170, health of maples improving: Millers, n.p.

page 170, "Sugar maple is doing well": from one-page photocopy of U.S. Forest Service statement supplied to the author by Gerard D. Hertel, Assistant Director of Forest Health Protection, U.S. Forest Service.

page 170, "There is general agreement": Pearson and Percy, p. 39.

page 173, fifteen thousand maple-sugar producers: Pearson and Percy, p. 76.

page 173, changes in sugar chemistry: Pearson and Percy, p. 22.

page 173, two-thirds growth rate for polluted trees: Pearson and Percy, p. 49.

page 173, crown conditions improved: Millers, n.p.

page 173, correlating nutrient loss: R. Ouimet and J.-M. Fortin, "Growth and Foliar Nutrient Status of Sugar Maple: Incidence of Forest Decline and Reaction to Fertilization," *Canadian Journal of Forestry* 22 (1992): 699–703.

page 174, "that the pattern of change": Orie L. Loucks, ed., "Pattern of Air Pollutants and Response of Oak-Hickory Ecosystems in the Ohio Corridor," unpublished monograph (Oxford, Ohio: Miami University, 1991), p. 37.

page 174, "short period of poor growth": Imants Millers et al., *History of Hardwood Decline in the Eastern United States* (Broomall, Pa.: U.S. Forest Service Northeastern Forest Experiment Station, 1989), pp. 4–5.

page 175: description of franklinia: James and Louise Bush-Brown, *America's Garden Book*, rev. ed. (New York: Scribners, 1967), p. 221.

page 176, discovery of chestnut blight: M. Ford Cochram, "Back from the Brink: Chestnuts," *National Geographic*, February 1990, p. 134.

page 176, history of chestnut blight: Ellen Mason Exum, "Tree in a Coma," *American Forests*, November–December 1992, pp. 20–21.

page 176, discovery of elm bark beetle: George Laycock, "There Will Always Be Elms," *Audubon*, May 1990, p. 61.

page 176, Dutch elm disease: Donald Culross Peattie, *A Natural History of Trees of Eastern and Central North America* (Boston: Houghton Mifflin, 1950; Riverside ed., 1991), pp. 244–245.

page 176, quarantine of imported trees and shrubs: Robert W. Stack and John G. Laut, "Dutch Elm Disease," in Jerry W. Riffle and Glenn W. Peterson, eds., *Diseases of Trees in the Great Plains* (Fort Collins, Colo.: U.S. Forest Service Rocky Mountain Forest and Range Experiment Station, 1986), p. 93.

page 176, extermination efforts and reemergence: Peattie, p. 245.

page 177, half of American elms killed: Laycock, p. 59.

page 177, new strain of fungus: Chris Bolgiano, "The Aliens," *American Forests*, July–August 1993, p. 53.

page 178: reduction of biological diversity: Orie L. Loucks, in *News From the Mother Forest* (newsletter of the Lucy Braun Association for the Mixed Mesophytic Forest), September 1993, p. 1.

page 178, stairway parts: Personal communication from Robert Byerley, manager, P.C., Inc., a custom woodworking sales organization in New Albany, Indiana, 2 November 1993.

page 179, infestation by adelgids: Mark S. McClure, "Control of Hemlock Woolly Adelgid," *Yankee Nursery Quarterly*, spring 1991, pp. 1–2.

page 180, description of adelgid attacks: M. S. McClure, "Density Dependent Feedback and Population Cycles in *Adelges tsugae* (Homoptera: Adelgidae) on *Tsuga canadensis*," *Environmental Entomology* 20:258–264. Also, Anne Raver, "Snow-White Insect Is Hemlock Poison," *New York Times*, 24 May 1992, section 9, p. 14.

page 180, adelgid compared to chestnut blight: Raver, p. 14.

page 180, experiments are "encouraging": D'Vera Cohn, "Shenandoah Hemlocks Under Siege," *Washington Post*, 4 September 1993, p. D3.

page 180, Mark S. McClure, "Nitrogen Fertilization of Hemlock Increases Susceptibility to Hemlock Woolly Adelgid," *Journal of Arboriculture* 17 (August 1991): 227–229.

page 180, "There is good reason to assume": Edward Whereat, personal communication to the author, 31 May 1992.

page 181, "No host resistance": McClure, "Control of Hemlock Woolly Adelgid," p. 1.

page 182, beech scale insect: Whiteford L. Baker, *Eastern Forest Insects*, U.S. Department of Agriculture Forest Service miscellaneous publication no. 1175 (Washington, D.C.: U.S. Govt. Printing Office, 1972), pp. 97–98.

page 182, "The fungus is entirely dependent": Baker, p. 98.

page 182, beech scale moving rapidly: Jay Cammermeyer, "Life's a Beech—and Then You Die," *American Forests*, July–August 1993, pp. 20ff.

page 182, beech thickets: Cammermeyer, p. 20.

page 183, beech tree lore: Peattie, p. 120.

page 183, beech distribution and description: Peattie, pp. 119–120.

page 183, "grand old American tree": Peattie, p. 120.

page 184, "more threatened than the American Chestnut": Rich Patterson, "Butternut Blues," *American Forests*, July–August 1993, pp. 22.

page 184, endangered species: "Summary of Forest Insect Disease Impacts," Great Smoky Mountains National Park, photocopied paper, 1 September 1993, p. 3.

page 184, now collecting "scions": "Summary of Forest Insect Disease Impacts," p. 3.

page 184, "ozone-like foliar damage": Briefing statement, Great Smoky Mountains National Park, 26 August 1993, p. 1.

page 184, "the park's defenses are down": Ned Burks and Chris Fordney, "Battle for the Blue Ridge," *Washington Post Sunday Magazine*, 10 October 1993, pp. 15–16.

page 185, "the strictest possible regulations": Burks and Fordney, p. 2.

page 185, definition of a tree: C. Frank Brockman, *Trees of North America* (New York: Golden Press, 1969), p. 13.

page 186, "They're dying": "Dying Saguaro Cactuses Are Bewildering Scientists," *New York Times*, 11 August 1991, p. 23.

page 186, symptoms on south side of plant: "Dying Saguaro Cactuses are Bewildering Scientists," p. 23.

page 186, a single chlorine atom: "Ozone," an information release by the Air & Waste Management Association, Pittsburgh, Pa., n.p., n.d.

page 186, a 2-percent increase: Al Gore, *Earth in the Balance* (New York: Plume, 1993), p. 87.

page 186, Mount Pinatubo: Boyce Rensberger, "Decline of Ozone-Harming Chemicals Suggests Atmosphere May Heal Itself," *Washington Post*, 26 August 1993, p. A10.

page 187, ground-level UV-B radiation: William K. Stevens, "Rise in Ultraviolet Rays Seen in North America," *New York Times*, 16 November 1993, p. C11.

page 187, "showed evidence that a portion": Orie L. Loucks, "Apparent Sun Scald on 1993 Foliage of White Pine (*Pinus strobus*) in Ohio," unpublished paper, 26 April 1994, provided to the author by Dr. Loucks; pp. 1–2.

page 188, growth reduction from UV-B: Victor Medina, Joseph H. Sullivan, and Alan H. Teramura (of the University of Maryland), grant application to USDA to investigate the implications of increasing UV-B radiation on loblolly pine and sweetgum, 1992, pp. 7–9.

page 188, "cell membranes": Ernest J. Sternglass, in Ralph Graub, *The Petkau Effect: Nuclear Radiation, People, and Trees* (New York: Four Walls Eight Windows, 1992), p. xx.

page 188, artifically created radioactivity: Ralph Graub, *The Petkau Effect*, p. 159.

page 189, "that could not be explained": Graub, p. 146.

page 189, "the toxicity of SO_2": Graub, p. 154.

page 189, TCA: Harmut Frank, "Airborne Chlorocarbons, Photooxidants, and Forest Decline," *Ambio*, February 1991, p. 17.

page 189, agricultural herbicides: "Herbicide Detected in Rainfall," *Land Stewardship Letter* (Marine, Minn.: Land Stewardship Project), summer 1991, pp. 1, 3–4.

page 189, Alaska cedar: Charles G. Shaw III, et al., "Decline and Mortality of *Chamaecyparis nootkatensis* in Southeastern Alaska, a Problem of Long Duration but Unknown Cause," *Plant Disease*, January 1985, p. 13.

page 189, Tongass National Forest: Robert Glenn Ketchum and Carey D. Ketchum, *The Tongass: Alaska's Vanishing Rainforest* (New York: Aperture, 1987), pp. 70–78.

page 190, impact of warming trend on Alaska cedar: P. E. Hennon, E. M. Hansen, and C. G. Shaw III, "Dynamics of Decline and Mortality of *Chamaecyparis nootkatensis* in Southeast Alaska," *Canadian Journal of Botany* 68 (1990): 661.

page 190, "Areas that today": "Looking On, Helpless, As Palm Trees Die Off," *New York Times*, 29 July 1992, p. A8.

page 190, "No credible claim": Committee on Science, Engineering, and Public Policy, *Policy Implications of Greenhouse Warming* (Washington, D.C.: National Academy Press, 1991), pp. 23–26.

CHAPTER 10: THE TREESAVERS

page 193, "Here the smooth Beach": As quoted in John Dixon Hunt and Peter Willis, eds., *The Genius of the Place* (Cambridge, Mass.: MIT Press, 1988), pp. 231–232.

page 193, "old word for sanctuary": James G. Frazer, *The Golden Bough*, abridged ed. (New York: Macmillan, 1958), p. 127.

page 193, savanna species: Richard E. Leakey and Roger Lewin, *People of the Lake: Mankind and Its Beginnings* (New York: Avon, 1979), pp. 17–76.

page 194, murder of Chico Mendes: Cândido Grzybowski, in Chico Mendes, *Fight for the Forest* (Birmingham, England: Third World Publications, 1989), pp. vii–viii.

page 194, death of Leroy Jackson: Jeffrey St. Clair, "On the Death of Leroy Jackson," *Wild Forest Review*, November 1993, pp. 4–5.

page 194, pipe-bombing of Judi Bari: Susan Zakin, *Coyotes and Town Dogs: Earth First! and the Environmental Movement* (New York: Viking, 1993), pp. 342–343, 388–394.

page 195, landscape preference study: Rachel Kaplan and Stephen Kaplan, *The Experience of Nature* (New York: Cambridge University Press, 1989), pp. 103–104.

page 196, one-fifth the land area: "Oak Woodland Facts," *California Oaks* (newsletter of the California Oak Foundation), fall–winter 1993, p. 5.

page 196, missions in midst of oak woodlands: James R. Griffin and Pamela C. Muick, "California Native Oaks: Past and Present," *Fremontia*, July 1990, pp. 5–6.

page 197, three million head of cattle: Robert A. Ewing, "How Are Oaks Protected? What are the Issues?" *Fremontia*, July 1990, p. 84.

page 197, "new natives": Judith Lowry, "Notes on Native Grasses," *Grasslands* (newsletter), July 1991, p. 1.

page 198, oak seedlings need moisture: K. J. Rice et al., *Ecology and Regeneration of Hardwood Rangelands: Influences of Water, Herbivory and Competition on Stability, Productivity, and Management Options* (Davis, Calif.: Dept. of Agronomy and Range Science, University of California, 1991), pp. 5–7, 12.

page 198, soil ecosystems changed: Bruce M. Pavlik et al., *Oaks of California* (Los Olivos, Calif.: Chacuma Press/California Oak Foundation, 1991), pp. 123–124.

page 198, few younger than seventy-five: Pavlik et al., p. 121.

page 198, "substantial recruitment": Rice et al., p. 3.

page 198, botanic name for oak: Pavlik et al., pp. 3–9.

page 198, Vancouver: Pavlik et al., p. 10.

page 199, "champion" valley oak: *National Register of Big Trees* (Washington, D.C.: American Forestry Association, 1992), pp. 11–12, 31.

page 199, 90 percent destroyed: Pavlik et al., p. 125.

page 200, 80 percent privately owned: Pavlik et al., p. 126.

page 200, between 23 and 46 percent: J. M. Welker and J. W. Menke, offprint paper, "*Quercus Douglassii* Seedling Water Relations in Mesic and Grazing-Induced Xeric Environments" (Davis, Calif.: Department of Agronomy and Range Science, n.d. [1987?]), p. 231. The offprint was provided to the author by Douglas McCreary of the University of California Extension Service.

page 200, "the efforts of": Pavlik et al., p. 121.

page 201, three acorns be planted: Lisa Bush and Rocky Thompson, "Growing Natives: Planting Oaks," *Fremontia*, July 1990, p. 105.

page 202, Visalia oaks: Ginger Strong and Alan George, "Visalia Is Saving Its Valley Oaks," *Fremontia*, July 1990, pp. 99–100.

page 202, more than one hundred cities and counties: Ewing, p. 86.

page 203, "may prove too costly": Pavlik et al., p. 127.

page 203, "Educational efforts": Thomas A. Scott, "Conserving California's Rarest White Oak: The Engelmann Oak," *Fremontia*, July 1990, p. 29.

page 204, "Long-scourged": Kenneth G. Lamb, "The Meridian Oak," *California Oaks* (newsletter of the California Oak Foundation), fall 1990, p. 11.

page 205, Hansen testimony: American Forestry Association, *Global ReLeaf* (Washington, D.C.: n.d. [1990?]), n.p.

page 205, benefits of planting trees: *Global ReLeaf*, n.p.

page 206, "We'll enter the 21st Century": R. Neil Sampson, "Cool the Greenhouse, Plant 100 Million Trees . . . ," *Los Angeles Times*, 16 October 1988, p. V1.

page 207, ReLeaf programs: R. Neil Sampson, "Global ReLeaf: Five Years of Progress—A Summary," draft paper (Washington, D.C.: American Forests, 1994), pp. 1–9.

page 209, "Only God": Ted Williams, "Don't Worry, Plant a Tree," *Audubon*, May 1991, p. 24.

page 209, "politely declined": Williams, p. 31.

page 209, "a more effective:" Williams, p. 27.

page 209, "bloated U.S. automaker": Williams, p. 26.

page 210, wood for energy: Neil Sampson and Tom Hamilton, "Can Trees Really Help Fight Global Warming?" *American Forests*, May–June 1992, pp. 13–16.

page 211, occurrence of ice ages: Wallace S. Broecker and George H. Denton, "What Drives Glacial Cycles," *Scientific American*, January 1990, p. 49.

page 211, shifts in ocean currents: Broecker and Denton, p. 49.

page 211, buildup of mountains: Gregg Easterbrook, "Return of the Glaciers," *Newsweek*, 23 November 1992, pp. 62–63.

page 211, "temperatures got a little warmer": Easterbrook, p. 63.

page 212, "as forests begin to die off": Joanna Campe, "Eden or Ice Age, Which Will We Choose?" *Remineralize the Earth*, winter 1991, p. 2.

page 212, "Within a few decades": "A Brief Perspective on Soil Remineralization and the Climate" (drawn from the writings of John Hamaker, Don Weaver, Larry Ephron, and Joanna Campe), *Remineralize the Earth*, spring 1992, p. 5.

page 212, massive application: Fred B. Wood IV and Fred B. Wood III, "A Call for Action," *Remineralize the Earth*, summer–fall 1991, p. 28.

page 212, healthful living microbes: Harvey Lisle, "Rock Dusts for Human Nutrition," *Remineralize the Earth*, spring 1992, pp. 35–36.

page 212, "showed four times the timber": Lisle, p. 5.

page 212, Fraser fir and red spruce test: Joanna Campe, "Making Communities More Sustainable," *Remineralize the Earth*, spring 1993, p. 30.

page 213, "Cyclone pulverizer": Joanna Campe, "The Cyclone Pulverizer: A Breakthrough Technology for an Affordable Rock Crusher," *Remineralize the Earth*, summer–fall 1991, p. 16.

page 214, "loony": Easterbrook, p. 63.

page 215, "On the Olympic peninsula": Jerry Franklin, "Toward a New Forestry," *American Forests*, November–December 1989, pp. 37–44.

page 215, "a new look at old forestry": N. Taylor Gregg, "Will 'New Forestry' Save Old Forests?" *American Forests*, September–October 1991, p. 51.

page 215, views of Professor Bill Atkinson: Gregg, p. 70.

page 216, "What you need": Rob Taylor, "Ecoforestry Causes a Stir," *Seattle Post-Intelligencer*, 10 June 1993, p. A4.

page 216, Wilkinson's selective cutting method: Taylor, p. A4.

page 216, "Natural selection ecoforestry": Ecoforestry Institute, *Special Report, July 1993* (Portland, Ore.: 1993), p. 1.

page 216, "through which 500,000 logging trucks": Alexander Cockburn, "Coercive Harmony: Clinton, Consensus, and Chainsaws," *Wild Forest Review*, November 1993, p. 6.

page 217, "It still leaves": Tom Kenworthy, "Revised Clinton Plan Saves More Forest," *Washington Post*, 24 February 1994, p. A5.

page 217, "The President's Forest Plan": James Monteith, "The Option 9 Lawsuit," a fund-raising letter, 22 July 1994, p. 3.

page 217, "parent plants": George Laycock, "There Will Always Be Elms," *Audubon*, May 1990, pp. 61–62.

page 218, the "Ross" tree: Joe Coccaro, "In Search of Cure for Diseased Trees," *Virginia Pilot*, 29 August 1993, p. 12.

page 218, hypovirulent fungus: Dennis W. Fulbright, "Treatment of the West Salem Stand with Hypovirulence," *The Bark* (newsletter of American Chestnut Foundation), May–June 1993, pp. 1–3.

page 219, "hypovirulent offspring": Donald L. Nuss, "Engineered Hypovirulence," *The Bark*, May–June 1993, p. 4.

page 219, "The first step": Mark Weiner, "Tasty Snail Unlikely Savior for Chestnut," *Syracuse Herald American*, 10 October 1993, n.p.; reprinted by State University of New York, College of Environmental Science and Forestry, n.d.

page 219, viable cultivar: Weiner.

page 220, paulownia: Veronica Byrd, "Hardwood: The Beanstock Approach," *New York Times*, 1 November 1992, section 6, p. 9.

page 221, "You are looking into fog": Ludwig Wittgenstein, *Notebooks, 1914–1916*, ed. G. H. von Wright and G. E. M. Anscombe, trans. G. E. M. Anscombe (New York: Harper Torchbooks, 1969), pp. 53–53e.

CHAPTER 11: ON CROSSING THE THRESHOLD

page 222, "no important change": Aldo Leopold, *A Sand County Almanac* (New York: Oxford University Press, 1949), pp. 209–210.

page 222, earlier version: Aldo Leopold, "The Conservation Ethic," *Journal of Forestry* 634 (1933): 635.

page 222, "We are remodeling": Leopold, *A Sand County Almanac*, p. 226.

page 225, Woodwell's point: Sandra Postel and Lori Heise, *Reforesting the Earth*, Worldwatch Paper 83 (Washington, D.C.: Worldwatch Institute, 1988), p. 44.

page 225, "The amount of carbon dioxide": Richard A. Houghton and George M. Woodwell, "Global Climatic Change," *Scientific American*, April 1989, p. 42.

page 226, carbon absorbed one-third greater: Tim Hilchey, "A Forest Absorbs More Carbon Dioxide Than Was Predicted," *New York Times*, 8 June 1993, p. C4.

page 226, oxygen content: James Lovelock, *The Ages of Gaia* (New York: Norton, 1988), p. 132.

page 226, decrease in oxygen "is consistent with": Ralph F. Keeling and Stephen R. Shertz, "Seasonal and Interannual Variations in Atmospheric Oxygen and Implications for the Global Carbon Cycle," *Nature*, 22 August 1992, p. 723.

page 226, "If the NCAR findings": Gar Smith, "More Trouble for the Earth's Atmosphere," *Earth Island Journal*, spring 1993, p. 20.

page 227, "When we reduce": "Global Ozone Down 10% Since 1969," *Washington Post*, 22 February 1994, p. A5.

page 227, "it just didn't pay": Martha M. Hamilton, "EPA Asks DuPont Co. to Make CFCs in '95," *Washington Post*, 18 December 1994, pp. C1, C8.

page 228, automatic destruction of ozone: Carl Zimmer, "Son of Ozone Hole," *Discover*, October 1993, pp. 28–29.

page 228, frogs dying in Cascades: "What the Frogs Are Telling Us," editorial, *New York Times*, 6 March 1994, section 4, p. 14.

page 228, "Researchers estimate": Emily Yoffe, "Silence of the Frogs," *New York Times Magazine*, 13 December 1992, p. 64.

page 229, decline of songbirds: Ken Emerson, "Seen Any Warblers Lately?" *New York Times Magazine*, 2 September 1990, pp. 26–27.

page 229, Shelbyville, Illinois: John Terborgh, "Why American Songbirds Are Vanishing," *Scientific American*, May 1992, p. 101.

page 229, "show a 50 percent decline": Orie L. Loucks, ed., "Pattern of Air Pollutants and Response of Oak-Hickory Ecosystems in the Ohio Corridor," unpublished paper (Oxford, Ohio: Miami University, 1991), p. 12.

page 230, tropical viruses: Richard Preston, "Crisis in the Hot Zone," *New Yorker*, 26 October 1992, pp. 58–81. The article was subsequently expanded to book length, in *The Hot Zone* (New York: Random House, 1994).

page 230, "becomes speckled": Preston, p. 59.

page 230, "When an ecosystem suffers degradation": Preston, p. 62.

page 231, Harvard entomologist: E. O. Wilson, "Is Humanity Suicidal?" *New York Times Magazine*, 30 May 1993, pp. 24–29.

page 231, "the elementary sin": Ludwig Wittegenstein, *Notebooks, 1914–1916*, ed. G. H. von Wright and G. E. M. Anscombe, trans. G. E. M. Anscombe (New York: Harper Torchbooks, 1969), p. 91e.

page 231, "If there were only 500 million": Lovelock, p. 178.

page 231, "The human species": Wilson, p. 26.

page 231, "The maladies of Gaia": Lovelock, p. 178.

page 232, "This kind of consensus": Union of Concerned Scientists, "World's Leading Scientists Issue Urgent Warning to Humanity," press release, Washington, D.C., 18 November 1992, p. 1.

page 232, Union of Concerned Scientists, p. 1.

page 233, "New studies suggest": William K. Stevens, "Poor Land's Success in Cutting Birth Rate Upsets Old Theories," *New York Times*, 2 January 1994, p. 1.

ACKNOWLEDGMENTS

I am grateful beyond measure to Max Gartenberg, literary agent and longtime friend, for setting me off on this quest to begin with; and to Carollyne Hutter, a valued associate and as skilled a collector of editorial research materials as I've ever worked with; Mindy Werner of Viking Penguin for her wonderful patience and sound advice, and Michael Cain for a thoughtful and thorough job of copyediting; Neil Sampson for crucial early guidance; Bill Rooney, editor of *American Forests* (a primary source for this book, as the notes show), for publishing some of my early adventures afield; Orie Loucks for instruction and counsel in the ecology and pathology of trees and forests; John Mitchell and George Thompson for consistently excellent literary advice (e.g., to keep everlastingly at it); Dick Beamish and Rachel Rice, Diana and David Dawson, Paul A. Clement, Nancy Vernon, Charles T. Little, Dorothy and Tom Pariot, Patricia Maida, Janice and Taylor Vernon, and Sarah and Roger Swearingen, for food, lodging, and fellowship during my research trips; Edward Whereat, forest ecologist and a scientific adviser during early stages of the project, whose contributions helped clarify for me some of the obscure technical corners of this story; Robert Bruck, Hubert Vogelmann, Dan Duriscoe, Nels Johnson, John Flynn, David Marvin, Dan Smith, and Lowell Dodge for reading portions of the manuscript; John Flynn (again) for moral support at every stage of research and writing, but especially when the air was filled with political shrapnel; my wife, Ila D. Little, for helping me through what turned out to be a very long siege; and all those, named in the text, who so generously granted me interviews and supplied me with written materials. They all did their level best to help me get it going, keep it going, and get it right. Any failures along the way, in comprehensiveness, fact, or interpretation, should be laid to my account, not theirs.

Kensington, Maryland
Placitas, New Mexico
1991–1994

INDEX